Judith Butler: Ethics, Law

CW00499020

Judith Butler is the philosopher who has invited us to think the subject as the effect of gender processes and practices. In this book, Elena Loizidou acknowledges the potency and influence of Butler's 'concept' of gender as process. But, instead of focusing on this well-developed and discussed position, she addresses a set of themes that, whilst central in Butler's work, have received rather less consideration. Loizidou traces how Butler comes to the themes of ethics, law and politics, analysing their interrelation and explaining how they relate to Butler's question of how we can have more livable and viable lives. And she argues that this possibility is articulated by Butler within the parameters of a sustained agonistic relationship between these three spheres. Critical legal scholarship has engaged with the question of 'life' by offering a disparate analysis of its ethical, legal and political dimensions. Loizidou suggests that Butler's rounded understanding of the interrelationship of these three spheres will enable critical legal scholarship, as well as critical theory more generally, to consider how the question of life's unsustainable conditions can be rethought and redressed.

Elena Loizidou is a Lecturer in the School of Law, Birkbeck College, University of London.

Nomikoi: Critical Legal Thinkers
Edited by Peter Goodrich and David Seymour

Nomikoi: Critical Legal Thinkers presents analyses of key critical theorists whose thinking on law has contributed significantly to the development of the new interdisciplinary legal studies. Addressing those who have most influenced legal thought and thought about law, the aim of the series is to bring legal scholarship, the social sciences and the humanities into closer dialogue.

Series editors: Peter Goodrich, Cardozo School of Law, New York and David Seymour, School of Law, Lancaster University, UK.

Judith Butler: Ethics, Law, Politics

Elena Loizidou

Routledge·Cavendish
Taylor & Francis Group
a GlassHouse book

First published 2007
by Routledge-Cavendish
2 Park Square, Milton Park, Abingdon, Oxon OX14 4RN

Simultaneously published in the USA and Canada
by Routledge-Cavendish
270 Madison Ave, New York, NY 10016

a GlassHouse book

Routledge-Cavendish is an imprint of the Taylor & Francis Group, an informa business

© 2007 Elena Loizidou

Typeset in Times New Roman by
Newgen Imaging Systems (P) Ltd, Chennai, India
Printed and bound in Great Britain by
MPG Books Ltd, Bodmin, Cornwall

All rights reserved. No part of this book may be reprinted or reproduced or utilised in any form or by any electronic, mechanical, or other means, now known or hereafter invented, including photocopying and recording, or in any information storage or retrieval system, without permission in writing from the publishers.

British Library Cataloguing in Publication Data
A catalogue record for this book is available
from the British Library

Library of Congress Cataloging in Publication Data
Loizidou, Elena.
Judith Butler : ethics, law, politics / Elena Loizidou.
p. cm.
Includes bibliographical references.
1. Butler, Judith, 1956– 2. Law – Philosophy. 3. Feminist theory. 4. Feminist jurisprudence. I. Title.

K230.B88L65 2007
340'.1–dc22 2006028481

ISBN10: 1–904385–45–1 (hbk)
ISBN10: 0–415–42041–5 (pbk)

ISBN13: 978–1–904385–45–5 (hbk)
ISBN13: 978–0–415–42041–9 (pbk)

In memory of Loizos K Loizides

Contents

Acknowledgements

A book happens. And this happening takes a lot – a lot of labour, a lot of enthusiasm, a lot of despair, a lot of elation – but above all it takes a lot of support.

Judith Butler: Ethics, Law, Politics would not have happened if Peter Goodrich and David Seymour had not agreed to include it in their series Critical Legal Thinkers. I therefore thank them for making this possible and for their support. Beverley Brown, then commissioning editor at Glasshouse Press, encouraged and wholeheartedly supported this book, so I thank her immensely for this. I would also like to express my appreciation to Colin Perrin, the current commissioning editor at Glasshouse Press, for giving me advice and encouragement.

In the course of the book, I have presented some of the chapters at conferences and seminars. I would like to thank Helen Baker, the organiser of the Feminist Theory stream at the SLSA conference at Liverpool in March 2005, who allowed me to present 'Ethical Sisters' there. Special thanks to the enthusiastic audience at Liverpool and especially to Ruth Fletcher for her engaging questions. I would also like to thank Davina Cooper, the AHRC director of Centre for the Study of Law, Gender and Sexuality at Kent Law School, for providing me the space to present 'Double Law' there. Similarly, I extend my gratitude to the Law School at Birkbeck College in all its entirety, for providing a most stimulating environment for research.

My extensive gratitude also goes to friends and colleagues who read and commented upon various draft chapters of the book: Sara Ahmed, Maria Aristodemou, Beverley Brown, Peter Goodrich, Piyel Haldar, Les Moran and Thanos Zartaloudis. Conversations over the year with Sara Ahmed, Maria Aristodemou, Brenna Bandar, Jose Belido, Lauren Berlant, Elizabetta Bertolino, Beverley Brown, Maria Drakopoulou, Peter Goodrich, Piyel Haldar, Nicoline Van Harskamp, Morris Kaplan, Les Moran, Anton Schutz, Vicki Thoms, Patricia Tuitt, Julie Wallbank and Thanos Zartaloudis kept the book and my life going. So I thank them all. But special thanks to Marty Slaughter and Nindi Samra who encouraged the cappuccino breaks that revitalised me. My thanks also to Marie Selwood who improved the quality of the manuscript.

I thank Sophie Petrou, Louise Storey and Jean Morris for their warm friendship. My immense gratitude goes to Chrystalla Loizidou and Christos Loizides for their understanding and love over the last eighteen months. And I thank Marike Van Harskamp above all for being there.

In the midst of writing, I found out that Bello, responsible for my early up-bringing in Nigeria, has passed away. I am indebted to him for teaching me that optimism is a condition of survival.

Table of cases and statute

Cases

Statute

Chapter 1

Introduction

> The public sphere is constituted in part by what can appear, and the regulation of the sphere of appearance is one way to establish what will count as reality, and what will not. It is also a way of establishing whose lives can be marked as lives, and whose deaths will count as deaths. Our capacity to feel and to apprehend hangs in the balance. But so, too, does the fate of the reality of certain lives and deaths as well as the ability to think critically and publicly...
>
> (Butler, 2004a: xx–xi)

Judith Butler is the Maxine Elliot Professor in the Departments of Rhetoric and Comparative Literature at the University of Berkeley, California. Her work has exerted great influence in a variety of academic and extra-academic environments since the publication of her book *Gender Trouble* (1990, 1999a). *Gender Trouble* set out to question those understandings of gender, in which gender is seen to be based on sexual difference, consequentially only recognising masculinity and femininity. Butler showed instead how gender is a process, and not some essence that pre-exists a subject's formation. As such, she introduced the concept of gender performativity into academia. The practice of gender performativity unveils the ways in which the above assumption prevents subjects outside the categories of femininity and masculinity from becoming culturally intelligible. Simultaneously, the notion and practice of gender performativity orients us to seeing that such preclusions and foreclosures reveal a certain resistance towards this totalising understanding of gender, thus enabling the possibility of so-called 'abjected' subjects to become culturally intelligible.

To date, *Gender Trouble* sold something like more than 100,000 copies and in 1993 inspired the creation of a fanzine called *Judy!*.[1] To understand the success of the book on purely market grounds will of course give us a rather impoverished understanding of why her thought has been influential. Sales are indicators of some kind (and they matter to publishers) and while they might explain the desirability of an object at least at the moment of purchase, they do not explain an object's afterlife. They fail, in other words, to account for how it triggers certain transformations or even, as exaggerated as it might sound, life itself. A friend conveyed to me how he first came across *Gender Trouble*: he found it lying discarded on a street in Amsterdam. We do not know whether the book has been dropped on the streets because the original owner found it unfathomable or because its carrying vessel was too overloaded causing it to fall out of it. The friend picked it up and began reading it, as the book had been frequently mentioned by his law professors in Australia but he had never before had the opportunity to read it. At an anecdotal level, his story captures the unreliability of sales as an index of how ideas get received, circulate and become influential.

The success of the book was also unexpected for Butler. As she writes, in its tenth Anniversary edition,

> I did not know that the text would have as wide an audience as it has had, nor did I know that it would constitute a provocative 'intervention' in feminist theory or be cited as one of the founding texts of queer theory.
> (1999a: vii)

But how then does she account for its success? 'The life of a text has exceeded my intentions . . . that is surely in part the result of the changing context of its reception' (1999a: vii). But this in itself cannot explain how it came to be so influential. It does, however, enable us to see that success and influence can be understood through the afterlife of a book. In order to understand how *Gender Trouble* had an afterlife and indeed succeeded in affecting so many academic fields and institutions,[2] we have to try to recognise both the direct or immediate contribution that its notion of gender as process has made and its more succinct intervention by problematising our living conditions.

It is thus *Gender Trouble's* critique of the way in which understandings of the relationship between 'life' and the institutions that promote, regulate and sustain it, that guaranteed its entry into different academic fields and spheres of life. The book appeared at the time when US feminism was influenced by the work of Marxist feminists such as Andrea Dworkin and Catherine Mackinnon, as well as European feminist post-structuralist thought. Dworkin's and Mackinnon's writings focused on the exploitation of women and the collusion of the State in producing unequal relations. At the centre of their critique stood their demand for the recognition of women's equality to men, one that would be enacted by the transformation of civil rights, criminal justice, employment, tort and contract law and other state-promoted institutions. Their diagnostic critique paid attention to the structures limiting women's lives, like the State or the law, yet this critique paradoxically came at the expense of presenting women as passive hostages to these structures. To be fair, this representation of women was unintentional; the result of their Marxist theoretical background which does not allow to escape such a position. French post-structuralist feminism, initially a post-1968 'French'[3] women's movement, invested its energy in critiquing the ways in which the lives of women, and 'woman' more specifically, were negated, by utilising for example linguistics, psychoanalysis and philosophy. Through these analytical tools they exposed the disavowal of women from public life and language; 'woman' was represented as the other of man, as a creature whose role in life was identified with procreation, care and domestication. Luce Irigaray for example, in *An Ethics of Sexual Difference* (1993b), addresses the absence of the feminine in western philosophical texts, focusing in particular on Plato, Kant, Hegel and Lacan. I use Irigaray as an example but it is important to remember that post-structuralist feminism did not expose the erasure of the feminine from the symbolic and linguistic field in a unilateral way. The importance of the movement lay in offering a sophisticated critique of the socio-symbolic and linguistic sphere and in producing a set of 'transformative' strategies aimed at creating an alternative space for women. In taking the difference of women from men, and in particular their 'sexual difference', as their point of departure they made feminine subjectivity the very ground of their politics. The movement, unlike the Anglo-American one which hoped that the State would provide equality to women, articulated that a transformation of the lives of women would necessitate an understanding of their difference to men and would have to be wider than any State-imposed changes. It would require the engendering of a feminine language, affectivity and 'symbolic'.

In taking to task Anglo-American and French post-structuralist feminism, Butler exposed the limits of their thought and politics. It is this intervention that explains in some way the success of *Gender Trouble*. Yet Butler was and still is also influenced by Foucault's work. *Gender Trouble* relied on his understanding of power (juridical, disciplinary, bio-power) to unveil the short-cuts of Anglo-American feminism's conception of power. In *Discipline and Punish* (1991a), Foucault addressed the misconceptions that Marxist thought had in relation to state power. Sovereign or juridical power (which we can loosely identify as power associated with the state in his vocabulary) was revealed as not being invested in transforming the lives of its subjects or citizens. On the contrary, sovereign power was seen by Foucault as being concerned with sustaining its own authority and territoriality. His genealogy of power explains this in more detail. Focusing on the sovereign's right to take a life or let one live, Foucault argued that this right is exercised in order to sustain the sovereign's authority and domination over subjects. It is therefore not concerned with the security and welfare of subjects. Foucault also identified two other modalities of power in his work namely disciplinary power and bio-power. These two modalities did not cause the disappearance of sovereign/juridical power in modernity; rather they became the more visible and potent modalities of regulating people and populations.

Through Foucault's critique of sovereign/juridical power, Butler argues that the Anglo-American feminist movement had to become more critical of the operation of State power if it was to progress its political agenda. It was pertinent to reflect on the operation of sovereign/juridical power as well as to consider to what extent woman, the subject of feminism, is embedded in the other two modalities of power. She indicates how sovereign/juridical power is unable to promote women's equality or encourage a wider political recognition of women's issues, as its paramount concern lies with sustaining its own authority and *not* in promoting the welfare of its subjects. Still the essence of

Butler's critique is not just in pointing out the suicidal attachment that this feminist movement had to the State or the law, but also in enabling feminist thought, preoccupied with questions of power and domination, to consider a different way of articulating how subjects are formed. Butler considers how disciplinary practices enable our formation. For example, the naming (an iterative practice) of somebody as either a girl or a boy at birth, reveals that such naming reproduces certain normative preconceptions of what it means to be a boy or a girl. To put it differently, the naming disciplines us into the subjects that we become. Moreover, in contrast to sovereign/juridical power, disciplinary power is not located in one space or in the hands of the ruler, but it is to be found everywhere. This affects our formation as subjects. In *Gender Trouble*, she considers how disciplinary power forms subjects and in particular gender subjects. Through this move Butler offers at least two fathomable observations: (a) it alerts us to the possibility that we are not outside power and its formative force; and (b) that we ought to reflect on the ways in which we become the subjects that we are. In doing so we need to form a genealogy of the subject of feminism and 'woman', and pay attention to the ways in which language and power form it.

Her intervention introduced a refreshing perspective in feminist thought. Women were not any more to be viewed as passive, repressed by power and waiting for the regime of power to alter, recognise and 'represent' them in order to be able to transform their conditions of livability. But as subjects embedded in power or, to be more precise, as subjects being formed by power and language, it meant that women could resist the conditions of their formation. Her outlook presents us with an un-static and active relation to our lives (and its constitutive forms: power and language). It would be wrong, though, to assume that *Gender Trouble* offers a transformative political blueprint for feminism. On the contrary, the whole point of her critique is precisely to trouble the idea of a transformative politics characterised by a belief in redeeming and liberatory political agendas, and instead to offer a more complex understanding of power and our productive relation to it.

Her quarrel with French feminism is of a different kind, as the state is not central to it. As I have already mentioned they argued that women had been excluded from the socio-symbolic sphere, and constituted as the Other, and worked via different methods towards promoting a feminine subjectivity based on the concept of sexual difference. *Gender Trouble* explores the limits of 'sexual difference'. To put it simply, the book argues that the marker of 'sexual difference' is grounded on a monolithic understanding of desire. Their genealogy did not account for those subjects whose lives could not be unilaterally encompassed within the 'sexual difference' marker, like those of gay men and lesbian women. 'Sexual difference' assumes that desire has always already been heterosexual. As a result gender becomes the cultural consequence of the male/female differentiation. Butler troubles this proposition and enables an understanding of gender, beyond the binary divisions of masculine and feminine that 'French feminism' offered.

The success of *Gender Trouble* is necessarily linked to the above critical interventions. But there is also another reason that, in my opinion, might explain the success of her work. In her critical account of these epistemologically different traditions, the first being based on Marxism and the other on post-structuralism, Butler synthesises a new way of approaching questions of formation, and especially of gender formation. This brought continental post-structuralist philosophy to the social concerns of the American feminist tradition. In the anniversary edition of the book, she alludes to this when she writes that her aim 'was not to "apply" poststructuralism to feminism, but to subject those theories to a specific reformulation' (1999: ix). Reformulation is inevitably concerned with the social issues dominating feminism. In critiquing both Anglo-American and French feminism, she sowed the seeds for the creation of a new academic discipline, namely queer studies. Queer studies found in Butler's work its own philosophical/theoretical grounding, which enabled the new discipline to bring to post-structuralism its own social concerns, to rework Bulter's own version of gender, expand it and ultimately criticise it (Eldeman, 2004; Prosser, 1998).

Gender Trouble was also the start of a series of related books by Butler herself. *Gender Trouble* had an afterlife. My narrative offers an explanation of its success based on her bringing together philosophical and social concerns. But at the same time it is worth mentioning that its subject matter and the way it was approached guaranteed this success. *Gender Trouble* puts life and its conditions of viability at its centre and provides a fresh outlook to the problems of life without offering the illusion that forms (identity) or institutions (state, law) could resolve them. The success of the book lays precisely in its interest in the unfinished and imperfect business of life and materiality. Putting life rather than gender as the subject matter of *Gender Trouble* might sound surprising, given that its analysis of gender formation seemed to have had the most impact in the academic world. Her reluctant endorsement of identity politics, or at least her troubling of the static-ness of identity discourses, however allows me to suggest that *Gender Trouble* is a book about the complexity of life, yet seen through the shades of gender. In dealing with the imperfection and unfinished state of life, *Gender Trouble* itself also unfolds these characteristics. Imperfection enables a space for potential investigation, for issues to be addressed later on, for an afterlife. In reflecting upon their earlier work, artists often refer to them as non-perfect or unfinished, whilst explaining that it is precisely 'that' that enabled them to continue producing works of art. Imperfection establishes precisely an afterlife of a work. It is the afterlife of *Gender Trouble* that *Judith Butler: Ethics, Law, Politics* is concerned with. As explained below, I take this book as a point of departure. I bring together Butler's subsequent work with contemporary critical non-legal thought in order to think and imagine how her work and the questions she raises concerning life relate to those of critical legal studies.

Judith Butler: Ethics, Law, Politics acknowledges the potency and influence of Butler's 'concept' of gender as process but instead of focusing on this, a well-developed, analysed and discussed position (see Chapter 6), it utilises the practice-based analysis of subject formation that she so incisively produced to excavate a different set of themes that are central to her work but have been less emphasised.

So what are these themes? The themes explicated in this book relate to Butler's conceptual understanding of ethics, law, and politics and their interrelation. The book traces how she comes to these concepts. Her inquiry into these concepts is threaded together by one question: 'How can we have more livable and viable lives?' The question is neither rhetorical nor normative. She does not raise this question for mere reasons of effect, nor does she ask it in order to provide us with an answer to it. Instead I suggest that her work reflects upon the agonistic relation between these concepts in their articulation not only of life.

Each of these expressions of life – ethical, legal, political – emphasises particular practices and expresses different aspects or ways of life. If, for example, we focus on ethics and not moral philosophy, or, as I explain in Chapter 3, on ethical theories deriving from the work of the philosopher Levinas, we could say that the question of life is addressed in relation to our response to the Other who asks for our help. It necessitates an impulsive reaction, one that takes place before any subjective considerations kick in either to stop me from responding or to respond because of them. Ethics, or a response to a life in need, requires within this scope of thought a practice of responsibility prior to any egoistic considerations. One could even say that the parameters of an ethical and viable life have to be considered within this proposition. The legal approach to the question of life will focus on the practices of judgment and decision. An understanding of life here is one that is legitimised via the authority of law, which is 'grounded' or represents itself as 'grounded' on rational and legitimate rules. As individuals, we ought to follow the law and any infringement of the law is seen as a violation of the expression of life that law represents, and at the same time an error of judgment. Law, in such cases, interferes to correct this, to offer a judgment on the error, via either punitive or private sanctions. We could say that it intervenes to readjust the imbalance that was created in the spectrum of life, or the image of a happy life that it represents.

But, as is clear from the above, these two conceptual accounts of life express diametrically opposing views. An ethical life necessitates that we strip ourselves of any presupposed knowledge and act spontaneously towards the call for assistance, while the life that law accounts for is somehow a calculative life, a life that could only be sustained through a calculative response: a response that above all else requires a knowledge and reflection upon the law. Put differently, one expression of life puts at its centre, or envisages the subject of life, a spontaneous pre-reflective subject (ethical subject) and the other the precise opposite (legal subject). The asymmetry of their account of life, or their aspirations for life (and inevitably our involvement in this process), creates an antagonism, a warring between these spheres of life. As I explain here, Butler does not merely represent this state of affairs. In addition, she alerts us to the problems we encounter, when one of these accounts, or competing expressions of life, totalise all the others. When, for example, the only account of life becomes that of law, then life itself is threatened, in the sense that what is squeezed out on such occasions is the very possibility of any dissenting account of life. Literally, no space is left for any form of dissent. In such a situation, the possibility of raising the question 'How can we have more livable and viable lives?' becomes difficult, if not impossible. Butler entices us into a reading of these different spheres or expressions of life, thus enabling us to foresee the conditions that allow one sphere of life to become totalising and at the same time signposts a way through which we can approach its undoing. In providing a convincing understanding of the relationship between these different spheres of life, she helps us to see that the answer to the question of a better life, a burning question in both of these spheres, lies specifically in recognising that their fight for autonomy, for becoming independent and totalising 'regulators' of life, will lead ultimately to their destruction and the destruction of life itself. Their survival requires sustaining their antagonism, their productive fight, and recognising that they are dependent on each other, for they both have as their goal survival and the creation of the conditions for a better life.

Throughout this book, this reading of her work is viewed through Butler's use of performative theory and Hegel's theory of recognition. In addressing the question of life, I propose that we read Butler through these two theoretical perspectives. It is her synthesis of these two theories that provides us with a fresh understanding of how we can begin to untangle this poignant yet enormous question. There are of course other theories and theorists appearing in her work. Butler talks to and with psychoanalytic theory; she engages with Foucault. But I contend that if we are to understand how these themes emerge in her work and how we can begin to account for the question of life, we are better off consulting her attachment to performative theory and Hegel. This combination allows us to understand how we might avoid suggesting that one of these expressions of life can provide us with a better answer to the question of life than another.

Life and the creation of better conditions for our survival, but also our recognition as intelligible subjects, is, as I already stipulated, the link between the themes that I introduced above. These themes also brought me to Butler as a critical legal theorist. Though of interest to a wider audience than the relatively small group of critical legal theorists, it is these themes that critical legal scholarship in the United Kingdom has engaged with. Students, researchers and academics who work in the field of critical theory have indeed been dealing with such topics, but I have to say that, despite the fact that my own writing, readings and influences take me outside critical legal theory, I wrote this book from the 'grounds' of my own disciplinary genealogy. Writing this book required at least two reading practices, namely those of interpretation and translation, if I was to transmit how Butler's ideas could contribute to the critical legal project. Below, I explain how these two practices have enabled the book and its writing.

As lawyers, academic and otherwise, we are more familiar with the first type of practice. Interpreting statutes and case law is our bread and butter. This is not to say that interpretation is a reading skill unique to lawyers. Interpretation is a skill exercised to read philosophical, legal, literary and religious texts. Interpretation deals with meaning. There are of course a variety of theories of interpretation but we may understand it as a practice that attempts to excavate either the intention of the author – the tradition that sixteenth- and seventeenth-century lawyers were trained in (Goodrich, 1986) – or to bring to the text a question that will address the text's answer to a question, but will, at the same time, provide a different meaning to the one intended by the author, a meaning that is the outcome of our (the readers) own cultural and historical concerns. This latter position (namely of privileging the meanings that may emanate from a text rather than actual authorial intention) as the aim of interpretation was, as is well known, put forward by Gadamer in his book *Truth and Method* (1975). The former aims at excavating the truth of the text that is sealed by the author's intention and, simultaneously, sees the practice of translation as an excavation of the past of a text. The second theory provides us with a link between the past and the present. Producing an understanding of a text is a productive enterprise; the reader brings to it their own concerns through which different meanings will emerge. In doing so, the past is linked to the present. Nevertheless, Gadamer maintains that our understanding of a text is not arbitrary. Rather, it is guided by tradition. As he explains, our reading is derived from the tradition to which the text belongs and to which we also belong. For the first theory, there is one possible truth that can be found if we unveil the intention of the author. For the second, meaning is unified by tradition and consequentially truth becomes the truth of a tradition. Gadamer never questions the possibility of the existence of more than one tradition, or more than one possibility of understanding the connection between past, text and present. In doing so, as Goodrich writes, past texts 'are treated as models of exemplary, classical existence which the interpreters of the tradition would have us, the readers, follow. Second is the assumption that tradition and the texts in which it is contained bear a "true" meaning which is their original meaning'(Goodrich, 1986: 133).

I thought that writing about the work of a critical theorist such as Judith Butler would entail a fair amount of interpretation. Her work is authoritative. It is well cited across disciplines, such as cultural studies, sociology, gender studies, film studies, legal studies, philosophy, political science, to name but a few and across the globe. And all this despite the fact that she writes from the standpoint of philosophy. I say 'despite' because it is more common for scholars to be cited or utilised within their own discipline. Or, more precisely, she writes within the American academy but within the tradition of continental philosophy, engaging in immanent critique (Butler, 1999a: vii). In considering the second assumption that Goodrich relates to the practice of interpretation, the search for truth either to be found in authorial intention or within the tradition, I ran into turbulent waters. How could I seek the hidden 'truth' in her texts if I, as a reader, was not a philosopher? My tradition, if I can call it that, is that of critical legal scholarship. Wouldn't this inhibit me from providing an accurate interpretation of her texts? Then, another concern arose. How could I unveil a hidden 'truth' from a theorist who engages with a type of theory that demystifies truth? Who traverses Austin's and Derrida's theories of performativity and citationality to argue with them but differently, that language does not report things or statements that are verifiable. If all language is performative, as Butler would like us to believe, then it goes against the spirit of her work even to consider the possibility of unveiling the truth of her texts. It would have been violent to do so. After all, as a lawyer trained in critical legal theory and engaged with deconstruction, I knew in advance that to interpret the 'hidden' truth of a text *was* impossible. A text does not hold one 'hidden' truth: it does not hold truth *per se*. Deconstruction, if it is considered to be an interpretive practice, shows that it is impossible to lay claim to a total meaning, as the universals of truth and law have been abandoned (Douzinas et al., 1991: 29–51). So if I was to interpret her texts, I would have to engage with a practice of reading that, instead of looking for the 'truth' of the text, would look for the effects that the texts were producing, the effects of performative language.

And this is what I seek to do here. I read *Gender Trouble* (1990; 1999a), *Bodies that Matter* (1993), *Excitable Speech* (1997b), *The Psychic Life of Power* (1997a), *Subjects of Desire* (1999b), *Antigone's Claim* (2000a), *Giving an Account of Oneself* (2003), *Precarious Life* (2004a), *Undoing Gender* (2004b) and a number of other essays and interviews that she has produced, with the aim of analysing their effects. It is well known that Butler has exerted and still exerts a tremendous influence on the terrain of conceptualising gender and sexuality. Her theory of gender performativity, as I have already mentioned, has enabled us to understand not only that gender is a process which unveils the foreclosure of passionate homosexual attachment, but also that political resistance emerges at moments of this exposition. Other effects become visible through this. These effects relate to our ethical, legal and political understandings of the world. They permeate our accounts of ourselves and communicate the impossibility of talking about gender and sexuality, and, moreover, the subject (which is after all what Butler's has revealed through the microscope of critique) without considering how ethics, law and politics relate to each other and to these concerns. It is precisely these effects that I proceed to talk about in the book.

But the practice of interpretation, even in the form of deconstruction, exposes the effects of texts and their limits, but...it is difficult to express clearly the hesitation that the 'but' above tries to infer. This 'but' relates to the connection that the book exposes between critical theory engaging with different forms of critique (emanating from various receptions of philosophy, political theory, gender theory and sexuality, cultural studies and sociology) and the work of Butler. This exposition could not have happened merely by using deconstruction, if we stick to an understanding of deconstruction as an interpretive practice. In order to relate her work to the wider themes and concerns of critical theory, critical legal studies being one amongst many others (concerns with ethics, law and politics), I had to engage with another practice or reading, which might sound very similar to that of interpretation, but nevertheless carries its own characteristics. I had to engage with the practice of translation.

Benjamin writes that 'a translation issues from the original – not so much from its life as from its after life' (1979: 71). Benjamin's essay 'The task of the translation', offers a very cryptic meditation on the mode of translation. The essay relates specifically to the bourgeoning business at the start of the twentieth century of translating classical texts, Greek and Latin, into German. It deals with what takes place when a foreign language is translated into an indigenous tongue. But, simultaneously, as I want to suggest, it provides a possible way of understanding the process of writing, in my case a book about the ideas of a philosopher and their relation or connection to critical legal studies. What takes place on this occasion is not a transmission of information – not a mere transmission of Butler's ideas on ethics, law and politics to my indigenous language, that of critical legal studies – but something different. What I seek to do is to provide an 'afterlife' for Butler's work and ideas. Translation, Benjamin suggests, does not concern itself with the original, though it arises from it, but rather it focuses upon the life that it takes on afterwards, in being put into a language that is foreign to it. And in doing so the translator is not looking for authorial intent but for something else. Benjamin writes that '[t]he task of the translator consists in finding that intended effect [intention] upon the language into which he is translating it in the echo of the original' (1979: 76–77). What is paramount in translating, therefore, is not to reproduce in the indigenous language (here the language of critical legal studies) a literal original (1979: 69), nor to simulate the poetics of the original (1979: 69–70), but rather to echo the original: to echo, to repeat in a quiet manner, the sound of the original, in the indigenous language, and the 'afterlife' of the text or texts. To understand this even better, let us look at the mythological story of Echo.

Echo, in Greek mythology, was the mountain nymph whom Zeus ordered to distract his wife Hera from spying upon him by insistently talking to her. When Hera realised his deceitful plan, she punished Echo. She robbed Echo of the power to speak complete words, allowing her only to be able to repeat the last syllable of every word she heard. Benjamin's essay allows us to comprehend translation in its mythical dimension. When Echo repeats the last syllable of every word that she hears she produces the 'afterlife' of a word. 'Translation' Benjamin writes, 'serves the purpose of expressing the central reciprocal relationship between languages' (1979: 72). Echoing the original in the indigenous language of the translator expresses the reciprocal relationship between the philosophy of Butler and critical legal studies. It is in the echo that the original sustains itself and continues its existence (1979: 71).

Benjamin clarifies this point when he considers the intention of a language and the intended object. The intended object in different languages, as Benjamin points out, is the same. So when in German the word *brot* is used and in French the word *pain*, the intended object, bread, is the same. But the mode of intention is totally different in both languages. The way they are used means different things in the two languages he exemplifies to describe this distinction. But as he points out:

> While the modes of intention in these two words are in conflict, intention and object of intention complement each of these two languages from which they are derived; there the object is complementary to the intention. In the individual, unsupplemented languages, meaning is never found in relative independence, as in individual words or sentences; rather, it is in a constant state of flux – until it is able to emerge as pure language from the harmony of all the various modes of intention. Until then, it remains hidden in the languages. If, however, these languages continue to grow in this manner until the end of their time, it is translation which catches fire on the eternal life of the works and the perpetual renewal of language.
>
> (Benjamin, 1979: 74)

We see that while the mode of intention is in conflict from one language to another, the object of intention nevertheless remains the same. Languages, we could say, echo to each other this precise impossibility, of one language being complete, or pure on its own. The original language may need the translated language to signify this. The translation signifies the foreignness of languages (1979: 75) in pointing to the incompleteness of each language that can only be achieved through bringing together all the echoes of foreignness, all the fragments that will enable the translation to be produced. In my own case, in translating Butler's work to the language that I call critical legal studies, I only aim to expose productively the foreignness of these two languages. 'It is the task of the translator', Benjamin writes towards the end of his essay, 'to release in his own language that pure language which is unclear under the spell of another, to liberate the language imprisoned in a work in his recreation of that work' (1979: 80). But this is not the only task, '[h]e must expand and deepen his language by means of the foreign language' (1979: 81). And all this must take place knowing that a translation is midway between poetry and doctrine (1979: 77).

In translating Butler's work, in putting it into themes that have preoccupied the critical legal studies movement in the United Kingdom since the early 1980s, I heard her as a critical legal scholar, an echo trapped in the usual interpretations of her work within the academy. Butler sounded not just as a theorist of gender and sexuality but something more. Her writing became, in my reading and writing, a critique of law, a critique of its production of subjectivity, of its re-evaluations of theories of ethics, and of the potential for a politics without law, a lawless politics.

In the sound of the question that I mentioned at the start of this introduction, 'How can we have more livable and viable lives?', I heard a way of revitalising the rich repertoire of critical legal studies. The question opened up, for me at least, new possibilities of understanding the ways in which law, politics and ethics operate with and against each other. For years, the movement has engaged with a critique of law, pointing out that the evaluations it produces and its representation of life and subjects tend to objectify them. Questions of ethics, politics and aesthetics are overseen, only to re-emerge via the interpretive practice of deconstruction from their repressed positions as the Other of law. Butler's question and work enable us to understand and see that these Others are by no means victims of the legal hegemony, are not subjugated to law, but are, rather, competing with law over the question of life. The ethical, political and legal subjects, and their prospective expressions of life, live or are animated or even gain their vitality precisely by retaining an agonistic relationship with each other. And it is this continuous agonism that caters for the survival of life *per se*. I explained what I meant by this at the start of this introduction, but I will explain it further below by focusing on the way in which the subject comes to be who he or she is.

Butler, throughout her work, talks about how subjects gain their agency and by this I understand her to mean the ways in which subjects become intelligible. Subjects become who they are through a long process by which they resist a variety of pre-existing knowledges and norms. This process begins at the moment we are called a name, when, for example, one is called a girl along with what this presupposes. These presuppositions, as she explains, are not grounded in anything but the utterance itself. But, throughout one's life, one challenges through various practices the meaning that the name 'girl' brings with it. These challenges do not merely resist a name, but also resist the presupposed dimensions of life that are expressed in the ethical, political and legal domain (amongst others, for example, economic, medical, etc.). We come to be the subjects that we are, we come to have an intelligible life, a life that makes sense to us and to our world, by resisting these expressions, or at least the significations and existential manuals that they provide. We become a girl in our terms, by resisting what it means to be a girl, for example, within the ethical, legal and political expressions of life. But this is not possible if one of these expressions of life totalises the other. When this happens our life is also threatened, or, more precisely, our ability to make our life intelligible is threatened. But, it is necessary to issue a warning here.

Butler is able to describe all this because she puts bodies at the centre of her analysis. It is bodies and the way they engage with the world, through practices, that enable us to see how subjects become agentic. And, since the body lives in at least two temporalities, a synchronic and a diachronic one, this process of becoming intelligible to ourselves and the world (as our resistance is responsive to the world) is very much an ongoing process. So ethical, political and aesthetic expressions of life, amongst others, are not the Other of law. To call them Others of law smothers them with the language of representation, which makes law the point of reference. The production of a critique of law based on this axiom ignores that the aforementioned expressions of life are not subjugated to law, but rather are competing with law. If we hear them as competing expressions of life, then law becomes immediately one amongst many such expressions and not the referent point. How can we have more livable and viable lives? A better life! This became the marker that enabled me to deepen the language by which critical legal studies in the United Kingdom travelled and still travels. But, in doing so I also hope that I have unleashed Butler, the critical legal scholar.

This book is organised in five interlinked chapters, each dealing with the ways in which we can come to understand how – the how of having a better life. As the whole aim was to bring Butler to critical legal studies and critical legal studies to Butler, each chapter does not confine itself to Butler's work, but also draws on other critical expressions that have an influence on her thinking and that of critical legal studies.

'Gender Performativity *as* Method', the second chapter, while tracing the genealogy of performativity – from Austin to Derrida to Butler – explains how the question of livability and viability for Butler is a question addressed through language. One comes into being through and by language. When one is being named, a performative speech act, one that cannot be verified as to its truthfulness or correctness, one registers his or her existence. While our survival depends on being named, whether this naming is injurious or not, Butler proposes our becoming agentic subjects, subjects that depend on the injurious naming but are more than that, relies on our resistance to this naming, in answering back to the question of 'Who are you?' The chapter explores this proposition by analysing and comparing her understanding of the performative in gender formation and injurious speech acts. Her unique method of analysis enables us to see, as I demonstrate, how subjects are both the products and the producers of existence.

For Butler, ethical life is not synonymous with a code of moral practices. Nor is it contained within the private sphere, as philosophers such as Hegel would have it. Her ethics unveil that at the centre of the question of how we can have a livable and viable life lies an inextricably connected agonism between politics and ethics. Philosophy tried to exclude the question of politics from the sphere of ethics. Nevertheless, this exclusion returns to haunt philosophy. Butler reveals the exclusive inclusion of politics to ethics and suggests that, in working within the parameters of this tension, we could begin to see the potentiality of human life. 'Ethical sisters', the third chapter of the book, deals with Butler's traversing of Hegel's concept of recognition. In doing so, she points out that at the moment we do not recognise ourselves in relation to our social and cultural norms (when, for example, one does not recognise himself as man or a woman in the way that we signify such markers) what is unveiled is that it is not we who constitute ourselves but rather our formation as subjects is dependent upon social and cultural norms. As a consequence, this challenges the more orthodox philosophical belief that the subject is the ground for ethics, the ground upon which either 'I' gives an account of its self or, deliberates or acts responsibly. On the contrary, this exposes that the subject is a problem for ethics: it troubles the way in which we understand any account of ourselves, deliberation and action. This troubling enables us though to inquire into how we come to form ourselves and how we act. It explains that a certain unknownness or failure of recognition is constitutive of us. Butler does not use this to offer an ethical code for action. Instead, as I explain, she explicates that the subject is never an 'I', relies on being addressed for its survival, and on precisely not knowing the shape and form which this address may take.

'Double law', the fourth chapter, engages with the two modes of power found in Butler's work: sovereign-governmentality and disciplinary power. Law is not portrayed as a category that exists in itself but, rather, our understanding of it comes through its relation to various modalities of power and the practices of such modalities. She suggests, by following Foucault, that disciplinary power is productive and vital in sustaining and revitalising life. On the other hand, sovereign-governmental power – as I explain by contrasting her understanding of this modality of power in 'Indefinite detention' (2004a) with that of Agamben – has the opposite effect on life and populations. Simply put, it hinders life's survival. This form of power instrumentalises law. It uses law to sustain the survival of the state and the sovereign with consequential effects on the lives of those that the state deems unintelligible. To avoid this dead end, she calls for a rethinking of the place of law when it falls into the hands of a status quo or state that totalises its uses. I indicate that, in such situations, if law is to sustain life, or at least produce the conditions for our survival, it might need to take a different role than the one it currently holds. It might indeed need to take up the task of the translator.

Butler's politics and understanding of 'the political' are expressed through her articulation of the body. As I explain in Chapter 5, Butler's embodied subject is the producer of the political. The body in its material and figural existence is not only rational but also affective. In coming into being, a body is enabled by norms, whether linguistic or otherwise, but its resistance to these norms, to the ought of how we can live our lives, allows different lives both to live and expose their intelligibility. Resistance enables the undoing of the very universality of norms and exposes the very possibilities that lives have. Her polis, if it is a polis at all, brings together the loci of the public and the private. In doing so, her polis and its political concerns open up a wider horizon, showing us the various dimensions in which bodies become politically intelligible and producers of life.

Chapter 6, 'Butler's reception', indexes the effects that her work has had on the wider disciplinary spectrum. In particular, it focuses on the hostile critique that her work received in Nussbaum's review in *The New Republic* (2000). I explain how this hostility stems from Nussbaum's attachment to law, her faith in this institution and her belief that law is the only expression of life that can enable the 'victim' to exit from its victim status. In exploiting this position, I argue that even critical legal scholarship at times hooks on to the figure of the victim to make claims about the nature of the law. I suggest that Butler's agentic subject deflects this position and offers us a potent understanding of how we account for our desire for a better life, without holding on to the figure of the victim to do this work for us.

These five chapters address some of the limits of critical legal scholarship. The question of life and its various expressions has not yet seen a sustained engagement: a simultaneous engagement with all these three dimensions of life (ethical, legal, political) that I explore here via Butler's work. This book, this translation, is meant to be a contribution towards such a journey.

Notes

1 http://www.theory.org.uk/ctr-butl.htm

2 In the Anniversary edition of *Gender Trouble* Butler tells how the book had prompted the American Psychoanalytic Association to 'to reassess some of their current doxa on homosexuality' (xvii). In addition due to the book and her subsequent work Butler was called to serve on the International Gay and Lesbian Commission from 1994–97. We are also told that her work bears influence in the visual arts. In respect to this Butler cites exhibitions that took place at the Whitney museum and the Otis School of Arts in Los Angeles (1999a: xvii).

3 The most notable women thinkers in this movement which is more generally described as 'French', Luce Irigaray, Julia Kristeva and Helene Cixous, had chosen France as their adopted country. Irigaray is Belgian, Kristeva is Bulgarian and Cixous Algerian.

Chapter 2

Gender performativity *as* method

> ...or Foucault, as for Nietzsche, cultural values emerge as the result of an inscription on the body, understood as a medium, indeed, a blank page; in order for this inscription to signify, however, that medium must itself be destroyed – that is, fully transvaluated into a sublimated domain of values. Within the metaphorics of this notion of cultural values is the figure of history, as a relentless writing instrument, and the body as the medium which must be destroyed and transfigured in order for 'culture' to emerge.
>
> (Butler, 1990: 130)

' "Speech," she said. "It is the gift of creation. For God created the world from speech and our speech too is the power to create" ' (Alderman, 2006: 246). These are the words Esti utters in a popular Orthodox Jewish Synagogue in Hendon, London. The community had gathered to commemorate the life of a distinguished rabbi, Rav Krushka. Esti, the wife of Dovid the succeeding rabbi, addresses the congregation on that day in place of her husband. Her measured, passionate and poignant speech unveils how silence congeals the community as it simultaneously undoes its foundations. When Esti was 15, she approached Rav Krushka to ask him whether having sexual fantasies about other girls was sinful. He pointed out that the Torah distinguishes between having a fantasy and acting it out: if one was to retain such desires in the realm of private fantasy, it was not sinful. However Esti had fallen for her best friend Ronit, who happened to be the Rav's daughter. And they did act out their desires.

Esti is the fictional character of Alderman's award-winning novel *Disobedience* (2006). At the congregation Esti is prompted to her speech by the gossip within the community regarding her desire for Ronit. The latter had immigrated to New York, marking her distance from her childhood in suburban Hendon. She is now a well-paid financial analyst, a lesbian who also has an on-off relationship with a married man who is her boss, dresses fashionably, smokes and, like most New Yorkers, has her own psychoanalyst. Ronit returns to Hendon to attend her father's funeral. Her visit stirs trouble, re-igniting Esti's desire for her to the extent that Esti clumsily kisses her in public. Witnessed by some community members, this starts disapproving murmurs. Esti's speech directly addresses the question of silence and the community's condemnation of her desire for women. It honours the Rav's final sermon which emphasised the world-creating power of speech and the role that people play in perpetuating this (2006: 244). In thinking critically about this, Esti points to a paradox within Judaic thought. If speech has the capacity to create worlds, to be constructive, then how come that one has to, as she was advised by the Rav, remain silent about her desire for women? And if speech is constructively creative, what are the effects of silence? Esti reflects saliently upon the effects of silence regarding this issue. She concludes that silence inflames poisonous murmurs, which in turn endorse the destruction of life, community and values. She concludes that it is not her desire for women that would jeopardise her faith and her survival in the community and consequentially the community's survival, but rather silence: 'I have desired that which is forbidden to me. I continue to desire it. I obey the Commandments. It is possible . . . as long as I do not have to do it in silence' (2006: 246).

Esti rewrites her own history through speech. In publicising her own desire for women, she minutely shifts the cultural norms of her Hendon Orthodox Jewish Community. The unorthodoxy of her act, taking the stage, making a speech, talking about desires that are better not addressed, alters the space at least momentarily: it induces it to confront silence, destructive of life if it is never being uttered, venomous if it takes the form of gossip, but above all non-conducive to constituting a community. In other words, her speech is a performative act in the sense that Butler understands it, which will be explained later. As a gender perfomative, it unveils that what is disavowed from the normative practices of the community, from its cultural constitution, is homosexuality. Simultaneously it exposes that homosexuality is at the heart of this constitution. As clear from Esti's speech, such acts do not transform the socio-symbolic sphere. Esti after all ends her talk by adhering to her beliefs, to her attachment to the Commandments, to the Torah and Judaism. Yet what is achieved, is the exposure of fantasies upon which communities and their cultures are built. Still, by addressing the murmurs of silence she transforms from this silent, shy person into a subject with agency. At the end of the novel, readers find out that Esti's speech has altered the numbers of believers attending that particular synagogue: they dropped drastically, although some remained and the synagogue continued to exist. More importantly Esti and her husband, the new rabbi, renew their lives in the community. Those remaining loyal to their congregation respect and support them. Their lives were revitalised. The community has sustained its normative values and itself.

Esti is a fictional character in a novel. Her speech is fictional. But her speech is effective despite its fictitious nature. The philosopher Austin (1962) was the first to bring to our attention that language is not only constantive but also adheres to the truth of statements. He introduced the concept of the performative: statements 'do what they say' without any need to be verified as to their correctness or truth. Even when assuming that Esti's speech is real (fictitious speech outright exclude us from considering it as performatitive within Austin's framework), it would still not fulfil some of the other six conditions that Austin provides for identifying performative statements, discussed in detail later, for example, his first two conditions (A.1 and A.2) where they postulate that a performative to be successful, needs to take place within the parameters of a conventional procedure and the person uttering has to be authorised to do so. Within Austin's framework, Esti's speech can't be considered as being performative. The procedure in which it took place was not conventional. The convention obliged the succeeding rabbi to make a speech in honour of his predecessor. In addition she was not authorised to address the congregation. Her speech had an effect nevertheless. The speech was to honour the rabbi. During her speech she repeatedly blesses the memory of the Rav and the public responds by echoing her blessing, a sign of the effect of the speech. So if her speech does not fulfil Austin's conditions, how can it still be considered as performative?

Derrida also addresses performative speech act theory, in which he focuses on precisely on what Austin deems a failed or infelicitous performative (Derrida, 2000). Derrida articulates that failure is structural to the performative. In excluding, for example, Esti's speech from being a performative, or considering it as a failed performative, Austin is able to define the pure performative. Derrida takes this a step further and points out that the infelicitous performative has citational effects: it recites the code but with *difference* (in difference and by differing). In this light, Esti's speech could be understood as being citational but *not* performative. In other words, it is able to differentiate itself from the norm (or the 'code' as Derrida refers to it) by citing it, *but* the speech act's effect is postponed. While the first mutation of *difference* could be easily identified in relation to our example from the novel, because Esti's speech cites the convention (giving a speech in honour of a beloved and dead rabbi), it differentiates itself from that by not being a rabbi. The second condition is more difficult to fathom. How can we explain that the congregation joined Esti in rejoicing the life of the rabbi? How can we explain that despite the fact that a large number of the synagogue members left, a good number stayed or that Esti continued to give occasional speeches at the synagogue?

Butler argues that if we take on board Derrida's critique of Austin's performative theory, our critique will remain at a structural level and fail to explain how subjects that are not authorised to speak by convention or norms, speak, gain agency and have effect (Butler, 1997b: 148). To put it differently, Derrida does not account for the bodies that *do* the speaking. He fails to provide a genealogy of the subjects that speak, the cultural norms that they inhabit and moreover the effects that such acts have on subjects. Esti had an orthodox Jewish upbringing that told her that she had to retain a silence regarding her love for other women. This silence condemned her to a melancholic and hermetic existence. Her speech in the synagogue shifted her life. She did not suddenly become an extrovert, non-Orthodox Jewish wife, but she was able to find a voice, one which at least some members of the community respected. Derrida fails to capture how such subjects find a way to break with the past or as, Butler put it, how they 'found[s] a future through a break with that past' (1997b: 159). Similarly the cultural norms of the community did not alter, indicated by the decrease in synagogue membership. Nevertheless in exposing the fantasmatic foundations of the community (that what is disavowed, the silence about private prohibited desires that are constitutive of the norm), it creates a future for some lives who have been disavowed, or reduced to silence, allegorised by Esti. In contrast to Derrida, Butler's point is that the infelicitous or inexplicit performative is embodied and its utterance is effective. What it exposes and resists might not shatter the whole socio-symbolic but it creates the possibility for more livable lives. As I explain in some detail below, Butler's notion of the performative and her articulation of its relation to the subject additionally unveils a challenging understanding of subject formation.

Butler's concept of performativity also pays attention to historical and social contexts. Performative speech acts expose that the past is constitutive of the present, and simultaneously that the past is not determinant of the present or the future. Bodies are integral in producing a break through the past, of producing a different genealogy and animating possibilities for the future. As performativity can be seen as a way of 'writing' history, this chapter will briefly describe some prominent historiography schools, thus also enabling a comparison. One of the differences between, say, the Annales school and a performative reading of the past lies in the way in which language figures in their analysis. The former considers language as a mere medium through which the past is transmitted. Performative speech acts, on the other hand, account for the active role played by both language and bodies in reconstructing the past and refiguring the future. Paying some attention to these differences allows an understanding of the differences between Butler's performative theory and those of Austin and Derrida, as well as an insight into the political significance of Butler's centralisation of the body and speech in her work. By putting bodies at the centre of analysis, she introduces a genealogical reading of culture, one that is able to succinctly unveil the fantasy of the norm, which is undoubtedly politically significant. To illustrate by returning once more to the novel and Esti's occasional speeches at the synagogue, in the reply to the murmurs regarding herself and Ronit, and the recognition of speech or language as a world-creating technology, Esti projects a different understanding of the function and formation of her community's cultural norms. And in doing so, she somehow alters her future and that of her community.

This chapter proceeds by making a connection between historical narrative, language and bodies. In Chapter 5, I explain Butler's understanding of the relation between bodies and language in some detail, so it suffices for the moment to say that she poses them as mutually constitutive of each other. The next section is a reminder that history is mediated through language. Rankian's and Annaliste, the two historical schools that I use as examples, undermined this. They either pay no attention to the way the historical is transmitted in language (Rankians) or even if when they do, it is by defending the use of 'I' in the narrative accounts (Annaliste), but still only to praise the historical objectivity of narration. Either way, the effect is that the claim to objectivity and the unattentiveness to language neglects to observe that language in itself is sedimented in/by the past. Moreover an emphasis on events (Rankians) and structures (Annaliste) obscures the significance of bodies in the formation of the past. This particular section introduces Butler's account of the past via her understanding of the role of language and bodies in its formation. In being less concerned with representing the past in objective colours, she provides a critical account of how it shields its fantasmatic character and the possibilities that might be attained for the future through speech and bodies that resist its normative claims. An additional and more supplementary reason lead me to address historiography here. Derrida's account of the failed performative as citational operates at the same structural level as the analysis of the past offered by the Annaliste. Unlike them, of course, he does account for the effective nature of language but in par with them he fails to assess the body in this process, leaving his analysis partial. To once more draw from *Disobedience*, Derrida draws on Esti's speech and forgets all about the woman embodying this speech. In order to engage with the various theories of the performative, thus, the chapter first needs to touch the topic of historiography.

Historiography, language and bodies

The earliest school of historiography, associated with its founder Leopold von Ranke, wrote about the past through the reconstruction of political history (events such as wars and revolutions and rulers). Consequently, their depictions ignored the role of social and economic factors in events and periods analysed. Their accounts of the past carried another important feature. The narratives left behind the use of 'I' and the use of affective language. Despite acknowledging that any historical writing would be by necessity a reproduction (depending always on what sources or records are available), their detached style of writing, aspired to produce a 'scientific' and 'objective' account of the past. So Rankians would have discarded the story of Esti (if she was a real person that lived in a particular time) from their representation of history from the start. But, as we have seen, her story tells us a lot about the rearrangement of the community and, her own life, as well the centrality of normative frameworks (symbolised by Judaism) in the formation of the present. If an occasion could be didactic and informative of the past, why should it be omitted from historical narratives?

This was partially rectified in the 1920s by the Annales school of history. This school, French in origin, included socio-economic, cultural and geographical factors in its account of the past and its effects on the present, and was critical of the presentation of history through grand political events (e.g. wars), people (e.g. kings) and short chronological periods. Its two founders, Bloch and Fevbre, emphasised that events should not be explained through their relationships to the past, but rather in relation to the moment of their emergence. Consequently these scholars looked at the role of structures (political, economic, geographical, cultural and social) in the transformation of the world and conducted analysis of historical facts over long periods. Like the Rankians, they paid little attention to the poetics of their language and epistemology of their discipline (Carrard, 1995: 111). Moreover, as Carrard suggests, even when they made statements relating to the role of the historian in historical writing, they retained an unquestioning assumption of objectivity (1995: 111). Despite their quest for objectivity, they distinguished themselves from the Rankians by explicitly using the 'I' in historical accounts. But still, as Bloch ensures us, this is not as obstacle to objectivity (1976: 138). The issue for Bloch is not the 'I' but rather the depiction of the past with impartiality and integrity. The process of historical analysis should be guided by resemblances or points of similarity, which enable historical categorisation and later on, in the midst of the emergence of 'new' material facts, the remaking of preliminary categorisations (1976: 143–156). Drawing a parallel to the novel, we can see that the Annaliste might be able to contain the structural information that Esti's story conveys. For instance, her speech act which challenges religious and cultural norms can be understood as a moment in history in which a new era emerges. If this was not to be deemed possible Esti's story would remain untold, an insignificant anomaly. But if it is deemed significant, the facts will be abstracted from Esti's body for the benefit of long history in which her body will become absent.

Returning then to the two historiographical schools, irrespective of their specific differences, we can still observe that their understanding of the representation of the past is based on a series of suppositions. First, such writing engages with the representation of the big picture of the past, a macro history as opposed to a micro one. Second, the relationship of events or structures with the past–present assumes a linear form (cause–effects), especially in the case of the Rankian historians. In the case of the Annalistes, this takes the shape of that of resemblance, as it is the resemblance between facts and events that allows the Annalistes to categorise their raw material.[1] In both schools of thought, there is no recognition of the writing/reconstruction of the past shaped through the inversion of cause and effect, in the case of the Rankians, or through asymmetry, in the case of the Annalistes. Third, language is the neutral medium through which the past is being both transmitted and analysed and this leads to, fourth, a scientific representation of the past. Finally, individuals are mere instruments of political events or structural indexes.

These historiographies embroider past and possible effects on the present with analyses and representations of detailed grand political events, geographical influences and cultural transformations but their embroidery is impoverished even, dare we say, *never* really made, as they neglect to bring to the textile the thread, the medium through which they will represent the past and present, namely language. Even if, for the Annalistes, language plays a significant role in the analysis of history, they remain silent as to the ways in which they utilise it and the way it affects their writing. Language is *never* considered as a highly valorised tool of writing.

In this line of thought, historians promote a representation of the past, and effectively an understanding of the present that is schematic, bereft literally and figuratively speaking of flesh and bones; *bodies*. Whether we talk about them figuratively (as representations in language) or literally (as materiality), bodies have voices, experience the past through the present and tend to forget or remember differently, reminding us through this process that claims to truth should always be considered as temporal stories that could always be retold and rewritten. Bodies, in other words, reverse the suppositions that the aforementioned historiography schools make. Above all, bodies present us with the possibility of understanding the past and its effects on the present through their affects and intelligibilities as well as the ways in which the everyday lives of bodies are lived. Moreover, they remind us that our writing enterprise, whether it is one of history or, let us say, legal studies, always plays an active and creative role in the telling of stories. The above opens up the space for a micro-bio-history, one that takes the telling of the history of political events or socio-economic and other indexes (macro-structural-history), as permutations or variations on the way we understand our present–past relationships.

Butler situates bodies (both literally and figuratively) at the centre of her analysis. Bodies are for her *vehicles*, to the extent that they enable her to understand the past and present in a relationship between the local and the universal, the cultural and the genealogical. The past acts upon bodies and constitutes them as culturally intelligible materialities. At the same time though, bodies act out, resist the very ways in which the past 'inscribes' them, or in some instances 'inscribes' as culturally unintelligible, allowing the exposure of historical limitations along with their political effects.

Butler's understanding of history is influenced by the work of Foucault. In the 1970s, he focused on a genealogical approach to analysing the past. Genealogy, as he writes, 'must record the singularity of events outside of any monotonous finality' (1980: 139), and as this suggests, it requires a shift in the way one observes the past. Instead of reading the past as a continuing interplay between cause and effect or in terms of resemblance and progression, the past could be seen as a series of facts that do not relate to each other, that are discontinuous, localisable and averse to any analysis that seeks origins. To do so, genealogy must seek events 'in the most unpromising places, in what we tend to feel is without history – in sentiments, love, conscience, instincts' (1980: 139–140) and moreover 'it must be sensitive to their recurrence, not in order to trace the gradual curve of their evolution, but to isolate the different scenes where they engaged in different roles' (1980: 140). Foucault's three volumes on the history of sexuality engage precisely with this mode of historical inquiry. He puts the body at the centre of his analysis and demonstrates how the sexualised body is produced culturally through the various regulative constraints that surround it. In analysing, without reference to scientific truth, just through affective language and records, he locates the emergence and proliferation of bio-power, the power to make life, that is located both at an institutional and a personal realm.

As Davis and Schleifer observe, this mode of 'historical inquiry leads Foucault to make closer connections between the public and private spheres of culture' (1991: 207).

Butler, as we shall see throughout this book, takes on board Foucault's genealogical approach and uses it strategically to produce a critical account of the formation of gender subjectivity and more generally cultural subjectivity. Foucault's genealogical project has been subject to criticism. Spivak, in her essay 'Can the Subaltern speak?' (Spivak, 1988: 271–313), for example, argues that while his genealogical approach attends to the representation of bodies or events that have been obscured from historical writings, eliminating in this sense our understanding of historical formation, he fails to address his own position as the investigator of these debates, obfuscating his own ideological position (1988: 273). Butler, on the other hand, takes on board precisely this problematic. Her cultural undoing of the gendered body is, as she says, part of her wider political project of unveiling the ways in which certain sexualised subjects are not recognised as part of public life and, in doing so, to demonstrate not only that heteronormative culture produces such foreclosures is founded upon the fantasy of the norm, but moreover to gesture towards alternative understandings of public culture (see Butler, 1999a: vii–xxvi).

While the New Historicism also drew on the work of Foucault, at the same time, it introduced its own dimension into the study of history. Butler's genealogical approach to gender's cultural formation is linked to this movement. Greenblatt, who coined the term 'New Historicism', and introduced it in a special issue of the journal *Genre* in 1982 on Renaissance writing, explained it as a new way of understanding the sixteenth and seventeenth centuries. The articles in the special edition were preoccupied with rethinking the ways in which texts from that period were connected and situated within the wider context of discourses and practices of the time.

At the time, the most common reading of literary history viewed the literary text as a mirror of the times in which it was created. The literary text in other words had a mimetic relation to the world. This new mode of historical reading as Davis and Schleifer point out 'encourage[d] literary critics both to view history as a species of language and to look beyond formalist aesthetics... in order to read literature in the context of power relations and practice' (1991: 212). Effectively, this at-the-time-new branch of literary criticism introduced into its analysis an understanding of narrative history as being full of gaps and interruptions. History therefore becomes the study of ruptures and discontinuities that are traced at the limits of discourse and practices. Butler's reading of gender formation at the limits of discursive practices of 'sex' (Butler, 1993) follows this path of historical analysis and provides a cultural 'history' of gender.

As I suggest, in a rather schematic manner above, Butler's 'use' of the body provides us with a genealogical and cultural analysis that enables a different understanding of the past than the Rankian and Annales schools of historiography. Her distance from the New Historicists can be located partially in her method of analysis (gender performativity/performativity) and partially in her concerns (who matters in the world and how they matter). In both instances, the figurative and material body plays an important role. For the purposes of this chapter, I will focus upon her method of analysis and the ways in which it facilitates the genealogical understanding of culture.

Butler is a feminist philosopher. As is well known, feminist scholarship (Ahmed, 1998; Cornell, 1992) including feminist philosophy (Grosz, 1994; Irigaray, 1985) promoted the body *as* knowledge. Philosophy has traditionally and frequently concerned itself with the mind and qualities associated with it, such as reason, memory and consciousness. The body was not altogether disregarded by western philosophy but it was discarded as an unreliable source of knowledge formation. As a result, any qualities associated with the body, such as emotions and passions, were denigrated from the epistemic realm and linked with the natural world.

One of the most influential proponents of the mind/body split was the Swiss philosopher Descartes. Descartes was successful in convincing philosophy of the separation between mind and body and, moreover, of the separation of the soul from corporeality or more specifically nature (Grosz, 1994: 6). This philosophical schema of thought dominated, and to some extent still dominates, western philosophy. Cartesianism had inevitably negative effects on the concept of 'woman'. 'Woman' came to be associated with corporeality and nature and was thought to be important only in the procreation of humanity and impotent and unreliable in contributing to knowledge and truth formation. Feminist thought championed the body as a source of knowledge by affirming the value of affects. But it is important to note here that for Butler, the body as a source of knowledge comes both in the form of a figure (constituted in language) and materiality (literal) and for this reason it is both intelligible and affective. This diverts slightly from the affective strand of feminism (Irigaray, 1985). Nevertheless, it is within this framework and through this political realm that Butler utilises the body in her work.

I will consider in detail the way in which she produces the body in Chapter 5. Here, instead, I will focus on the way in which the body, and more precisely a bodily practice of *gender performativity*, becomes the way in which Butler explains our relationship to the world or, put another way, her explanation of how we connect to our past and how the past connects to us.

The section that follows gives a detailed explanation of her use and reception of the concept. It is worth noting at this early stage, however, that *performativity* is a practice of citationality by 'which discourse produces the effects it names' (Butler, 1993: 2). *Gender performativity* is also a practice of citationality, though this time discourse produces bodies 'as already sexed' (Ahmed, 1998: 113), that is as having a sex prior to naming. As you can see from the above, language, and more specifically a critical analysis of the way language operates is at the centre of Butler's method. The term *performativity* is a linguistic term that Butler takes from Austin (1962) and Derrida (1992a, 2000)[2] and adapts to gender, although

I hope to demonstrate by the end of this chapter that 'gender performativity' as a method could be used productively to analyse alternative issues to gender and more precisely that it relates to the more general idea of the subject and its formation. There is one other point that is worth noting at this stage; Butler manages through *gender performativity* to bring together the historical and the cultural. The third section of the chapter will explain how this succeeds.

Gender performativity and its genealogy

> I originally took my clue on how to read the performativity of gender from Jacques Derrida's reading of Kafka's 'Before the Law'. . . . In the first instance, then, the performativity of gender revolves around this metalepsis, the way in which the anticipation of a gendered essence produces that which posits an outside itself. Secondly, performativity is not a singular act, but a repetition and a ritual, which achieves its effects through its naturalization in the context of a body, understood, in part, as a culturally sustainable temporal duration.
>
> (Butler, 1999a: xiv–xv)

Judith Butler introduces the concept of *gender performativity* in her book *Gender Trouble* (1990). However, the most interesting manifestation and citation of this concept takes place in her subsequent books *Bodies that Matter* (1993) and *Excitable Speech* (1997b) (in this latter book she uses primarily her own concept of performativity as it emerges from gender performativity). Her concept of performativity in general – a radical variation, as I explain later, of Austin's theory of performativity – has been used by her to explain how gender is formed, how racist, sexist, hate speech operates and how institutions more generally exclude, torture and terrorise individuals and construct them as the enemy (2004a). I explain here her concept of *performativity* via Austin's *How to Do Things with Words* (1962), and Derrida's essay in *Limited Inc* (2000) 'Signature, even, context'. These two texts influenced Butler's understanding of the performative. I am drawing upon the genealogy of the method because it enables us to understand how her concepts of *gender performativity* in particular and *performativity* more generally were formed and developed. Methods, like ideas or people, have attachments to what went before them (past) but simultaneously they differ from what they left behind. As will become explicit, *gender performativity* and performativity as practices of citationality perform precisely this attachment and detachment with the past. Therefore, by tracking their pathway one is able to perform or execute the very method that one is describing.

How to Do Things with Words (1962) is the book version of the William James Lectures that Austin gave at Harvard in 1955. We are informed that the ideas he promotes in the book were formulated as early as 1939 and he made use of them in an article on ' "Other minds" published in the Proceedings of the Aristotelian Society, Supplementary Volume XX (1946), pages 173 ff.' (Austin, 1962: v). *How to Do Things with Words* (1962) addresses, as he says in 'Lecture I', a widespread phenomenon in language (one that had already come to the attention of grammarians and philosophers who had not become preoccupied with the difficulties that it raises) (1962: 1–2) namely, that not all statements are constative. In other words, not all describe or report things and so cannot be verifiable or falsified (1962: 4–5).

Since not all statements are constative, it follows that utterances must have the capability of being something else. Austin explains that utterances are performative, they indicate 'that the issuing of the utterance is the performing of the action' (1962: 6). Performative utterances don't describe things, they can't be verified as to their truth or falsity (though they can be void) but they simply do what they utter. Austin provides us with four examples of performative utterances, namely: 'I do', an utterance in a wedding ceremony, a confirmation from prospective spouses that they agree to marry each other; 'I name this ship the Queen Elizabeth'; ' I give and bequeath my watch to my brother'; 'I bet you sixpence it will rain tomorrow' (1962: 5). As we can see, his examples of performative utterances *do* what they *say*. If we look closer at the second example for illustrative purposes, we can clearly see that the utterance does what it says it, names the ship Queen Elizabeth. As Austin points out the intelligibility of an utterance does not rely primarily or solely on whether it is true or false. If we stay for a second with the above example and consider the possibility that we have not been authorised to name the ship, or if the name that was to be given was other than the one used, then the utterance will be effectively void but not false. We can therefore make sense of a sentence, such as the one used in our example above, by examining how effective it is. In other words, language is not only used to make constative statements. Austin thought all utterances were performative and consequently his concept of the performative is applicable also to 'all ceremonial acts, not merely verbal ones' (25).

Nevertheless, despite the claim to the universality of the concept, it is clear from the very start that for him a successful performative must fulfil certain conditions. This allowed some of Austin's interlocutors (Benveniste, 1971; Searle, 1969; Sedgwick, 2003) to argue that his performative is not universal. Nevertheless, I am not concerned here with whether Austin lays a universal claim upon the performative but rather with drawing the links between his idea of the performative and that of Butler. It becomes therefore pertinent to consider the conditions that, as Austin opines, give rise to a performative utterance.

In 'Lecture II' he sketches the conditions that can enable a happy or *felicitous* performative. Performatives that fail are *infelicitous*. They fail because they breach any of the following conditions:

(A.1) There must exist an accepted conventional procedure having a certain conventional effect, that procedure to include the uttering of certain words by certain persons in certain circumstances, and further,

(A.2) the particular persons and circumstances in a given case must be appropriate for the invocation of the particular procedure invoked.

(B.1) The procedure must be executed by all participants both correctly and
(B.2) completely.
(Γ1) Where, as often, the procedure is designed for use by persons having certain thoughts or feelings, or for the inauguration of certain consequential conduct on the part of any participant, then a person participating in and so invoking the procedure must in fact have those thoughts or feelings, and the participants must intend so to conduct themselves, and further,
(Γ2) must actually so conduct themselves subsequently.

(Austin 1962: 14–15)

As he explains 'if we sin against any one (or more) of these six rules, our performative utterance will be . . . unhappy' (15). The two lectures that follow, are dedicated to explaining how a breach of the above conditions produces different types of infelicity. An infelicity, he suggests, is nevertheless embedded in every performative utterance, or as he put it 'is an ill to which *all* acts are heir' (18). Irrespective of whether a performative is felicitous or not, Austin considers utterances to be performative (21–22) only if they are 'issued in ordinary circumstances' (22).

Simultaneously, he explicitly excludes the 'doctrine of the infelicities' (14), speech acts that have been uttered either accidentally or under duress or misunderstanding. Such utterances, as he suggests, might appear to possess infelicitous characteristics but nevertheless their unhappiness corresponds not to the conditions in which a performative emerges but rather to 'extenuating circumstances' or to the (diminished) responsibility of the speaker. Put otherwise, such utterances are considered to be external to the conditions of possibility of a performative utterance and therefore incapable of producing an infelicity, since an infelicity can only be produced as a breach of the aforementioned six rules (conditions of the performative). It is important to emphasise that all this allows us to read Austin's infelicities as being contextual or circumstantial rather than structural.

At this stage and for our purposes, the following observations can be made in relation to Austin's performative: (a) it has to be ceremonial, in the sense of a well-established, repeated and recognised procedure; (b) it has to be serious as opposed to being theatrical (Austin is adamant that an actor's stage utterance can't be performative (21–22)); (c) its intelligibility does not depend upon its falsity or truth but rather on successfully doing what is being uttered (based on the fulfilment of the six conditions I quote above); (d) an infelicitous utterance can't be a performative primarily because it is detached from the intentions of the speaker.

So far I have given the impression that *How to Do Things with Words* sets out to provide us with a clear and uncomplicated list of the type of utterances that do what they say. Undoubtedly, Austin's treatment of the infelicitous utterance might allow us to come to such a conclusion. On the contrary though, Austin's journey queries in general the possibility of compiling an exclusive list of performative utterances but, more specifically, on the basis of grammatical rules. In 'Lecture V', he explains how a constative and a performative utterance cannot be differentiated through the use of grammatical rules. Additionally, halfway through the book, we are made aware that an exclusive and therefore pure list of performative utterances is impossible.

Nevertheless, Austin maintains throughout that an explicit performative brings us nearer to a pure or clear performative utterance (73). I suggest that by this he means that, while we might not be able to have a pure performative, we can observe a set of rules that can bring us as close as possible to it. Moreover, while he generally suggests that grammar is not helpful in his quest for a proximate pure performative, he nevertheless does not completely abandon grammatical tropes. The 'first person singular present indicative active' utterance, as he states, enables us to distinguish a performative from a constative (67). The advantage of the above utterance lies in the fact that it makes the performative explicit. In the absence of 'the first person singular indicative active' and where the second and third person can be used, Austin suggests that the 'pronoun "I"... will be referred to in one of two ways' (60): (a) by physically being the person doing the uttering; (b) in cases where the performative comes in written form, by having the signature of the author attached to it (60–61). Even when the pronoun 'I' is not explicitly attached to the sentence Austin explains, as I have elaborated above, that it can still be present. Its presence is being affected through other means.

Austin goes on to demonstrate the distinction between an explicit and a primitive performative utterance through the following example. The utterance 'I shall be there' is what he understands as a primitive performative while 'I promise I shall be there' introduces the explicit performative. The explicit performative, in contrast to the primitive one, not only says what it does but additionally clarifies how we should take this utterance, or as Austin puts it, the 'force of the utterance' (73). An explicit performative makes us take the *doing* more seriously. In the conclusion of his book, Austin explicitly indicates that in reality, all utterances are performative (132–146, 147–149) while simultaneously he notes that not all utterances or acts are pure or explicit performatives.

Throughout the lectures, he ponders the possibility of deploying grammatical rules in constructing a list of performative explicit verbs but concludes, as I explained earlier, that such a task is not useful so turns his attention to creating another list; a list of affective speech acts. This attempt, an attempt to archive the ways in which 'language constructs or affects reality' (Sedgwick, 2003: 7) and to track down the meaning of an utterance in the expression that the act performs (force of the utterance) turns him to the linguistic tropes of illocution and perlocution. As becomes obvious, the use of illocution and perlocution tightly links with his differentiation between constative utterances and performative utterances. You will recall that constative utterances have an attachment to truth and inevitably to the source of truth, the author of speech. Illocutionary (where speech performs an act, for example, a threat) and perlocutionary speech (where speech has as its aim some act, for example, persuasion) are instead forms of speech that, instead of revealing truth, aim to do something else, to affect somebody. Explicit performative acts, utterances that are closer to the ideal of the 'pure performative' are, as Austin suggests, of these two types.

In 'Lecture XII', he provides us with examples of such utterances. These examples are divided into five classes: (a) verdictives are utterances that pronounce a verdict and, although they are to be uttered by authorised agents, for example, judges, they are not characterised by finality (e.g. Austin includes appraisals as verdictives); (b) exercitives 'are the exercising of powers, rights, or influence. Examples are appointing, voting' (150); (c) commissives 'commit you to doing something', that is, promising (150); (d) behabitives, 'they have to do with attitudes and social behaviour. Examples are apologizing, congratulating' (151); and (e) expositives explain how our utterances fit in the total conversation. Utterances such as 'I postulate' or 'I assume' (151) are examples of this class of utterances.

The overall contribution of *How to Do Things with Words* lies in its demonstration that statements are not merely descriptive and verifiable as either true or false but that they are also, and more so, performative, and as such are effective. In doing so, as we have seen, Austin sets up a set of conditions that are constitutive of the felicitous performative. Simultaneously, he warns us of the impossible 'explicit' performative but nevertheless suggests that illocutionary and perlocutionary speech acts bring us as close as possible to this, as long, of course, as the performative is serious, that is, conventional.

Austin's speech–act theory has been deployed in various disciplines and in different ways. Sedgwick (2003: 5–6), for example, classifies Austinian performativity by reference to the ways it has been deployed in different epistemological projects. She points out that Benveniste's (1971) and Searle's (1969) uses of Austinian performativity take a positivistic shape, pertaining to the logical structures of language and inevitably to grammatical organisation, as a means of understanding meaning. As for Derrida's and Butler's use of Austinian performativity, she reminds us that they emerge from the deconstructive project and give rise to an anti-essentialist epistemological commitment. Sedgwick alerts us therefore to the fact that interpretations of texts, such as Austin's *How to Do Things with Words*, are not necessarily attempts to reach the truth of the text. In other words, they are not concerned with the meaning of texts but rather with using texts effectively. This shift from truth in texts to *effects* of texts allows one to see how epistemological projects are also strategic projects. Sedgwick's observation reminds us that, for example, Butler's concept of 'gender performativity' is not just a methodological tool but also a strategic tool, developed and deployed to offer a critique of essentialist feminist thought and theoretical/practical commitments to ideas of 'origin', propriety and causality. It is not surprising then that Butler's reading of Austin to a significant extent follows Derrida although, as will become clear below, the latter is more interested in the proper performative, not the primitive or inexplicit one, while Butler orients her interpretation towards the inexplicit and infelicitous performative.

In 'Signature, event, context' (2000: 1–23) Derrida sets out to evaluate Anglo-American speech–act theory and, more precisely, John Austin's work. Sedgwick crudely and poignantly captures Derrida's critique when she writes: 'You can caricature Derrida as responding to Austin's demonstration of explicit performatives by saying, "But the only really interesting part of it is how all language is performative" ' (2003: 5–6). Indeed, Derrida is interested in Austin's work because it introduces the performativity of language. Derrida begins his analysis by turning to the practice of writing. Writing, he says, irrespective of its form[3] in order to sustain being called writing has to

> continue to 'act' and to be readable even when what is called the author of the writing no longer answers for what he has written, for what he seems to have signed, be it because of a temporary absence, because he is dead or, more generally, because he has not employed his absolutely actual present intention or attention, the plenitude of his desire to say what he means to be written in his name.
>
> (Derrida, 2000: 8)

As the quote demonstrates, Derrida invokes from the start a post-structuralist anti-essentialist strategy. He argues that for writing to be called such it has to be independent of its author. Here Derrida invokes Barthes's pronouncement of the 'death of the author' (a variation on Nietzche's well-known announcement of the 'death of god'). For him, writing can still be readable and effective even if the author is no longer present in it. This, as he says, is also possible even in relation to the oral word. He explains this possibility by invoking the trope of iteration. A word, he explains, is detached from its author by the practice of citation or reiteration. Additionally, a citation detaches the author from the word. A 'grapheme' (anything that can be detached from the signified, including the oral), he goes on to state, can be cited or iterated (2000: 10). Iteration or citation then annihilates the possibility of reaching the referent or the origin, that is the author. Citationality creates events as effects of the citation, constantly swirling around a past that can't be presented. To return to the first line of this paragraph, something that is cited is also detached from the referent and in effect can be called writing even if it is in an oral/vocal state.

Can anything that is cited be called writing? Derrida turns to Husserl in order to answer this question. Husserl observes that there are certain utterances that are agrammatical, that have no meaning. Husserl indicates this by referring us to phrases such as 'the green is either' or 'abracadabra' (2000: 11). Derrida observes that Husserl 'considers that there is no language any more, or at least no "logical" language' (2000: 11). Grammar, or the grammaticality of a phrase, understands that meaning arrives or is reached through the cognitive faculties of our minds, and in particular through the faculty of reason. Consequently, Husserl argues, language can't be language unless it disseminates some 'reasonable' meaning or signification. Derrida finds Husserl's position limited. Phrases such as 'abracadabra', he notes, are not bereft of signification. Such phrases, even when they are de-contextualised, signify at the least agrammaticality.

It is in this respect that Austin's performative is of interest to Derrida. As we have seen, Austin's performative speech acts attempt to introduce philosophy to an analysis of language, one that is bereft of attachment to truth. And as Derrida writes, 'the performative is a "communication" which is not limited strictly to the transference of a semantic content that is already constituted and dominated by an orientation toward truth' (2000: 13–14). Austin, as explained above, develops this theory by differentiating performative from constative utterances (2000: 13). Performative utterances aim to have an effect through the practice of speaking (2000: 13). Constative utterances are assertions that aim at 'communicating' nothing but the truth or falsity of the claim. Moreover, he explains 'a speech act is produced in the total situation in which the interlocutors find themselves'[4] and is attached *totally* to the present (2000: 13).[5] Speech acts, as a result, can be analysed only on the basis of their effects or in terms of the *force* of the speech. Let me explain this a bit further. If x pronounces 'I promise I shall be there', this sentence relates totally to the present situation of the interlocutor (and not to any past). X promises to somebody else, whom we may call for our purposes y, that x will be at a certain place (there). The intelligibility of this utterance does not rely on the truth of the statement (remember that the concept of truth attaches itself to an author which in turn relates to an origin, a past), but rather on its effect, namely on y waiting for x at the place where x promised to be.

As I have already mentioned, Austin uses two linguistic tropes, namely, those of illocution and perlocution to explain this effective characteristic of language. Illocutionary (where speech performs an act, that is, a threat) and perlocutionary speech (where speech has as its aim some act, for example, persuasion) are forms that act effectively. When Derrida evaluates the use of these linguistic tropes in Austin he correctly observes that Austin does not consider that failure is structural to any of these two performative speech acts. We have seen above that we may interpret infelicities as being the result of the context in which the performance takes place. An unhappy verdict according to Austin is the result of a breach of any of the six conditions that I mentioned earlier. For example, a verdict of guilt might not be effective because the person that uttered it might not be authorised to do so. Nevertheless, Derrida observes that Austin fails to consider

> what . . . in the structure of *locution* (thus before any illocutionary or perlocutionary determination) already entails that system of predicates I call *graphematic in general* and consequently blurs [*brouille*] all the oppositions which follow, oppositions whose pertinence, purity, and rigor Austin has unsuccessfully attempted to establish.
>
> (2000: 14)

Locution, Derrida concludes, anamorphosises[6] Austin's argument. Austin relies on illocutionary and perlocutionary speech acts to demonstrate how we can come close to the pure performative utterance. These two linguistic tropes are pure performative speech acts, because they are attached to an intentional subject. As I already suggested, this enables Austin to suggest that any failure or infelicity is contextual. Nevertheless, Derrida insists locution (the style in which our utterances are conveyed) is also predicated upon the intentional subject. The transmission, for example, of the sound of a threatening voice or an authoritative sentence is attached to a subject, albeit an intentional one.

This precise revelation enables Derrida to point out that infelicities are not necessarily context specific but rather structural to performative utterances. For example, if the sound of a threatening sentence is not communicated as such to its recipient it has nothing to do with whether there is a violation of any of the six rules (context) that Austin has provided for us. The irony is, of course, that Austin (as Derrida reminds us) accepts that infelicities are structural to the performative (2000: 15). In particular, infelicities are part of conventional or ceremonial performatives. Despite all this, Austin dismisses the structural failure as being accidental and not intentional (2000: 15). This paradoxical dismissal enables him to promote a theory of performative utterances that is far from general (2000: 16) in nature. In other words, Austin, crudely speaking, is saying that not all language is performative. Derrida, on the other hand, by exposing that infelicities are structural to performative utterances is also claiming that all language is performative in character.

Austin cements the idea that not all language is performative by excluding from the formulation of the performative speech act all non-serious utterances (2000: 16). Derrida writes:

> Austin thus excludes, along with what he calls a 'sea-change', the 'non-serious', 'paracitism', 'etiolation', 'the non-ordinary' (along the whole general theory which, if it succeeded in accounting for them, would no longer be governed by those oppositions), all of which he nevertheless recognizes at the possibility available to every act of utterance.
>
> (Derrida, 2000: 16–17)

A successful performative is, according to Austin, a 'serious performative'. The stage (as a theatrical space) does not produce a performative but rather a failure, an infelicity. Derrida incisively points out that what makes the performative a performative is what it excludes, the non-serious or impure (2000: 17). It is at this point that Derrida provides us with both a criticism of and a supplement to Austin's speech–act theory. For Derrida, performative utterances recite the infelicity (through its exclusion) and through this recitation the appropriate/felicitous performative utterance is created. The above obviously may imply that every utterance can give rise to the performative. Still, Derrida questions this implication. For a speech act to be performative it needs to be attached to an event or a happening. An event is defined as a singular and present happening and at the same time entails 'the intervention of an utterance [*énonce*] that in itself can be only repetitive or citational in its structure, or rather...iterable (2000: 17–18). Derrida understands the event as something that is singular and present. What gives the event its 'eventness', its essence if you like, is the very fact that it makes itself recognised through the interruption of language, iteration and citation, repeating with *différance*[7] (in difference and by differing) what is already there, what Derrida calls the 'coded'. This may echo the words of Austin.

Unlike Austin, though, Derrida suggests that when the 'performative' does not repeat a culturally specific code, such as the opening of a meeting, but is, rather, impure, but can still be cited. In this sense, a 'theatrical play' or a 'philosophical reference' might not be performative but might still be citational. Derrida still manages to hold like Austin to a performative that is pure and in some obscene manner real. The performative remains for him an utterance that recites an already established code. Of course, he suggests that it is not useful to pit the performative against the citational and that

> one ought to construct a differential typology of forms of iteration, assuming that such a project is tenable and can result in an exhaustive program, a question I hold in abeyance here. In such a typology, the category of intention will not disappear; it will have its place, but from that place it will no longer be able to govern the entire scene and system of utterance [*l'énonciation*].
>
> (Derrida, 2000: 18)

On the one hand, Derrida is urging the creation of a different typology of forms of iteration, one that does not set up citation in conflict with the performative. But, at the same time, he insists that intention (the 'I' behind the speech act) remains central to this new order of forms of iteration. Derrida is confident that in such a situation intention will not be able to organise the scene of iteration but just be present to it.

Still, his insightful invitation to rethink the terrain of forms of iteration is unfortunately problematic. Derrida fails to see that the 'doer' is an effect of the performative and the citational. Derrida fails to see that there is no intentional subject (even if his intentions do not organise the terrain of speech happenings) behind the speaking. The consequence of this is that it fails to read the subject as an endless effect of the practices and process that bring it into being. Perhaps Derrida, unlike Butler, as I explain below, wants to hold on to a prelinguistic subject that is also pre-political, holding on in this way to the subject of enlightenment. While this interpretation of Derrida's citational utterance may appear ungenerous, since his aim was precisely to invoke a different 'I', an 'I' that is constantly in deferral, it still remains the case that it is impossible, at least in this particular text, to understand his 'I' as an effect of the doing. Derrida's desire is to see this 'I' displaced, unable to organise the field of iteration in reference to itself, but paradoxically what is sustained (at least in *Limited Inc*) is this precise 'I' as the organiser of iteration. Derrida's hold on the differentiation between the performative and the citational locks him into this paradox. Butler on the other hand, both enables and sustains his desire. Her performative, as you will be able to observe in due course, breaks this attachment with the 'I' (or intention). For this reason, I argue that it is possible to find indications of pathways through which we can walk away from the subject of enlightenment.

Butler's understanding of the performative, as already mentioned, is derived from Austin via Derrida. As Sedgwick points out, Butler is interested in the non-explicit performative (what Derrida calls the citational utterance) (Sedgwick, 2003: 6). The inexplicit utterance is for Butler more performative and, it is 'more' of a performative when such utterance is not 'embodied in actual words' (Sedgwick, 2003: 6). Like Derrida, considers infelicity the structure of utterances and, therefore, she does not seek to provide an analysis of pure performative utterances. Consequently, she also believes that all language is performative. Her adaptation of speech–act theory aims at explaining how we are formed as subjects and above all how we come to be gendered subjects. Existence is inextricably linked for Butler to language and its disparate discursive practices. Our calling into being, our naming in other words, is one such discursive practice that is performative in character. As I explain below, she develops her concept of the performative in relation to gender formation and consequently offers us the concept of gender performativity. In later work, her concept of gender performativity mutates into a more general concept whereby it is used to explain how subjects are formed in and by language. Butler's concepts of gender performativity specifically and performative utterances in general are different from those developed by Austin and Derrida. Unlike criticisms to the contrary,[8] I want to suggest they are transgressive. She inverts and adulterates the rather un-material, un-discursive and textual interpretations of Austin's speech–act theory offered by Derrida. What do I mean by the above? As you will now be aware, Derrida like Austin understands performative utterances (whether explicit or implicit) as being predicated on an intentional subject. Additionally, he understands them as singular, embedded in the moment that they are uttered. As a result, he confines his criticisms to contradictions of Austin's text. This eliminates from his analysis the possibility of considering the performative as a practice, a discursive practice, which as such is both historically and culturally produced. Of course, his intention was to deconstruct the foundational and essentialist claims that Austin made, but as a consequence he fails to consider the effects that performative practices have in their performance. This is what Butler considers and what provides her adaptation of performative speech–act theory with material significance.

What follows is a description of Butler's understanding and use of the concepts of gender performativity and the performative. I examine them through two of her books, *Bodies that Matter* (1993) and *Excitable Speech (*1997b). Of course, one can trace the life of these concepts back to *Gender Trouble* (1990), however, I find that the concepts crystallise and render themselves more productive in her later work.

In *Bodies that Matter*, Butler states that

> performativity must be understood not as a singular or deliberate 'act', but, rather, as the reiterative and citational practice by which discourse produces the effects it names. What will, I hope, become clear…is that regulatory norms of 'sex' work in a performative fashion to constitute the materiality of bodies and more specifically, to materialize the body's sex, to materialize sexual difference in the service of the consolidation of the heterosexual imperative.
>
> (Butler, 1993: 2)

Butler first uses the concept of performativity in relation to gender. For her, gender performativity is understood as a citational practice whereby it produces the 'subject as already sexed'. Nevertheless, this citational practice is fantasmatic; it creates the illusion that the subject pre-exists its calling into being, its citation. Gender performativity becomes the practice by which genders are constituted as materially intelligible. In other words, gender performativity produces as intelligible those genders that 'institute and maintain relations of coherence and continuity among sex, gender, sexual practice, and desire' (Butler, 1993: 17); it produces 'subjects as already sexed' in order to sustain intelligible genders and, thus, maintain the hegemony of heterosexuality. This comes into effect through the foreclosure or disavowal of identifications that are not intelligible. Such identities are produced as 'abject beings', beings that are not yet subjects (Butler, 1993: 3) although, Butler argues, the 'abject' subject remains '"inside" the subject as its own founding repudiation' (1993: 3). Thus, the 'abject' is not outside the 'subject' but is rather part of its foundation; that which is refuted or disavowed in order for a subject identification to be formed. The 'abject' that is internal to the foundation of the subject is of primary importance in Butler's work because it helps to demonstrate the limits of gender performativity and also opens up ways by which embodiment can be reconfigured through these limits. In order to demonstrate the possibility of reconfiguring embodiment through these limits, I will turn to 'Critically queer', Butler's last chapter in *Bodies that Matter*.

In 'Critically queer', Butler sets out to read 'the contentious practices of "queerness"…not only as an example of citationality, but as a specific reworking of abjection into political agency' (Butler, 1993: 21). In this chapter, she reads the figure of the melancholic drag queen. The figure of the drag queen, as she explains in the 1999 preface of *Gender Trouble* (1999), was not analysed so as to be celebrated 'as the expression of a true and model gender' (1999: xxiii) but instead to, demonstrate that gender could neither be fixed nor assumed (1999: xxiii–iv). The melancholic drag queen takes the place therefore in her analysis of the example that amongst other things allows her to show that gender is not something constant and fixed. When Butler writes that '[i]f drag is a performative, that does not mean that all performativity is to be understood as drag' (1993: 230–231), she alerts us to the figure of the melancholic drag queen, as an example bereft of any universality, something that shows its singularity. And in doing so she is not suggesting that gender performativity is to be understood as drag (1993: 230); rather, she reads the performativity of the melancholic drag queen as an allegory of the fantasies that stabilise gender. The melancholic drag queen signifies, or rather, allegorises heterosexual melancholy:

> the melancholy by which a masculine gender is formed from the refusal to grieve the masculine as a possibility of love; a feminine gender is formed (taken on, or assumed) through the incorporative fantasy by which the feminine is excluded as a possible object of love, an exclusion never grieved, but 'preserved' through the heightening of feminine identification itself.
>
> (Butler, 1993: 235)

Gender identification, Butler argues, is formed through the disavowal of same sex love. The drag queen performs this disavowal. The performance signifies a lack of 'cultural conventions for avowing the loss of homosexual love' (Butler, 1993: 236). Due then to the lack of cultural conventions that avow the loss of homosexuality, heterosexuality is produced, in such a way that 'the straight man becomes the man he "never" loved and "never" grieved; the straight woman becomes the woman she "never" loved and "never" grieved' (1993: 236).

At the core of Butler's analysis of gender identification lie two significant observations. First, Butler shows how gender is formed or (re)produced through the disavowal of same sex 'passionate attachment' – 'it is not the sameness that forecloses difference, it is (the desire for) difference which forecloses (the desire for) sameness' (Zizek, 1999: 270). As a result, the man who loves another man is identified as a failed gender (Butler, 1993: 238).[9] Second, Butler suggests that same sex passionate attachments are not attachments which suddenly emerge and are then censored or foreclosed; rather, they are there from the start. This is significant because it shows that heteronormativity is (re)produced through the disavowal of the already existent homosexual desire while homosexuality is (re)produced through the lack of cultural norms avowing the loss of same sex passionate attachments.

Butler's analysis of gender formation and gender identification shows that gender performativity fails to be transgressive in a traditional sense. It fails to transform the normative logic of the system because it is caught within the discourses that produce it as a practice. Nevertheless, it succeeds in exposing the interrelation between what is produced as 'abject' (e.g. homosexuality) and the processes by which the 'abject' becomes the mode by which gender becomes fixed and identified. While this might not radically transform the whole field of sustained systems, or, while it might not necessarily open up the possibility of a 'pure' re-appropriation of power, it does create the potential for an alternative mode of power, namely one that exposes and resists the fantasmatic character of gender formation and identification.

Her reading of the performative in *Bodies that Matter* is radical in the way it approaches the Austinian concept. By comparing Butler's interpretation of performativity to Derrida's, we can identify, as suggested above, a slight transgression, and even cheekiness, in her reading. One way of understanding her interpretation of performativity is to say that Butler offers us a way of reading those impure and inexplicit performatives (in the Austinian understanding), in other words those practices that can be cited but cannot be performative. Austin, as we know, was wholeheartedly opposed to the possibility that theatrical performances occupy the space of a performative for they lack ceremonial and conventional status and, therefore, seriousness. Derrida, on the other hand, granted such practices and utterances a denigrated status; theatrical and philosophical utterances, for example, are read as citational and not performative practices. As I argued above, Derrida holds to a limiting and exclusive understanding of the performative, one that excludes any utterances that are not explicit. The effect of this is that he understands as performative only those utterances that are intentional and are attached to the speaker. Butler, however, in using the theatrical performance of the melancholic drag queen, is demonstrating that such practices are not only citational but they could also be performative. Butler thus focuses on those practices, textual or discursive, that, as Derrida suggests, belong to the genre of philosophy or drama, and thus can't be a code. So one can say that Butler's choice of the melancholic drag queen precisely recites that which is impure but can still be at the foundations of the coded. The melancholic drag queen allegorisation of heterosexual melancholy can be translated in a Derridean language as that infelicity which through a recitation creates an appropriate performative, one that splashes out of the limits of heterosexuality as a cultural norm and gender formation. But, the above interpretation is limited to Butler's contribution to the performative. I argue below that this contribution is much more radical than the interpretation above allows.

Derrida's adaptation of the performative puts 'out of place', outside the broadway[10] or the public space, anything that is staged, anything that falls outside the cultural hegemony of the code. At the same time, his reading is limited or strangled by his understanding of the parameters of appropriateness, felicity and sobriety and bourgeois-ness. Think of the examples he uses (or recites from Austin): the wedding ceremony, the christening of the ship. ... Butler's adaptation of the performative does precisely the opposite. The melancholic drag queen performs on stage, on the broadway, and recites through this her resistance to the loss of pleasure and the loss of same sex love that heterosexual hegemony feeds upon. The melancholic drag queen is precisely this cultural materiality that brings the speech act, the performative utterance of Derrida, face to face with its limitations. It re-appropriates the 'exclusion', what both Derrida and Austin exclude, and puts it on centre stage or on the broadway. It shouts, to risk a pun, 'bodies matter' and they matter publicly. Moreover, it demonstrates more strongly than Derrida can that the exclusion is always already there, constantly producing fleshy, voluptuous utterances that can shake the code.

In addition, as I noted above (pp. 37–38), there is no agent prior to the performative, the 'I' (intention or agency) comes through the performative speech act. It is this that also allows Butler to read the political into theatrical, philosophical and similar practices/discourses. The political, like the subject, comes into being at the moment of the utterance.

Butler's performative (and, in this respect, the political) relates to gender. This locates her work within a particular academic project, that, of course, of feminism and gender studies. Nevertheless, such a description situates her work narrowly. Butler's investment in gender is one that offers an understanding of the concept of the subject and politics that arise from what is 'repudiated', forgotten or put aside. As such the idea of 'gender performativity' gives us a reinterpretation of speech–act theory that considers the inconsiderable, namely those political moments that western philosophy and its subject of the enlightenment set aside and considered *unintelligible*. Butler's gender performativity provides us with a way of making intelligible those discourses and practices that can be thought as infelicitous and, therefore, unintelligible. How can this be achieved? Let me offer a guide to Butler's pathway: (a) first we have to understand that performativity (gender performativity) in its very activation (iterative speech act) brings the subject into being; (b) inevitably there is no 'I' behind the subject; (c) this performative relates to any form of activation (iterative speech act); (d) this performative both conserves and reconfigures the code (normative realm); (e) the reconfiguration comes at the moment of resistance of the process of bringing a subject into being; (f) this very resistance also brings into the fore the 'I' (agency, intention) of the subject and; (g) it is through this very moment (note the temporality of this resistance) of resistance that the unintelligible becomes intelligible. What is interesting in relation to her formulation of intelligibility is that it belongs both to a cognitive and a sensual realm. The material and voluptuous subject that she produces does not distinguish between these two realms.

Even more, as I intimated at the beginning of this chapter, Butler's performative utterances, either as used in *Bodies that Matter* as gender performativity or as used in *Excitable Speech* (1997b) as injurious speech, bring together the past and the present, the historical and the cultural. Derrida, as we have already seen, argues that a performative breaks from its context. It is in this sense that he argues that an infelicitous performative, in Austin's terms (such as a theatrical play), can still be citational though not an authoritative performative. This allows Derrida to read the performative as something that is bereft of an 'origin' and therefore unauthorial. The historical, as an attachment to a past is cut off from the performative. Of course, Derrida's performative, the performative without a context, still retains an attachment to time, and this time is temporal and present, rather than past and original. Butler's reading of the performative, on the other hand – whether it is the performative of 'gender performativity' of whether that of the 'injurious speech'– is one which is not cut off from the historical but does not nevertheless present the historical as the original. As we have seen in *Bodies that Matter*, the melancholic drag queen recites that heterosexual hegemony is constituted through the disavowal and foreclosure of same sex love. This, as I explained, exposes heterosexual hegemony as fantasmatic. When the melancholic drag queen recites her melancholy, at the moment of the effective act (for Butler, Derrida and also for Austin the performative cannot be confined to speech, it is also a bodily act) as the symbolic order orders relations, there is a hegemonic heterosexuality that is presented as original and therefore our past. At the same time, what the performative does is to unveil the fantasy of this hegemonic ordering by exposing that it is founded upon the infelicitous, same sex love. Gender performativity then brings together the so-called original (sex, heterosexual hegemony) and a re-articulation that unveils that its 'originality' relies upon a fantasy.

You might ask how this *really* differs from Derrida's articulation of the performativity. After all, at the end of the day the re-articulation of the 'original' allows the performative to break from its context. If we carefully observe her construction of gender performativity, we can clearly observe that Butler holds a strong conviction that what is being re-articulated relies on the recitation of the coded. This not only differs from Derrida drastically *but* at the same time is a more radical reading of the performative as it allows for the possibility of the subject that is being effected by it to *resist* its very calling into being, an effect of performative speech act and performative practices.

In *Excitable Speech*, she considers a different dimension of the performative speech utterance. Here she looks at the type of claim that one makes when an individual says that they have been injured by language. Pornography, racist chanting and 'hate' speech directed most often against women, men and women of ethnic and minority groups and homosexuals are the types of speech act that she considers. Such infelicitous speech acts, she argues, while unwanted are at the same time one of multiple ways in which the subject is inaugurated. She reminds us that our entry into language and into the world relies on the speech act of being named, being called into being, and this primary call is prima facie injurious (for we have not chosen the name that brings us into being) (1997b: 26). This primary performative act is, however productive. It brings us into being and signifies our existence through being named. Through the utterance of naming, which can be both vocal and bodily, the subject becomes recognised (1997b: 26). The call for legal regulation of injurious speech acts through censorship, as Butler points out, curtails the possibility of the subject being both recognised and recognisable (1997b: 5). Of course, Butler is aware of the injurious nature of hate speech and as such she writes:

> To be addressed injuriously is not only to be open to an unknown future, but not to know the time and place of injury, and to suffer the disorientation of one's situation as the effect of such speech. Exposed at the moment of such a shattering is precisely the volatility of one's 'place' within the community of speakers; one can be 'put in one's place' by such speech, but such speech may be no place.
>
> (1997b: 4)

Nevertheless, she argues that the censorship of speech, if it were possible, no matter how injurious it is, will kill the subject both literally and metaphorically. Butler proclaims that the allowance of injurious speech provides the subject with the possibility of resisting its calling, injurious or otherwise, for through the limits of language the subject attains its agency (1997b: 26). The interpellated subject can speak back. This speaking back is enabled because the effects of the performative speech act are not momentary or temporary. She writes:

> Thus, the gap that separates the speech act from its future effects has its auspicious implications: it begins a theory of linguistic agency that provides an alternative to the relentless search for legal remedy. The interval between instances of utterance not only makes the repletion and resignification of the utterance possible, but shows how words might, through time become disjoined from their power to injure and recontectualised in more alternative modes.
>
> (1997b: 15)

The fact that naming can injure, Butler tells us, lies in the history of the name (1997b: 36). By this, she alerts us to the possibility that responsibility for injurious acts should not be addressed to individuals but to the social and the way that it constitutes normative values. This history of the name though could be re-appropriated. The effects of the performative utterance or act are not always the ones anticipated and they are not always instant or temporal. Language, or more precisely linguistic existence, allows one to reconfigure and resist a name or being named. Again, as we can see, Butler's performative theory holds to the dialectic between the historical and the cultural in order to produce a different modern subject (1997b: 161).

The performative method that Butler develops enables us to see how our naming, whether as women, foreigners, idiots, etc., is produced. This explicates that we are products of both a past that precedes us and a cultural context in which we find ourselves. To be named a woman, for example, means that there is a historical understanding of who is a woman, but to become one, to re-appropriate that naming or to resist the historical way in which that naming is uttered, produces us as subjects of a contemporary culture.

Her interest in the performative, as I hope I made clear, goes beyond the mere demonstration of what is or is not a performative. On the contrary, it engages with what a performative does and how it affects the way in which we come to inhabit the world. It holds within it a potentiality that is not present in Austin or Derrida, the potentiality to answering back, of reversing the naming and thus present it to a presence that has not been calculated or articulated in advance by the subject that utters it. This performative (which is impure, inexplicit) renders language hostage to the possibility of being alive. For Austin, the pure performative is successful because it is attached to an intentional subject, which in turn is an appropriate subject. The subject is, therefore, intentional in advance, intentional before he/she utters the speech act. For Derrida, the subject gains its intentionality at the moment of the ceremonial utterance. Austin's understanding of how we come to be is one that is not affected by language, on the contrary language is the medium through which we transmit that we are and, we are somebody, a judge for example (who will utter a sentence). Derrida on the other hand impliedly suggests that to be a judge, to be named as such, happens at the moment when I utter a sentence, when I name somebody a criminal. Language in other words is the medium through which my existence is constituted and my existence is effected at the moment of my utterance. One is therefore not necessarily independent of language. For Butler though, neither the one that is being named nor the one that names are independent of the performative utterance. When I am named as a criminal, I can always resist that naming, resisting therefore not only the name but also the authority of the one that names me as such, the judge or the police officer. The subject therefore 'gains' its intentionality at the moment of resistance, an intentionality nevertheless that can always be in turn resisted or re-appropriated by the one doing the naming. Intentionality therefore becomes an attribute that is highly unstable and therefore intentional only as a fantasy. Her allegory of the melancholic drag queen demonstrated that naming is fantasmatic. Gender performativity functions as that practice that enables us to see or read that the infelicitous is at the foundation of performative utterances. Her analysis of performative speech acts in *Excitable Speech* takes us a step further, demonstrating that every naming holds within it the possibility of answering back, suggesting in this way that infelicities are potentially productive when understood as the product of a social and historical past. While Austin, on the one hand, kills the potentiality that language has to produce and Derrida, on the other, kills the potentiality in speak back, Butler sustains a vitality in language by understanding performative speech acts as a dynamic dialectic between the past and the present, the one that names and the one that is being named.

As I will explain in the final chapter of this book, Butler's performative method has important implications for legal studies. For example, it allows feminist legal studies to read the productive character of gender discourse. More generally, though, it can enable a productive reading and interpretation of sources of law, enabling us to see not only the limitations of judge-made law or enacted statutes but, additionally, it can offer us a way in which we can critically evaluate assumptions as to justice and ethics, the very subject upon which the critical legal studies movement is predicated.

Notes

1 For a critique of resemblance as a modality of categorisation see Deleuze (1994).
2 It is worth noting that Judith Butler in the Tenth Anniversary edition of *Gender Trouble* (1999a) states that she 'took . . . [her] clue on how to read the performativity of gender from Jacques Derrida's reading of Kafka's "Before the Law"' (1999a: xiv). You can find Derrida's essay in Derrida (1992a).
3 Derrida includes as writing anything that is written, pictures as well as text, if one can make this differentiation (Derrida, 2000: 7).

4 This quote is cited by Derrida in 'Signature, event, context'. It is taken from the introduction to the French translation of Austin's *How to Do Things With Words*. It is in this respect that speech acts are defined by Derrida as possibly being a-contextual. The context is created in the process of communication.

5 As I explain later on in this chapter, Butler interprets the performative as a citational practice that both repeats and resists the past. Derrida, on the other hand, understands such practices as being constitutive of a present. Derrida's overall philosophical project endeavoured to find ways whereby the present could be written. By insisting that a performative speech act exists in the total situation in which the interlocutors find themselves, Derrida aimed at detaching speech from a historical past, which conventionally is understood as being the foundation or the origin of the present. Butler's performative, as I will explain, despite its 'attachment' to the past, does not understand past as being totally authorial to the present.

6 The word anamorphosis refers to the sixteenth-century artistic practice whereby an image looks distorted unless it is viewed from a specific side. Holbein's painting *The Ambassadors* is paradigmatic of this type of artistic practice. The painting features an elongated skull at the bottom of the picture. The skull looks 'normal' if the painting is looked upon from the right.

7 *Différance* captures the double meaning of the French *differer*, meaning both difference and differal or postponement. See Derrida, *Margins of Philosophy* (1984) and Spivak (1976) 'Translator's preface' in Derrida's *Of Grammatology* (1976).

8 See, for example, Slavoj Zizek, *The Ticklish Subject* (1999) and Judith Butler, Ernesto Laclau and Slavoj Zizek, *Contingency, Hegemony, Universality* (2000b).

9 Butler suggests that homosexuality operates in such a way as to produce stable and fixed genders. Homosexuality is read by heterosexuality as a failed gender; for example, the homosexual is often referred to as being feminine. Butler does, however, state that we need to have a non-causal connection between sexuality and gender.

10 I am alluding to an understanding of the broadway as a public space whereby any form of practice can be read as an effect of a political iteration. A performance, such as the one by the melancholic drag queen, both conserves and resignifies the code (normative values) and as such produces a public space. For an elaboration on this concept see Michael Warner, *Publics and Counter Publics* (2001).

Chapter 3

Ethical sisters

> I've worried that the return to ethics has constituted an escape from politics, and I've also worried that it has meant a certain heightening of moralism and this has made me cry out, as Nietzsche cried out about Hegel, 'Bad air! Bad air!' I suppose that looking for a space in which to breathe is not the highest ethical aspiration, but it is still there, etymologically embedded in aspiration itself, and does seem to constitute something of a precondition for any viable, that is, livable, ethical reflection.
>
> (Butler, 2000c: 14–15)

Historically, people have underlined the need to live life according to appropriate moral or ethical standards. Discussions about this need, about ethics, seem increasingly prevalent these days. For example, a Sunday newspaper supplement, *The Observer Magazine* (OM), runs a regular column in its life section on 'ethical living'. On 6 February 2005, the column featured an article entitled 'Kids are alright' (56) in which Lucy Siegle stated that today's youth is active in supporting a diversity of issues from 'greater global HIV fund' to anti-capitalism. Apart from illustrating a possible proliferation of the use of the word 'ethics', the offside also signposts that because of this proliferation, or perhaps despite of it, it has become difficult to form a clear understanding of what is meant by the term *ethics* today. For example, why is young people's stance against capitalism described as ethical rather than political? If capitalism dominates our lives, then how comes that an antagonistic relation to it is not identified as politics? What enables this differentiation? Are there particular markers that allow a distinction between political and ethical conduct? Avoiding the impossible task of defining ethics definitively, I instead use Siegle's magazine article as the starting block for explaining some of the meanings attributed to ethics and their limitations. Such an exploration will enable a better understanding of Butler's concerns regarding ethics and the moralisation of life, as highlighted in the opening quote of this chapter.

Butler's ethical discourse undoes differentiations between ethics, politics and ultimately law. This undoing or deconstruction points out that when ethics becomes the dominant or totalised expression of life, it can no longer sustain its hold on life. It cannot hold that actions are merely ethical as in doing so their political side is revealed. Building on this, Butler goes on to demonstrate that the subject can no longer be seen as the ground of ethics, but instead as its problem. It is worth stressing that her argument arises from her analysis of universality embedded in historical practices (Butler, 2003: 11; 2000) that challenges abstract universal claims. Acknowledging similar arguments by other theorists such as Adorno and Foucault (Butler, 2003: 65), Butler takes this a step further and states that the subject cannot be presupposed or have any of its qualities (reason, understanding, knowledge of oneself) fixed. In her undoing of ethics, a subject emerges that is different or opposing to the one presupposed. Put otherwise, any abstract and universal claim regarding the subject de-solidifies when it encounters the concrete.

Returning, then, to Siegle's article about 'ethical living' we see that she attributes an ethical framework to the conduct of youth. In doing so, she presupposes what an ethical subject is, yet she cannot sustain it without relating to some understanding of the political. Siegle forms the differentiation between the political and the ethical by pointing out that young people are interested in supporting and being active in promoting *specific issues* rather than supporting political agendas (poverty, the environment, availability of AIDS drugs in developing countries and corporate abuse). In doing so, she differentiates between the political and the ethical. The political subject endorses and sustains coherent and longstanding manifestos that might support unjust projects, such as the proliferation of nuclear power or global capitalism, while the ethical subject acts on the basis of a private conscience to support ad hoc, but nevertheless 'morally right' issues. That Siegle imagines ethics to emerge from one's conscience is underlined when she draws from everyday life examples: 'Young adults', she writes, 'are notoriously attuned to corporate misbehaviour, as a friend of mine discovered when she suggested to her 13-year-old son that they go for a burger. At her mere mention of visiting the Golden Arches, he was ranting and sneering like a mini Michael Moore' (2005: 56). At precisely this point, Butler's critique of ethics, reflecting not only philosophy but also the everyday, is astute. Butler's reading of Siegle's positioning of ethical conduct in the private realm would point out that Siegle fails to acknowledge the transformation in political practices (i.e. reacting to interests rather than holding on to deeply rooted ideological concerns), but also that this 'ethical youth' can be seen as political precisely because of its resistance to publicly normative assumptions about the 'good life'. In their conduct, a subjectivity emerges that challenges or becomes the problem for what is commonly understood as an ethical subject. Put differently, it is through the youth's practices that we can see that what comes to be described as an ethical subject is more ambivalent than Siegle assumes. Butler takes such ambivalence and draws the contours of the subject unfolding within it. The problem for her is neither the ethical nor the political, but rather the problems arising in privileging one over the other, or when one seeks to totalise the other. When this occurs, the object of their concern, namely life is endangered. In putting life at the centre of this debate, Butler articulates the contours of a subject that could enable life's survival.

This indexical and rather compressed understanding of Butler's account of ethics will be followed by a more elaborate one to enable a better view of how Butler arrives at this account. Consequently, this chapter is divided into three sections. The first section offers a cursory and by no means exhaustive introduction to the philosophical use of the term and locates Butler's ethics within post-structuralist critical theory. One of the reasons for doing this is the existence of a post-structuralist tradition of addressing ethics within legal theory which pleads for, and privileges an ethical perspective in law (Diamantides, 2000; Douzinas and Warrington, 1999). Butler instead offers a critique of post-structuralist approaches to ethics. Here, particular attention is given to the ways in which ethics is distinguished from politics in the writings of Levinas, who foregrounded a unique understanding of ethics within post-structuralist philosophy with which Butler engages critically.

The second section of the chapter focuses on the concept of the 'subject'. The 'subject' is often misused or used in its lay or colloquial sense, often presented as synonymous with the word 'person'. In philosophy, of course the 'subject' carries a different meaning. The word 'subject' has its roots in Latin and is the translation of the Greek word *hypokeimeon*. Aristotle introduces this term in both *Physics* and *Metaphysics* (Critchley, 1999: 51) to designate that which 'lays under' the 'soil' upon which assertions, accidents and qualities rely. In the Aristotelian vocabulary, the subject remains unchanged through the passing of time and operates like matter (Critchley, 1999: 1). As such, any assertion or predication about ethics requires an understanding of what 'lays under' it, namely the subject. In order to understand Butler's critique of ethics, we require foremost to grasp her conception of the subject. This necessitates at least some understanding of its history. To this effect, the second section focuses on mainly Nietzche, Heidegger, Levinas and Foucault, whilst paying close attention to Hegel's phenomenology which has been the predominant influence on Butler's conception of the subject.

Finally, the third part discusses Butler's approach to ethics by focusing on three of her texts, namely the essay 'Ethical ambivalence' (2000c), *Antigone's Claim* (2000a) and the collected lectures *Giving an Account of Oneself* (2003). One of the most important points to be raised in this chapter is that Butler's ethical discourse is one that finds itself interwoven with political and legal discourse. Unlike Hegel or Levinas, she locates ethics within the public sphere, which could mean that her philosophy of ethics is really a philosophy of politics or law. While such a claim can be disputed, the importance of Butler's evaluation of ethics remains precisely that ethics are not pre-political but rather emerge as matters of public and political concern of imperative interest to the city. Classical Greek philosophers such as Plato and Aristotle of course already sought to establish an integral relationship between philosophy and the public interests of the city, primarily achieving this by turning philosophy into a science. Ethics inevitably became the 'scientific' study of how individuals can become good. In doing so, they elevated both philosophy and ethics as branches of an authoritative discourse concerning the *truth* of being and life, matters of interest to the city. At the same time, Aristotle's *Nichomachean Ethics* (1976), for example, argues that excellence and the good life could be achieved only by those who have access to the public political arena, thus excluding women, slaves or workers. This creates a marked separation between those who could be ethical and have access to public life and those who remain eternally positioned within the realms of private life. As we shall see, Butler's writings contest this separation, demonstrating that the distinction between private and public is unsustainable. This, ultimately, opens up a space where we can observe not only that ethics is politicised but, in addition, that such distinctions impose limitations to the quest for a livable and viable life. Implicitly, this evaluation of ethics offers a critique of the universality of truth proposed by Aristotle.

These points will be explicated in my reading of *Antigone's Claim*, where there will also be emphasis on Hegel, whose work influenced Butler's understanding of the 'subject' significantly. Hegel not only kept ethics in the private sphere, according to Butler, but moreover understood philosophy, and thereafter ethics as a branch of it, to be able to grasp reality and sought to establish the process in which this is achieved as a science (Findlay, 2004: v). Consequently, the truth about this reality of being and life is produced as universal. Butler, in contrast sets out to demonstrate this relationship between the city and philosophy by showing us that philosophy can provide an index to a livable and viable life despite the truth, or more accurately despite the search for an original and certain truth. A livable and viable life could be achieved if we pause searching for the meaning of life and focus on how life is lived. Her critique of ethics, as will become clear, offers us this possibility.

Ethics: a brief genealogy

> The welfare of the greatest number and the welfare of the few represent opposed points of view on value: to hold the former as of intrinsically higher value may be left to the naïveté of English biologists. ... From now on, all disciplines have to prepare the future task of the philosopher: this task being understood as the solution of the *problem of value*, the determination of the *hierarchy of values*.
>
> (Nietzsche, 1998: 38)

As the introduction above suggests, the term ethics is being used in a variety of ways and in disparate contexts. This creates a number of difficulties. As I have already insinuated, one such difficulty is that it complicates our understanding of what *is* ethics. The first part of this section aims at addressing the question: What is ethics? In doing so, it engages with essays and dictionaries that seek to describe the concept. Nevertheless, as I found out and as will become evident, such a journey leaves us with a sense of dissatisfaction. It does not, for example, address how we come to the conclusion that a certain action belongs to the sphere of ethics or how we determine with certainty that some action is good or bad. These are addressed in the second part of the section. Here, I ask the question: How can we come to understand ethics? This question opens up the relational aspect of ethics, allowing us to see how an ethical action is considered and how it might differ from other forms of actions, such as political and legal actions. The *how* question is linked to the philosophy of Emanuel Levinas, who provides us with a useful and challenging guide to contemporary ethical concerns and philosophy.

What is ethics?

Laurence Buell (2000) in his useful essay 'What we talk about when we talk about ethics' taxonomises the different ways in which the term ethics is utilised within the academy today. Buell, writing about the influence of discourses on ethics upon contemporary literary studies, names four categories:

(a) *Ethics as earnest noise*: this category emphasises the way in which literary interpretation and criticism *ought* to be conducted; the interpreter or critical theorist (who is thought to be an expert in their field) is to use the highest standards in approaching a literary text (3–6).
(b) *Ethics as relationship*: literature, is presented either as a space where ethical reflection takes place as opposed to 'formal reasoning' or as a practice where the reading of literature encounters 'an ethics of difficulty' (6).[1]
(c) *Ethics as imperative*: in this context ethics becomes the sign of authoritative common and shared principles (7).
(d) *Ethics as professional conduct*: in contrast to Buell's first category (where the emphasis is on the relationship between the reader and the text), this category focuses on the practice of ethics in the context of institutional practice; the professor/teacher of literature therefore engages in his/her work taking into consideration obligations towards students, the academy and society (10).

Buell's categories can be very easily related to other academic fields. If we take, for example, the discipline of law we can locate Richard Weisberg's *Poethics* (1992) within the fourth category. Weisberg's overall argument has literary representations of legal ethics resembling those of legal professional pedagogy. Buell's category of 'ethics as relationship' can also be traced within the context of legal studies. For example, the UK movement of critical legal studies has utilised continental philosophy's contributions to ethics (more precisely the work of the philosopher Emmanuel Levinas) to suggest, amongst other things, that they provide us with a critique of law's judgments. Diamantides' *The Ethics of Suffering* (2000) and Douzinas and Warrington's *Justice Miscarried* (1994) are perhaps the most interesting contributions within this category.

As we can see, Buell's categories usefully convey the varied ways in which ethics has been used in the late-twentieth and early-twenty-first centuries within literature. Nevertheless, this is not without its limits. It doesn't clarify, for example, why Siegle's article is about ethical living and ethics. To put it simply, it doesn't provide us with the indexes that could enable us to decipher the meaning of ethics. Therefore, in order to begin unknotting an understanding of the term I turn to a dictionary of philosophy.

The Cambridge Dictionary of Philosophy (2001) initially describes ethics tautologically as 'the philosophical study of morality' (284). A page later, the Dictionary qualifies ethics in the following way: 'the general study of goodness and the general study of right action, constitute the main business of ethics' (285). Before I raise my eyebrow and question how one deciphers 'goodness' and what is 'right action', the dictionary elaborates on this. 'Goodness' has been treated 'either as a question about the components of a good life or as a question about what sorts of things are good in themselves' (285). The study of goodness, as John Deigh the contributor to this section of the Dictionary suggests, leads us either to the study of well-being or to a theory of intrinsic value. Well-being is assumed as the natural and universal aim of all beings. While this is not the case with the intrinsic value theory, it nevertheless believes that if a thing is good in itself, beings find it worth pursuing (2001: 285). What underlies both positions is an *agreed* understanding of what is good or bad.

As for ethics as a study of right action, the dictionary stipulates that it concerns:

> the principles of right and wrong that govern our choices and pursuits. In modern ethics these principles are typically given a jural conception. Accordingly, they are understood to constitute a moral code that defines the duties of men and women who live together in fellowship.
>
> (*The Cambridge Dictionary of Philosophy*, 2001: 286)

What we learn from the above is that 'right-action' is based on duties, which in modern times have their roots in the juridical order and aim to bind and create a sense of community and sociability. It is also suggested that such duties in the West originate in the Christian faith.

In both circumstances, however, the Dictionary does not explain either how the good life and goodness are produced, or how it has come about that certain duties are more right than others. In failing to address how we arrive at such conclusions, the Dictionary is simultaneously unsuccessful in addressing what ethics is. I turned to the *Dictionary of Philosophy* in my quest to discover what makes something ethical after I reviewed Buell's essay. This journey has also left me no wiser. We can conclude so far that both, *The Cambridge Dictionary of Philosophy* and Buell's essay enabled us to see that ethics can be generally described as the study of how we *ought* to live and consequently we have an abundance of philosophical perspectives that address this question.

What still remains unanswered is how the issue of how we ought to live our lives has become an ethical question. The how question, addressed below, provides us with a more meaningful understanding of what we mean by ethics and how it differentiates itself from other spheres of life.

The how *question*

As we have seen so far, ethics is understood as the normative framework through which we ought to live. So far we have also become aware that in philosophy there is a plethora of schools of thought that explicate this. Since this is the case then, it becomes pertinent to look into some of these philosophical schools, or at least look into that school of thought that is more proximate to Butler's work. So I begin my inquiry into the meaning of ethics by looking into post-modern or post-structuralist ethics. Post-structuralist ethics is primarily associated with the work of the philosopher Emmanuel Levinas. This will additionally enable us to distinguish at least provisionally the difference between ethics and politics. In the course of this section, I will explain how this distinction cannot be upheld and the implications that this has for life *per se*.

Critchley writes that Levinas's ethics are not concerned with the 'justifiability of human action' (1993: 3). As we have seen so far, the study of ethics has been described as being preoccupied with either the attainment of well-being or with justifying the judgments or codes of human action/conduct. Levinas criticises this understanding of ethics and argues that this type of philosophical inquiry is *not* concerned with ethics but rather with morality. How are we then to perceive this distinction? Critchley explicates that:

> Ethics, for Levinas, is critique; it is the critical *mise en question* of the liberty, spontaneity, and cognitive emprise of the ego that seeks to reduce all otherness to itself. The ethical is therefore the location of a point of alterity, or what Levinas also calls 'exteriority' (*exteriorité*), that cannot be reduced to the same . . . moral consciousness is not an experience of values 'but an access to exterior being' (DL 409).
>
> (Critchley, 1993: 5)

If the dictionary definition of ethics, moral ethics in Levinas's terms, is preoccupied with ethics as goodness and right conduct, that raises normative and universal standards, Levinasian ethics is concerned with 'undoing' the normative and universal standards that moral philosophy raises. But what is the significance of his critique?

Before I draw on the Levinasian critique, its ethics and finally its effects, I will elaborate on the characteristics of moral philosophy. As we have seen, moral philosophy addresses the question of how lives ought to be lived and, if a good life and right action are the aims of an ethical life, it appears to suggest inexplicably that there are universal and unquestionable standards for these.

If we take as an example right action, it is evaluated on the basis of whether human action meets such duties. The assumption that follows is that the meeting of these duties constitutes an ethical life. Any deviation from these duties is considered an abrogation of right-action and good life and is conduct that cannot be justified.

If we look at the area of omissions in UK criminal law, we have as a set of duties (statutory, contractual, relationship, assumption of responsibility, self-creation of a dangerous situation) that turns one's inaction into action. If one fails, for example, to act upon a stranger's call to for help when that person is in danger of drowning, that failure to act is not an omission in UK criminal law, which does not impose upon citizens a general duty to act and therefore this inaction is considered right and therefore ethical.

Underneath this particular understanding of ethics lies, as we noted earlier, the *subject*. The Dictionary failed to explain how moral philosophy interprets the subject. Nevertheless, the nature and content of the descriptions that we have can allow us to form at least a general understanding of this. We can observe, that its subject is a closed reflexive self-consciousness which reduces the world outside it (exteriority) to itself and thus to interiority and sameness. How do we then come to this conclusion? If the right action, saving a relation's life when they are asking for help when drowning, produces ethical human conduct, this presupposes that there are duties that are considered as such. When we ask the question 'What is a right action?', the answer seeks to reveal what we already know. A right action is supposed to be something strived for and comprehended universally, given to us, as we have seen above, via UK criminal law by a set of duties. This correspondence between duties and conduct produces or presumes a subject. This subject is ordained with particular characteristics: it is self-conscious, rational and able to reduce its conduct to a preordained understanding of a right-action, what we might call sameness. This subject is rational, for it responds in a calculative way to the call of help. It measures the call against the set of duties that require it to act, and decides as to whether to react to the call. In doing so, it becomes conscious of what is morally required of it and finally it reduces the exterior call to a standard of duty, reducing in this way the exterior to the universal, the duty that orders it to act only if the call comes from (as in our example) a person that it relates to and not a stranger. This process, which relies heavily on a calculating subject, according to our Dictionary definition (moral philosophy), provides us with ethical contact. Such contact will also be considered as 'just' as it is in compliance with the law. But at the same time, such conduct will be considered as normative because it both imposes and requires a uniform code of practice. It is in this respect that we can say that moral philosophy corresponds to moral normativity.

The quote from Butler at the start of the chapter explains her unease with a return to ethics (and it is important to note her uncertainty in relation to whether critical thought has returned to ethics (2000c: 15)). Her unease is directed to moral philosophy and its universalised presuppositions of what is considered the good life and right action. It is these concerns that bring her close to Levinas's critique of moral philosophy. Admittedly, she also holds reservations regarding post-structuralist ethics but, as I will explain, her reservations stem from her fear that a so-called return to ethics might displace and privatise political concerns relating to questions of life.

Post-structuralist thought critiques moral philosophy. At the start of this discussion, I suggested that Levinas's ethics is concerned with undoing the subject of moral philosophy. He argues and demonstrates how the subject of moral philosophy is not an ethical subject, or at least it is not ethical according to his own understanding of ethics. Ethics requires, he writes, a subject that is spontaneous, unreflexive, uncalculative and does not reduce exteriority to universal standards, but rather retains its difference. Let us turn our eyes to the paradigm of the stranger who calls upon us to save him from drowning. According to our definition of moral philosophy, if we don't save the stranger from drowning then our act will be considered legal since it complies with the duties imposed by UK criminal law. Such an act, to repeat myself, will also be considered just; because it adheres to the universal values (justice in accordance to the law) that underwrite criminal law. But, for Levinas, this conduct, will not be ethical for we have not acted responsibly towards the call of the other. Responsibility and justice become in his view two distinct areas of action. The first belongs to the sphere of ethics, the latter to the sphere of politics. Before explaining how ethics and politics are distinguishable in his work, I will elaborate further on how Levinasian ethics differs from moral philosophy.

Levinas's ethics, as we have seen via Critchley, addresses differentiation and the inscription within the discourse of ethics of the possibility of addressing exteriority, the possibility of engaging with what he calls the Other, without reducing this exteriority to pre-given understandings. In order to achieve this, he offers a critique of moral philosophy by deconstructing what lies beneath it, the concept of the subject as reflective and the same. Levinasian ethics addresses the issue of responsibility, of how one acts towards one's fellow humans and asks if this necessitates the undoing of the subject as sameness, reflectivity and consciousness. As Critchley suggests, Levinas's ethics occurs at the moment when the ego is brought into question (1993: 4). When I answer a call for help from a stranger to save him from drowning, I act ethically and responsibly according to Levinas because I have acted spontaneously, *despite* my ego or a duty-bound law. Spontaneous conduct puts aside considerations of duty, or calculating concerns such as the risking of one's own life in trying to save somebody. Because one acts, despite oneself and despite the commands of universal law, one does not reduce the call of the other to the same (universal law, ego). The subject that lies beneath such conduct, is one who is not self-conscious, not reflective and not calculative, but rather a subject that retains its difference from the other precisely by rejecting its ego. The conduct in this respect might not be just (breaches a duty) but it is responsible, as it does not abandon the drowning stranger to the wrath of the sea. We might say hyperbolically that the difference between moral philosophy and Levinasian ethics is the difference between the death and the survival of the one that calls for assistance.

As we follow his distinction between moral philosophy and post-structuralist ethics, we can begin to see that the use of ethics in Siegle's column in *The Observer Magazine (OM)* is concerned with adhering to conduct that is responsive to some universalised understanding of rightness and wrongness and not to sustaining the difference of exteriority. The question of how we understand ethics has so far familiarised us with the differentiation between moral philosophy and ethics. We can get a deeper sense of this, as well as its effects, if we turn to another set of differentiations that I address within the same parameters of the *how* question.

Critchley stresses that Levinas's understanding of moral philosophy corresponds to politics (1993: 4). Politics, for Levinas, is the place of *the* question of judgment, and the 'place of contestation, antagonism, struggle, conflict and dissension on a practical or empirical domain' (1993: 189–190). In contrast, ethics is presented as the place of responsibility. This distinction is drawn from Levinas's 'Subjectivity and infinity', the fifth chapter of *Otherwise than Being* (1998). I address in detail this distinction below, nevertheless, if we keep to the indexical distinction between ethics and politics raised above it makes absolute sense to say that the column in the *Observer* falls within the field of moral philosophy and not ethics. The cited article recognises that teenagers, contrary to popular opinion, are not politically apathetic. Teenagers have political interests that are antithetical to the dominant capitalist ethos. Nevertheless, their conducts or actions take place within the parameters of a calculative, self-reflexive and egoistic subject that reduces any call for action to their own concerns and values, denigrating every exteriority to the same universal laws that they believe in.

Returning to the Levinasian distinction between politics and ethics, we can crudely say that the political subject acts without questioning whether it reduces the outside to the same, to its ego. The political subject is a reflective subject. The ethical subject, at least within the Levinasian context, is unreflective, it acts *despite* the ego. This distinction between politics and ethics is of course tentative as it relies heavily on Levinas[2] and, as you will become aware, his ethics encounters limitations. But despite the fragility of his ethics, his understanding of politics is well embedded and worth considering. By this, I mean that his discourse on ethics and politics offers a critical evaluation of western philosophy's engagement with the political. Arendt in 'Philosophy and politics' (1990) reminds us that the distinction between philosophy and politics emerges in the aftermath of the trial of Socrates and dominates the writings of Plato and Aristotle. Philosophy emerges as a field dominated by the distinction between *doxa* (opinion) and truth in Plato or, *phronesis* (political insight) and *nous* (philosophical spirit) in Aristotle. Central to this distinction are the mode of address and the number of communicators. According to this, the philosopher, and hereafter philosophy *per se*, uses a dialectical mode of communication to address questions such as the meaning of life, death or, more pertinently to us here, the question of being. In doing so, the philosopher arrives at a truth that arises out of the labour of questioning. This form of communication requires only two communicators, the philosopher and another, a dyad, and results in reaching the truth. In contrast, politics is understood to utilise rhetoric and what is communicated is based on *doxa* (opinion). Politics is also considered as a place where communication happens amongst a plurality of participants. Nevertheless, as she demonstrates, these distinctions do not hold. These distinctions, driven by philosophy's desire to become once more central to the concerns of the city, are based on the Socratic statement, 'I know that I do not know.' What does this suggest? Plato and Aristotle described the philosophical mode of inquiry, which begins with wonder and continues with raising questions that can't be answered completely, as based on a dialogue. The dyad is its modality of communication. Nevertheless, as she persuasively argues, the Socratic 'I know that I do not know' exposes the philosopher as being one-in-two; in the sense that if one is to acquire self-knowledge one engages with oneself, which in turn reveals that the philosopher is always in contradiction or contestation with their own self. Consequently, the philosophical claim to the dyad of the dialectic shows itself as a plurality. If the philosopher is already a dyad (a split-self), then his/her dialogue with another is always going to be dialogue with plurality and, as Arendt, concludes 'the escape of the philosopher from the realm of plurality always remains an illusion' (1990: 86). The distinction between philosophy and politics, therefore, proves to be a non-distinction. As Arendt writes at the end of 'Philosophy and politics', philosophy needs to take seriously its rhetorical proclivities and rethink the practice of philosophy and how it engages in speech. Levinas's understanding of politics is invested in this debate. Politics and speech intervene after ethics and responsibility. As he writes, ethics is 'a responsibility of the same for the other, as a response to his proximity before any question' (Levinas, 1998: 25–26). Our responsibility towards the other takes place before any question, before speech, or, as we will see below, before the *said* and, since politics is configured as the sphere where questions are raised and judgments are declared, then Levinas does address, despite his allegiance to a separate sphere of ethics, the poignant quest raised by Arendt, that philosophy should consider itself as political philosophy. The question of justice, or more precisely what to do with the question of justice, becomes the question of political philosophy.

In this way, Levinas addresses the deadlock that Greek philosophy imposed and lays claim to the importance of politics within philosophy. Philosophical discourse addresses politics via the question of justice. The question of justice for him is imposed within or from the community. Ethics and responsibility relates me (the same) to the other, a dyadic (private) relationship, prior to any question of justice and prior to speech. Consequently, a response to the call from the Other for help, gives rise to a relationship of inequality, since it requires the ego to submit to the Other, elevating the Other to a higher position than the ego. But politics involves contestation that emerges from the community. Nevertheless, while 'my ethical relation to the Other is an unequal, asymmetrical relation to a height that cannot be comprehended, but which, at the same time, opens onto a question to the third and to humanity as a whole – that is, to a symmetrical community' (Critchley, 1993: 226).

Levinas might set ethics as a first philosophy, one that addresses the specificity and difference of my fellow human beings (something that, as we have seen, moral philosophy or politics does not address) but philosophy still can't escape from addressing politics. While ethics addresses my relationship to the Other, politics acts as a reminder that conduct does not only take place between me and the Other but also between me, the Other and the community. Levinas sustains the distinction between philosophy and moral philosophy as a distinction between ethics and politics, but simultaneously he does not deny that politics is pertinent to philosophical inquiry. The political subject, the subject of sameness, reflection and self-consciousness, addresses the question of justice which he understands as raising issues surrounding equality. But there is a worrying effect of Levinas's attitude and understanding of politics. He appears to locate politics within the public sphere and ethics within the private sphere.

Such constructions as Berlant and Warner suggest betray heteronormative sensitivities (1998: 547–566). Heteronormativity, as they convincingly demonstrate, places the intimate sphere within the private realm. Ethics can be seen to relate to this sphere of intimacy. The sphere of the public and of politics is construed as the place where crisis is resolved. The subject is imagined as fleeing from the intimate sphere to the political at the moment of crisis and returning back to it when the crisis is resolved. If Levinas's politics takes place and strives for equality within the sphere of contestation, the sphere in which the crisis of inequality can be resolved, then it becomes impossible to see how his ethical subject, the subject prior to the question of judgment, for him resides in the public sphere. Berlant and Warner poignantly argue the differentiation between ethics and politics, or the intimate and public sphere proves to be imaginary. They demonstrate this through analysing practices and, in the cited piece of work, by analysing sexual practices. In doing so, they alert us to the fact that while affects such as love, hate, disgust and compassion have traditionally been located as a matter of private relations, they are not completely so.

Such matters are and have been politicised (see also Berlant, 2000). Levinas's ethics, that promotes responsibility, a stretching of one hand to help, despite one's ego, privatises affect and ignores the very politicisation of affect. The effects of this are significant. Levinas reproduces the classical divide between public/private allowing in this way issues such as sexual violence and aid to be resolved within an interpersonal sphere. The work of Berlant and Warner argues that since affect is not privatised, such issues can only be resolved within a sphere of indistinction, the public intimate sphere. Moreover, their analysis produces a more complex subject: a subject that is both intelligible and affective simultaneously.

Butler, as I will elaborate, takes this critique in a different direction pointing out that, as we have seen, the subject is both constitutive of and constituted in language. This means that one comes into being through language, but at the same time one is able to undo its calling into being. So when the Other calls for me to assist him/her, he/she does not only do so through language, either in a phonetic or silent way but simultaneously his or her calling brings me into being, necessitating me to question who I am. Language, since it pre-exists subjective formation and is the medium through which the subject is transmitted and (dis)organised, is public. Levinas's private ethical relation proves not to be private, precisely because it is communicated (despite the effects of such communication) through language. Butler, as we will explore later on in the chapter, locates ethics within the public sphere.

Nevertheless, before conclusively rejecting Levinas's understanding of ethics it is important to consider his work in more detail. Levinas argues that philosophy has been primarily interested in addressing the ontological question of what it is to be something (a rock, a human being, etc.). This philosophical preoccupation accordingly reduces exteriority (a rock, a human being, etc.) to the same or interiority, understood as self-consciousness, the knowing subject and the ego. For example, if one asks the question of what it is to be a rock, that question will be based on pre-existent knowledge that the subject doing the questioning has about rocks (colour, shape, etc.) and on the use of faculties such as that of reason and reflection, all of which are internal to the questioning subject and therefore the external object is reduced, the rock in our case, to an already pre-existent configuration.

Levinas's philosophical project is concerned with establishing ethics prior to ontology or metaphysics, to give to philosophy a pre-reflective subject. One of its main difficulties remains with thinking of a subject outside language. Derrida in 'Violence and metaphysics' (2001: 97–192) points out that his emphasis on the face-to-face relationship, an attempt to escape the emphasis on speech and to this effect language that dominated western metaphysics, is in itself a sign of metaphysics. Western metaphysics privileged presence. Philosophy from Plato onwards, in its journey to find the meaning of being, has privileged the temporality of the now, immediacy, proximity, contact. Speech becomes the medium in which thought is transmitted without lapse of time and without mediation. Derrida, like philosophers before him (e.g. Heidegger) critiqued the privilege of presence in western philosophical traditions. His critique focused upon the opposition between speech and writing. While western metaphysics privileged speech, Derrida argued that this ignored the effects of writing. Writing remains effective, despite the absence or literal death of the author. We have seen this position explained in Chapter 2 in relation to his understanding of citationality. Levinas's attempt to escape language, or rather the presence of language, by saying that the face-to-face relationship takes place *before* language, brings him right within the metaphysics of presence (see, in particular, Derrida, 2001: 125–127). This is crudely the core of Derrida's deconstructive reading of Levinas's *Totality and Infinity*. Levinas addresses this criticism in *Otherwise than Being* (1998).

He uses the typologies of the 'saying' (an ethical language that is irreducible to ontological language) and the 'said' (ontological language) to explain the possibility of an ethically responsible language (Crtichley, 1993: 7–8). Critchley uses the linguistic tropes of performative and constative to explain this. The 'saying' is to be understood as a performative (as doing what it names, which does not rely on the verification of its validity to be intelligible) while the 'said' can only be verified as to its truth or falsity. Additionally, the 'saying' is the action of response to the call of the exterior and it is an impossibility to ignore or refuse that call (1993: 7).

Critchley's translation of Levinas's concepts of the 'saying' and the 'said' into linguistic tropes is useful, but this disguises Levinas's philosophical moves, especially his critique of Husserl's phenomenology. While I am not planning to engage with this here, it is important to track in more detail the moves that Levinas makes in 'Intentionality and sensing' (1998: 23–60) in order to demonstrate how his 'saying' is presented as being pre-ontological, exterior to ontological language which has at its core the revelation of 'truth'.

He begins his journey by exposing that the philosophical questions raised through the questions of 'What' (what shows itself) or 'Who' (who looks) stage the metaphysics of presence. When one asks, for example, the question 'What is a tree?', the answer presupposes or has recourse to what the question wants to discover, the *meaning* of the tree. Similarly, when one asks the question 'What is a "being"?', the answer already has recourse to what it seeks to discover or reveal. The 'being' 'discovered' is the *intelligible* being. This tautology that produces the 'being' as intelligible corresponds to the question of *what* with the one who is looking (conscience) (1998: 24–27). The problem with this is that it presents 'being' as synchronic, unchangeable through space and in time and consequently *constantly* identical to itself. The tree, for example, would be always the same, it does not contain a differentiation between this tree *or* that tree, nor a differentiation between a blooming and a dead tree. Ontology, as Levinas suggests, forgets the event – the event of *being* a tree or *being* a 'being'.

The verb 'to be' reduces all exteriority to the same and does not express the event of '*being*'. But, Levinas reminds us that names are either verbs or nouns. For example, 'being' is the noun of the verb 'be'. This observation allows him to write that the noun 'being' discloses two things: (a) that the verb 'to be' freezes the name in a temporality and spatiality that does not correspond with the name, since time always 'disfigures' the name; and (b) that it exposes us to the event of being something, precisely what the verb 'to be' conceals. Moreover, he uses this to make a bigger claim: to suggest that the noun exposes us to the experience of the event before language, or more precisely before the linguistic desire to transfix being to grammar and a meaning that can reveal the truth; before the

Other is petrified into a symbol of language; before consciousness returns the phenomenon, the object, to itself. The 'saying' relates precisely to this. The 'saying' is the prelinguistic moment where subjectivity relates to the Other and responds to its call, *prior* to any reflection that will end in reducing it to the 'I'.

When, Levinas writes that 'the responsibility for another is precisely a saying prior to anything said' (1998: 43), he invokes a language made of a series of nouns that show us that there is something else prior to reflection, there is the experience or the event that draws us towards the call of the Other, that disrupts precisely the ontological being, the being of consciousness. The pull towards the other happens before any questioning, before the question of 'Who am I?' The 'saying' falls therefore within language only in so far as it unveils the event of language, only in so far as it breaks the *intentionality* that is installed in the 'said' (Levinas, 1998: 48). Consequently, this exposes that language is not always about intelligibility, language is also *sensible*. More precisely, if the face-to-face encounter with the Other happens before grammar then what moves me towards it is not my intelligence but rather my sensibility.

We can see why Critchley correlated the concepts of 'saying' and 'said' with Austinian linguistic theory (see Chapter 2 for an analysis of this), but nevertheless this does not capture the subtle movement of Levinas's thought. While Austin suggests that performative speech acts or any other form of acts have an effect without an attachment to truth, he does not analyse this through the *experience* of the event. Levinas of course talks of the effect of 'saying' bereft of truth, but he does this via the concept of *experience*. Levinas's theory of ethics is thought provoking. But there are limits to it. I have already talked about its heteronormative tendency. There are more criticisms that relate to his philosophy of ethics.

As you are no doubt aware by now, the 'saying' and the 'said' are linked to each other. Levinas does not deny this (1998: 43). After all, the 'saying' comes in the form of a critique to the 'said', the ontological (1998: 44). However, this raises an important question, the question of boundaries, chronology and transmission. Levinas suggests that the experience of the event, the magnetic pulling towards the other that suspends reason, comes *before* consciousness, before the thematisation of phenomena. But to say this, he relies precisely on the fact that there is a consciousness that thematises phenomena, that reduces the noun to a verb, 'being' into 'be'. In doing so, he invokes a chronology that relies on what happens afterwards. He reconstructs experience *after* he considers consciousness.

So we might ask, to what extent can one have an experience that is not thematised or not appropriated from consciousness? Levinas's answer to this relies upon the suspension of knowledge: the experience of the event breaks away from knowledge and reason. In doing so, he invokes tacitly a form of agnosticism (that we don't reason when we answer the call of the other) sustained by gnosticism itself (that we know that this is the case). Put differently this invokes Socrates's 'I know that I don't know'. We can see that Levinas is able to say this precisely from the place of consciousness, from reason, from knowing that one doesn't know. 'Being' and not 'be', 'saying' before 'said' signifies at the very least Levinas's 'not knowing'. But even if we consider the above as sophistry, there is another way of problematising this. According to him, when I move towards the Other, when I give despite reason and even more when sometimes this giving requires me to suffer without reason, I do so passively, without labouring, instead of having in mind my own preservation or, as he puts it, *despite* life. How does he *know* this is possible?[3] Knowledge, according to him, is suspended from the realm of responsibility. But still, paradoxically, the 'saying' *labours*, critiques the very notion of the 'said'. 'Saying' exposes the limits of the 'said'. Can we not say then that the very action of critique *labours*? Of course! For Levinas, this very 'saying' contours a passive movement towards the Other. This signifies its inaction. But still, doesn't the cancellation of reason in passivity rely on an *invisible* labour? Let's see how Levinas answers this question:

> The corporeality of the subject is the pain of effort, the original adversary of fatigue, which arises in the upsurge of movement and in the energy involved in labor. In order to describe the passivity of the subject, one should not start with its opposition to a matter which resists it outside of it, or resists it in the body with which it would be incomprehensibly afflicted, and whose organisation gets out of order. Nor should one start with the opposition between a man and a society that binds him to labor, while depriving him of the product of his labour. This passivity is, to be sure, an exposedness of the subject to another, but the passivity of the subject is more passive still than that which the oppressed determined to struggle undergoes.
>
> (Levinas, 1998: 54–55)

The above suggests that Levinas is not opposed to the idea of labour. Labour, though, is reconfigured outside the parameters of market calculability (see also Diamantides, 2006). He simultaneously does not differentiate between materiality and soul. Nevertheless, even if we could sustain the proposition that our movement towards the Other is bereft of calculability and intentionality, his understanding of labour leaves unanswered how we can escape the body returning to itself. How can we escape the pain or the joy that the body senses from returning back to itself (Nancy, 1994) and to that effect consciousness? Doesn't our senseless pain for the other always consist of a return of senselessness to the body and therefore intelligibility? Levinas fails to address this. As we will see, Butler's ethical subject, if we can call it that for the moment, addresses this limitation. The possibility of a livable and viable life for Butler takes place within the realm of intelligibility. Responsibility for the other takes place within the parameters of two questions: the *who* question and also the *how* question. Ethics for her takes place within the field of language and politics.

My aim here was not to take cheap shots at Levinas's philosophy. On the contrary, I wanted to show that his philosophy of ethics enables us to understand the concerns of ethics and politics. Additionally, we have seen that the investigation into the *how* question, has unveiled that the distinction between ethics and politics proves to be a non-distinction. We can say that Siegle's article on ethical living touches precisely this zone of indistinction between ethics and politics. Responsibility towards the Other issues, the environment for example, necessitate a response to difference as well as contest beliefs that denigrate their importance. This requires a conflation of Levinas's ethical and political subject. Our journey into post-structuralist ethics enables us to understand that questions of responsibility, when left or assigned to the private sphere, create precise political effects that affect our lives. If we are to be able to have livable and viable lives, lives that will be free of the burdens of universal moralism, differentiation and exclusion then we need to think of the subject along Levinas's lines (as his subject, ultimate desire, is the inclusion of difference), but within the zone of indistinction of the public/private. What follows is a very brief, history of the concept of the 'subject' within western modern philosophy and its effects to clarify this further.

The briefest history of the subject

Critchley writes in *Ethics, Politics, Subjectivity* (1999) that the 'subject' has its origins in Latin and translates as 'that which is thrown under as a prior support or more fundamental stratum upon which other qualities, such as predicates, accidents, and attributes may be based' (1999: 51). Consequently, the external world, the world that lies outside the boundaries of my body, is mediated through this idea or concept of the subject. So when we ask the question of what it means to be something, the question of metaphysics, it has at its underbelly the concept of the 'subject'. The 'subject' has a long history and a variety of figurations sketched in a very brief philosophy history below. This will lead us to Butler's own conceptualisation of the subject and her understanding of ethics.

Descartes, in particular in 'First meditation: about the things we doubt' (1968: 95–101) and Kant, especially in *Critique of Pure Reason* (1982) have talked about the subject differently. However, they both attributed similar qualities to it. Their subject was to be one of reason. Reason, unadulterated by anything external, enables a truthful life. The mind, as opposed to the body, is the location that will deliver us to this. Their notion of the subject can therefore be described as disembodied and synchronic (unchanged through and by time). Hegel's subject is slightly more complex. In his *The Phenomenology of Spirit* (2004), self-consciousness is inextricably linked to desire, producing an embodied subject (Taylor, 1999: 144). Butler elaborates upon this connection eloquently in the *Subjects of Desire* (1999b):

> Hegel claims that 'self-consciousness in general is Desire' (167), by which he means that desire signifies the *reflexivity* of consciousness, that it

> becomes other to itself in order to know itself. As desire, consciousness is outside itself; and as outside itself, consciousness is *self-consciousness*.
> (1999b: 7)[4]

Understanding Hegel is vital in grasping Butler's ethics, so I offer below an extensive analysis of his notion of the subject.

Hegel, like Kant and Descartes before him, sets out to defend philosophy's claim to universal truth.[5] This claim of being able to grasp the meaning of being, of being something, and of being in the world, rivals the theological and scientific monopoly to such a claim. In doing so, Descartes, Kant and Hegel resort to demonstrating that philosophy's claim to universal truth has a scientific basis. Hegel's *Phenomenology of Spirit* (2004) is a masterful elaboration of this. Here, he underscores that any claim to truth is predicated upon the subject–object antagonism, a dialectical relation,[6] through which self-recognition can be achieved. It is important to note that his subject is not only the human subject but also that of philosophy. His analysis of this process therefore operates on two levels, namely that of the human subject and the subject of philosophy. The process itself is multifaceted consciousness (sense-certainty, perception and understanding, which are analysed below, are stages that move towards consciousness), self-consciousness, reason and spirit. Each facet or step of this process accordingly reveals to the Other that its grasp of 'being' is 'deceptive' or 'fictitious' (Butler, 1999b: 21–24). This unconcealment, though, is not bounded, it does not take place *within* the parameters of each facet, but rather when one progresses from one facet to another, for example, from consciousness to self-consciousness and so forth. To put it otherwise, the process of becoming a subject identifies the fiction of each stage once it looks back from the stage it has arrived at to the one that it has left behind.

It is evident, as Butler (1999b) and lately Nancy (2002) amongst others[7] before them point out, that Hegel is tracing a history of these fictions, whereby their unity can result in the Absolute (self-knowledge of philosophy itself, as itself and ultimately knowledge of the subject as itself and itself).[8] Effectively, Hegel produces a moving subject or, to use Nancy's term, a 'restless' (2002) subject. Butler uses the phrase 'Substance is subject' that is found in the 'Preface' of the *Phenomenology of Spirit* to suggest that 'the "is" carries the burden of becomes' (1999b: 18) exemplifying as such that Hegel's subject is a moving subject.[9]

Before engaging with each one of these facets, I want to draw your attention to something else. As we noted, this retrospective look enables thought to grasp that its previous facet is a fiction or a deception. One of the effects of this process is that it grasps each facet in *negative* terms, *as what it is not*. So when the subject moves from consciousness to self-consciousness, to take one example, this subject realises that the way it understood the world in the first place was as it was not, the world in other words is *lesser* than it was when first encountered. What follows is a brief exposition of this movement between the different facets that contributes to the production of the 'restless' subject and ultimately the Hegelian Absolute.

Hegel begins his journey contemplating our immediate encounter with the world, the object that we are to grasp, understand, and ultimately make universal truthful claims about. Our first encounter with the world, he writes, is immediate and unmediated. We think that we grasp 'This' (our object or the world as our object) in its fullness (2004: 58). Our consciousness of the world appears at first instance to be unmediated. This gives out certainty of our sense of the world, what Hegel calls 'sense-certainty'. This doesn't last. The observer soon realises that there is mediation: there is a sense of the world itself ('This' as object) and a sense of the world as is grasped by the observer ('This' as I) (59). Hegel proceeds to question the correspondence between the object and sense-certainty:

> 95. It is, then, sense-certainty itself that must be asked: 'What is the This?' If we take the 'This' in the twofold shape of its being, as 'Now' as 'Here', the dialectic it has it will receive a form as intelligible as the 'This' itself is. To the question: 'What is Now?', let us answer, eg 'Now is Night'. In order to test the truth of this sense-certainty a simple experiment will suffice. We write down this truth; a truth cannot lose anything by being written down, any more than it can lose anything through our preserving it. If *now*, this *noon*, we look again at the written truth we shall have to say that it has become stale.
> 96. The Now that is Night is *preserved*, ie it is treated as it professed to be, as something that *is*; but it proves itself to be, on the contrary, something that is *not*.
>
> (Hegel, 2004: 59–60)

Through this, he alerts us to the mediated nature of reality or truth (through language) and that the correspondence between sense-certainty ('This' as 'I') and object ('This' as object) can only be figured as a negative. Sense-certainty's universality can be captured by the concept of 'not-This'. Moreover, reality or truth can only be revealed in the *movement* of the unity of language and object and not within the sense-certainty of each one separately. Kojeve explains that: 'The concrete Real (of which we speak) is both Real revealed by a discourse, and Discourse revealing a real. And the Hegelian experience is related neither to the Real nor to Discourse taken separately, but to their indissoluble unity' (1980: 178). Kojeve goes on to explain that 'truth' or 'reality' in Hegel is temporal: 'What can be said, except that real being can transform a human truth into an error – at least in so far as the real is temporal, and Time has a reality' (187). Time's reality enables us to 'see' that the truth about truth, if you like, lies in its inability to capture the 'now'. Let us reconsider Hegel's thoughts regarding this in the above quote. Hegel suggests that, once thought, the thought of 'Now is night' is penned down and reconsidered at another time, at noon, and we observe that it negates its immediate temporality and becomes past. History reveals to us the truth about our relation to the world, its constant overcoming. This movement of thought into language demonstrates that the 'not-This' is spatial as well.

'Not-This' signifies that the being that contemplates the truth about the world has moved away from the place (the truth in itself or identity) that it initially started from in order to get to the truth, as captured by the 'not-This' (Kojeve, 1980: 200). Sense-certainty's sense of the world is revealed as fictional. Sense as a modality or image of thought to capture 'truth' is defeated or, more precisely, it 'reveals' that the truth is not revealed in sense-certainty.

The cycle of consciousness then moves from sense-certainty to perception. Perception both supersedes sense and at the same time preserves it (Hegel, 2004: 68–69). In other words, the universality of sense-certainty as 'not-This' is now transformed or appears in the form of property (68–69). The object is perceived as having properties. For example, a tart could be described as sweet and soft. An object is here described by: (a) the set of properties that it has in itself or more precisely that come together to form the thing itself; (b) but also again in terms of space–time (the way in which properties such as the sweetness and softness of the tart differentiate from each other) and; (c) properties as universals having qualities independent of the object itself (sweetness and softness as qualities existing outside the actual tart itself).

As perception moves on, consciousness realises that the object is made up of an amalgamation of properties that both stick to each other *and* are separate from each other. Consciousness, Hegel professes, at first blames itself for being unable to grasp the unity of the object and its properties. It is important to remind ourselves that by this stage consciousness realises that perception is mediated through the 'I', which in turn is mediated through language. It is this that causes the initial self-blame of consciousness. Soon though, consciousness grasps that an object is inherently contemporaneously in itself one *and* more than one. Consciousness then stops blaming itself for being inadequate in grasping the object in its oneness. This becomes even more apparent when consciousness realises that objects are also identified through their differentiation from other objects. A tart, for example, is soft and sweet because is not a tree, which could be described as being green, brown and hard. Hegel concludes that objects supersede themselves, in the sense that not only can they not contain the unity of their properties internally but, additionally they cannot hold the diversity of their properties internally. Objects constitute their properties through an internal and external movement. Like sense-certainty, perception proves to be illusory, the unity or truth that it reveals in relation to an object is ambiguous; a thing is one but also more than one, both internally and externally constituted. Hegel writes that it is naïve to hold on to perception as a medium of truth revelation, as naïve as the type of knowledge that is possessed by the proto-scientist who fails to situate himself/herself in the knowledge production (77).

Understanding is proposed as the type of thought within consciousness that can produce truth by situating the 'I' in its production. Understanding ultimately supersedes perception (while of course sustaining it as an illusion). As noted earlier, each facet is sustained and negated within the one that supersedes it.

When Hyppolite writes: 'Perceiving consciousness has been transcended. Since the thing is contradiction, it dissolves as thing equal to itself and becomes phenomenon' (2000: 116), he captures precisely the movement from perception to understanding. This movement, as he later on explicates, affects thought's relation to the object. The object decomposes from one that is constituted through its properties to one that invokes the very question that, as we know, troubled metaphysical philosophy, namely the question of what it meant to be an 'entity' (Hyppolite, 2000: 116). The question of 'being' for Hegel relates not only to the meaning of 'being-in-itself' but also to the meaning of 'being-for-another' (Hyppolite, 2000: 117). Understanding, therefore, becomes that process (a dialectical process) whereby thought reflects back to itself the sensuous world, that an object is being-for-another and being-for-itself and only in this sense does it becomes a unity and therefore take a universal form (Hyppolite, 2000: 117). At the end of the process of understanding, consciousness becomes conscious of itself or self-conscious. As self-consciousness, it understands that 'the I is absolutely other, and yet this other is the I. . . . Beyond certainty, truth is posed in that very certainty' (Hyppolite, 2000: 139). True subjectivity is revealed as being one that overcomes the 'I', but nevertheless at the same time sustains it in the form of 'not-I', in its negativity.

This journey in search for truth continues in the chapter on 'Self-consciousness'. As we have seen consciousness discovers its own universality, in the form of self-consciousness but, so far, Hegel has not related it to the Real or the world. This takes place when two self-consciousnesses meet. With this he reminds us that our world is not made up of just insular self-conscious beings. For Butler, as I will elaborate later on in this chapter, it is language, or more precisely our coming into being through language, that evidences this.

But let's stick with Hegel a bit longer. Desire plays an integral part to this encounter. Indeed, chapter 4 explicitly mentions desire for the first time. Nevertheless, it is important to note as Butler did (1999b: 24), that the concept of desire was already there in the *Phenomenology*, working its way through the previous chapters. To understand this suggestion, we must remind ourselves of Hegel's method. As I have explained earlier, each facet of thought overcomes the one before it but at the same time it maintains or sustains the previous facet as an illusion. This method of writing or explaining how we come to the truth suggests that what appears later on, in this case in the next chapters of the *Phenomenology of Spirit*, must have already been present, even as just a mere trace. To put this otherwise and in more everyday terms, for Hegel nothing exists out of nothing but rather things, even concepts come into being through something, they are, in other words, contingent to their history. But while the method of Hegel's writing might allow us to see this, Butler goes a step further, suggesting that the object of the *Phenomenology of Spirit* can be located around the concept of desire. The reason for this is that desire in itself embodies its own ambiguity and, more precisely, that desire reflects ambiguity. Truth, or Absolute Knowledge in Hegel, embodies precisely this point, that truth is neither immediate (found in the object itself) nor mediated (found in the 'I'), but rather that it can be found through the movement of this two. The subject, as touched upon earlier, is the underbelly of any questions relating to ethics and responsibility and so far is conceptualised by Hegel as this movement between immediacy and mediation. Desire is precisely what captures this movement and the ambivalence of the subject. So despite the fact that desire reveals itself in the fourth chapter as an afterthought, it is nevertheless what constitutes the subject. Butler explains:

> For Hegel, the preconditions of desire are the object of the inquiry itself, for desire in its articulation always thematizes the conditions of its own existence. When we ask, what is desire 'after', we can give a partial answer: the illumination of its own opacity, the expression of that aspect of the world that brought it into being. This is part of what is meant by the *reflexivity* that desire is said to embody and enact. Eventually, the reflexivity enacted by desire will be identical with absolute knowledge itself.
>
> (Butler, 1999b: 24)

So far, we have seen how desire is fundamental in Hegel's conceptualisation of the subject. We will now focus upon Hegel's explanation of how desire operates in the production of truth and inevitably in the production of the desiring, self-conscious and reflexive subject.

His fourth chapter narrates what happens when two self-consciousnesses meet. As we know, self-consciousness is the reflection of thought back on itself, whereby it realises that the 'I is absolutely other' but nevertheless 'otherness is the I'. When self-consciousness A, let us say, meets self-consciousness B, Hegel suggests that their initial desire is to maintain their identities. Soon enough, they realise that this identification is constituted as a negative, A = not B and B = not A. Similarly, B recognises its identity in negative terms, B = not A, and A = not B. Their identification relies on recognising each other.

The process of self-identification, though, can only happen when A or B notice that they both have as a goal to be recognised as autonomous and self-consciousness. When this occurs then A, for example, recognises its beingness (as opposed to its animality)[10] in the other. What we can observe so far is that A and B depend on each other for identification, for truthful identification. Parenthetically, it is important to note that Hegel observes that this process, which we can call dialectical, creates an unequal subject–object relationship, represented later on in chapter 4 of the *Phenomenology* by the figures of the master and bondsman. As the story goes, each individual self-consciousness desires the annihilation of the other as it is only in this way that its own autonomy or independence (as a negative, as not-the other and therefore being for itself) is to ensue.

But, autonomy or being-for-itself can only be achieved if one's own life is risked (Hegel, 2004: 113–114; Kojeve, 1980: 13–14). For Hegel, this risk captures also the overcoming of one's attachment to the sensual world and therefore it allows one to reach truth, truth as notion. But the story takes a different turn when the two adversaries realise that if they kill each other what gets killed is consciousness itself (since, as we have said, what each self-consciousness recognises in the other is notion itself or, put otherwise, the negative of the sensual), the aim of their agonism. Also, since one of the self-consciousnesses dies while the other survives, the surviving consciousness would lose its identity (consciousness), for identification is achieved through the other (external self-consciousness).

As a result of the above, the desire to annihilate the other is overcome by consciousness itself. Therefore, Kojeve writes 'it becomes clear to Self-Consciousness that animal-life is just as important to it as pure self-consciousness' (1980: 15). So for life to ensue, both self-consciousnesses need to preserve each other. Accordingly, in this process the desire that the subject has to be an undivided unity is abandoned, as self-consciousness realises that that is what it is *not*. Hegel's subject is one that comes into being, through a dialectical movement, or movement *per se*, one that is as much consciousness (internal) as body (external), and one in this respect that is both self-consciousness and desire, both idea and matter.

This conclusion might appear paradoxical since, as we have already mentioned, Hegel's main aim was precisely to reach truth by overcoming the senses. There are still remnants of this intention in the same chapter where Hegel uses the master and bondsman analogy to explain this process of recognition. To be more specific, Hegel suggests that the bondsman or slave reaches pure consciousness (2004: 117–118). The story of these two individuals, the master and bondsman, is a story that can be best described as a story of interdependence. The bondsman is the body that through his labour produces the goods that sustain the master. In this respect, he appears initially at least to have given up his mind in order to maintain his own survival. The master, on the other hand, in owning the body of the slave, survives through the labour of the slave. The master is the mind in the production of goods. When the bondsman realises that he can never own his own goods, he gives in to his desire to be the owner of the goods and his fear of his lord and puts his energy into disciplining himself to create goods. In this way, he becomes the owner of the goods for the goods become an extension or reflection of him. Thus, he reaches recognition for himself. The lord's relationship to the goods, on the other hand, is one of pure enjoyment and therefore a dependent one (upon the bondsman's production of the goods). Since the bondsman achieves his independence through the creation of the goods, through this he also achieves pure consciousness and ultimately truth.

Butler insists that desire does not disappear at the moment of recognition. On the contrary, it is maintained in a different form. To understand this point, she writes that we have to see the antagonism between the lord and the bondsman as a war between a desire to live and a desire to be autonomous. The lord learns that he can't transgress need by simply abdicating the task of production to the bondsman. The bondsman learns that he can't be free by simply resisting the lord. What they both realise is that their desires, the desire to live and the desire to be autonomous are always going to be dissatisfied. She concludes that desire is always going to be integral and constitutive to the process of recognition of the subject (Butler, 1999b: 55–59). The story of the lord and bondsman captures the general problem of life (Butler, 1999b: 55): the struggle between life and freedom. Then if we are to survive, desire has to give in and transform itself into work, the work of surviving (1999b: 57). Desire, and along with it, materiality remain, they can't be dispensed by consciousness. Hegel's subject, as Butler puts it, 'emerges not only as a mode of intentional enthrallment and the reflexive pursuit of identity, but as a desire that requires Others for its satisfaction and for its own constitution as an intersubjective being' (1999b: 58). As such, it is a subject that, in requiring the other to constitute itself, exists/comes into being within the parameters of the community. To conclude, 'this new subject is still desire, but one that seeks metaphysical satisfaction through the articulation of the subject's historical place in a given community' (Butler, 1999b: 58). It is precisely this historical communal desiring subject that becomes for Butler, as I will elaborate in more detail, the vehicle to think the problem of life, the struggle between living a viable life and self-determination. This problematic is one that requires her to think of ethics within the parameters of one's historical existence, sensibility and intelligibility.

The Hegelian subject, the subject that gains its truth through labour, that is conscious but at the same time material and therefore desiring, that is mobile and ecstatic (in the sense that it maintains its attachment to the external material world), that is historical and collective, has been at the centre of critique ever since. Nietzsche, in *On the Genealogy of Morals* (1998), sets out to criticise philosophy's attachment to scientific, religious or any form of values. He exposes the terrorising effect of the master–slave mentality, dominant in the nineteenth century and the claims to truth it carries. Unlike Hegel, Nietzsche points out that the master's truth and values dominate and subjugate the bondsman. Thus he promotes a resistance to this type of moral subject. The resistance comes in the form of creativity and poetics, that through them the individual attains a 'will to power' and the possibility of producing an individual moral code for life. Creativity is contrasted to Hegel's labouring subject, whom Nietzsche sees as being subjugated to the moral codes of the master and therefore unable to escape enslavement.

It is important to note here, as Butler did (1997a: 35), that while the lord might delegate production or labour to the bondsman he is also responsible for the bondsman's production. This makes Nietzsche's critique of the Hegelian subject more acute. Nietzsche's subject comes into being through action and language (Nietzsche, 1998: 29). This subject becomes conscious of itself at the aftermath of the injuries it sustained from the value system that it inhabits. It is only after it overcomes these injuries and becomes conscious of itself that it can give an account of itself (be creative) and take responsibility for its actions. Thus, when he writes: 'there is no "being" behind doing, acting, becoming; "the doer" is merely a fiction imposed on the doing – the doing itself is everything' (Nietzsche, 1998: 29), he alerts us to this. Without a master behind our doing, then we become free, self-creating and truthful subjects bereft of any attachment to the burden of collective and slavish values. In this respect, the ethical subject, is one that is critical towards any slavish morality and morality as slavery.

The history of the concept of the subject within western philosophy sees its most powerful critique in the work of another German philosopher. Martin Heidegger in multiple works[11] addressed the problems of western philosophy and their discourses of 'being' or, to use more familiar terms, their engagement with the question of what it means to be an entity, human or otherwise. Heidegger's 'Letter to Humanism' (2004), eloquently sums up his critique of western metaphysics.

Heidegger criticises western philosophy from Plato onwards for its account of what it means to be a human being, what he calls the 'Being of beings' (226–227). In pursuing the meaning of being, philosophy 'does not ask about the truth of Being itself. Nor does it therefore ask in what way the essence of man belongs to the truth of Being (226–227).

If we apply this critique to Hegel, we can see that in focusing upon the process in which being itself comes to thought, in his attempt to subject the animal being (desire to live) to consciousness (autonomous from desire or *extentia*, materiality) he fails, according to Heidegger, to capture the essence of being. For Heidegger,

> man essentially occurs only in his essence, where he is claimed by Being. Only from that claim 'has' he found that wherein his essence dwell. Only from this dwelling 'has' he 'language'; as the home that preserves the ecstatic for his essence. Such standing in the clearing of Being I call the ek-sistence of man.
>
> (227–228)

To grasp the human subject, we need to understand it as a subject that dwells in language, that its coming into the world coincides with its coming into language. This is what we need to grasp first if we are to understand the meaning and 'essence' of 'man'. It is the essence of 'man' that will bring us closer to its understanding. But, we should be careful not to suggest that language can capture absolutely the essence and truth of 'man'. The reference to language as a dwelling of 'man' demonstrates the proximity of language to the latter but simultaneously sustains that the essence of 'man' remains a mystery, it can't be wholly captured by language (237).

Heidegger's philosophical insights are of tremendous importance to metaphysical philosophy. Metaphysical philosophy focused primarily on capturing the substance of things. Substance is the *what* of a thing, for example, being a man is universal and therefore unchangeable through time. Essences, on the other hand, address *how* an object is, in other words how we account for an object. An essence, according to Aristotle, can't sustain a universal status on its own. An account of how man is, for example, can only gain universality by attaching itself to the essence of what it is to be a man. Essences, we might conclude, were considered to be both temporal and particular.

As we have learnt, Hegel's *Phenomenology of Spirit* demonstrates that the substance of man and community is not static, in other words it can't be sustained unchangeable through time. His historical dialectics pervert the metaphysical understanding of subject and allow him to produce a discourse of a desiring reflective self-conscious subject. Essence is treated as incapable of on its own capturing the truth of an object. While language plays an important role for Hegel and he is of the opinion that the truth of objects is always mediated, nevertheless, he demonstrates that the universality of being takes place between the dialectic of the object and the subject itself. However, language, as we can see, is the medium that enables him to see, as the auditor of this dialectic, that the subject is reflexive. Heidegger, on the other hand, proposes that the linguistic dwelling of the subject abrogates its essence as reflective but nevertheless sustains its restlessness or movement. The true essence of the subject lies, as he writes, in his 'ek-static' condition. What does this mean? For him being is an entity that is thrown into language. The projection into language seals man's entry into the world. This casting is described as ek-static, as a projection towards an unknown future. Our entry into the world produces the subject as potentiality, a non-reflexive subject that is thrown into the mystery of its future. There is more to write and say about Heidegger's theory of the subject, but at the moment, suffice to say that, if ethics exists for Heidegger (and he is critical of metaphysical ethics), it lies in the 'destru-ktion' of the attachment to a reflective ontology of being and thus an inauguration of the subject as ek-static.

Butler draws on Foucault in formulating a critique of universality and ethics. Michel Foucault was not a philosopher, although as a historian he has influenced our understanding of the subject. A number of his essays written from 1954 to 1984, collected in *Ethics, Subjectivity and Truth* (1997), his three volumes on the history of sexuality[12] and his lectures on parrhessia which were published as *Fearless Speech* (2001), all deal with ethics. In the introductory essay of *Ethics*, Paul Rabinow, the editor and one of Foucault's interlocutors, writes that Foucault thought that philosophy's journey into the question of being and effectively philosophy's dismissal of bodily practices, community and care was 'our biggest wrong turning' (Rabinow, 1997: xxv). As he was critical of metaphysical endeavours, he found comfort and intellectual vitality in understanding ethics or our relation to ethics by looking at the ways in which ethics has been practised. In 'The ethics of the concern for self as a practice of freedom' (1997: 281–302), he is concerned with unravelling the relationship between the subject and truth. As the essay progresses, he explains that at the foundation of ethics lies an analysis of a set of practices through which the subject will gain its freedom (284). At the foundation of ethics lies the idea of 'freedom'. He goes on to say that practices of care of the self aim at providing the subject with knowledge of oneself and consequently with the truth of oneself (285). It is the practice of care of oneself, which will result in 'freedom', 'the ontological condition of ethics' (284), that provides him with the link between ethics and truth. As such, if we are to understand the relationship between the subject and truth as one of ethics, we have to understand that ethics is not a theory but it rather entails a series of practices that are embodied (286). The subject is not substance (290), but instead a reflexive entity, constituted by the truth games of the periods in which it finds itself (297). Additionally, as he explains, the question of ethics is located at the crux of philosophy and politics (293). Politics, for Foucault, relates to the different modalities of power and the practices of government. Finally, he writes that philosophy could be understood as a practice with different aims to those of politics.

It is expedient to see how all this connects with our concerns relating to the concept of the subject. Foucault provides us with a way to understand the subject, not as a noetic production (as our philosopher above did), but instead as one that is produced through the historical practices of truth, power and care. This subject, while it is restrained by the conditions of its production, is still able to produce itself, or more specifically the truth about itself, by resisting those practices that subjugate it. The resistance is both practical and linguistic. His posthumously published lectures on parrhesia are exemplary of the latter. I don't want to spend a lot of time on them but it is necessary to draw at least briefly upon them as Butler's *On Account of Oneself* (2003) has been influenced by them. Fearless speech tracks down the use of parrhesiatic speech in Classical Greek and Roman texts. Parrhessia appears for the first time in Euripides and is roughly translated as 'free speech' (2001: 11). Later on, he describes parrhesia more precisely as

> a kind of verbal activity where the speaker has a specific relation to truth through frankness, a certain relationship to his own life through danger, a certain type of relation to himself or other people through criticism (self-criticism or criticism of other people), and a specific relation to moral law through freedom and duty.
>
> (2001: 19)

This provides us with the conditions through which truth-speaking emerges (frankness, risking oneself, criticism). In addition, Foucault informs us that in order to risk something, your status or position must be lower than that of the person you are criticising. Nevertheless, parrhesia could also be a form of self-criticism. In tracing the classical trends in parrhesiatic speech, Foucault observes that we can find it in various spaces and in different shapes. There is political parrhesia whereby citizens had the duty to speak the truth in the agora of 'democratic' ancient Greek states. In not so 'democratic' states, the vezir or advisor to the sovereign undertook this role. There is also philosophical truth-speaking whereby the philosopher had the role to speak the truth about the world to politicians and kings, and also an individual truthful account of oneself. Truth-speaking came from the tradition of the cynics who understood it as something that can be taught, as an askesis or pedagogy, and it comes in the form of scandalous events and provocative discourse. There is much more that could be said about Foucault's *Fearless Speech* (2001) but it is sufficient to note that the importance lies in his concerns with how one reaches liberation from moralism through various practices and techniques of truth-speaking. For Foucault, to give an account of oneself requires a practice of risk taking where one undoes any previous knowledge of oneself. The ethical subject is a subject that is vested in these practices. Of course, as you might have guessed, the 'truth' that Foucault invokes is not a pure truth but specifically a truth that emerges out of or in relation to power.

As we have seen, there is a long history within and without philosophy on the constellation of the subject. I intimated at the start of this section that at the basis of an ethical discourse, as understood through the critiques or evaluators of western metaphysics, is a requirement for reconsideration, or to use Heidegger's term, a de-struktion of the way philosophy, since Plato, constituted the subject. Levinas's critique of western metaphysics offered us an important lesson. We have learned that if we are not to regress into morality, if we are to have an ethical relationship with the Other, we are required to establish ethics as a first philosophy. This requires a reconception of how we understand ourselves. It necessitates the deconstruction of the ego or knowing self when the Other, the one that is external to me, calls upon me. Levinasian ethics, calls for a language of and response to ethics that is outside the parameters of metaphysics and its attachment to reason or logos, presence and universality. In some respects, the call for this type of ethics could also be a description of moments when my ego, my self-knowledge, is reconstituted via the call of the Other, where I fail to reduce the Other to myself. Within legal theory, Diamantides' *The Ethics of Suffering* elaborates on this. There are a lot of criticisms in relation to this type of ethics and some of them have been addressed earlier in the chapter. There are, though, poignant observations that have influenced philosophical thought since Levinas. It becomes paramount that if we are to talk of ethics, bereft of moralisation, we need to think of the subject as, unreflexive, not-knowing, a surprise, non-identical and particular. As is by now apparent, Levinas's critique of western metaphysical philosophy could be comfortably directed towards Descartes and Kant.

The Hegelian discourse provides us with another dimension of the subject. Hegel suggests that a truthful universal subject is restless, ecstatic, desiring, collective, material and self-reflexive. It is more or less constituted or produced through its historical conditions. Nietzsche called for a self-creative subject, that challenges, resists its conditions of serfdom and, inevitably, collective values. Heidegger's subject moved us to consider the subject that is thrown into the world, that is ecstatic and at the same time represents potentiality or future. Foucault, as we have just seen, provides us with a subject that through parrhesia can reach an ethical abode. Hegel, Nietzsche, Heidegger and Foucault in their own different ways produce the subject as non-self-identical. In this respect, no matter their diversities or limitations, they all share to some extent Levinas's critique of moral discourse.

Butler's philosophical evaluation of ethics formulates a *synthetic* subject, that draws from the work of Hegel, Nietzsche, Foucault, Levinas and less overtly – in the sense that she does not explicitly refer to his influence – Heidegger. In doing so, she reformulates the quest for ethics. The quest for her is simply the desire to establish the preconditions of a 'viable, livable and ethical reflection' (Butler, 2000c: 15). However, suffice to say here, that her concern with how to articulate the conditions for a viable and livable life does throw her right into a discussion of the subject and an inquiry into the best place for this to occur. Her discussion of the subject, as we shall see, is inherently influenced by the aforementioned philosophers. One might correctly be concerned that her subject is the outcome of such disparate philosophical perspectives. We can even ask how is it possible to synthesise all these perspectives and still have a coherent, competent and philosophical perspective. I do not claim that I can fully argue the plausibility of providing an exhaustive answer. Nevertheless, I can suggest that her synthetic subject comes out of her attachment to Hegelian thought. As I have explained Hegel's quest for the Absolute, for establishing philosophy as a science that produces truth, the truth of being or moreover philosophy *as* truth, lies in his auditing of the dialectical discourse that articulates western metaphysics. This required him to observe the ways in which a thesis (for our purposes we can say a starting philosophical position about the subject) is contested by antithesis (conflicting positions about the same issue) to produce universal and absolute synthesis (a compilation that is the struggle of these positions). I have also demonstrated that Hegel's synthesis is historical, in the sense that it emerges out of the conditions that make it possible. As the auditor of dialectical discourse he was able to put together a conception of the subject that corresponded with both his times and the concerns of his time. Having the latter in mind, we can say that any contemporary discourse on the subject has to take into account the positions that have gone before it.

As I explained in Chapter 2, Butler's utilisation of performative theory explains that the subject is not constituted by constative speech and practices, but rather by performative ones. Without repeating what I have already said, this effectively tells us that the production of the subject does not reside in acts that lay claim to truth but rather in acts that are effective or forceful. This pursuit corresponds with the deconstruction of truth claims in philosophy, promoted by philosophers such as Nietzsche, Austin, Derrida and historians of thought such as Foucault. Effectively, they acknowledged that truth is neither Absolute nor pure but rather the product of conflicting values, discourse, language and power. As the auditor of what has gone before her in philosophy, Butler is compelled to produce a synthetic subject that corresponds to her time but with the additional caveat that such a subject does not correspond to truth but is rather the effect of speech or other acts. This enables philosophy to address the particularity of each subject and expose at the same time that claims to a universal subject or universal truth are violent towards the particularities of the subject. I think this provides a possible understanding of how she is able to come up with a coherent and useful discourse about the subject. But at another level, it enables her to address the question raised by Heidegger, the question of how a subject comes to occupy material life. Her analysis of the processes through which the subject comes into being addresses 'the truth of Being' which for her is that the subject comes into being through the fantasy of truth *per se*.

Before engaging with Butler's work, it is pertinent to provide a set of indices for guidance with regards to the quest for an ethical subject. For the possibility of ethics to be, we need to be aware that exteriority ought to be sustained, that the Other ought not to be reduced to the same and that claims to universal truth are not only mythical but also violent towards the subject, and temporal. Either overtly or subtly, these indices are addressed through the question of how can we have livable and viable lives? While she provides an answer to this question, it remains unclear or ambivalent at the moment as to whether Butler sees this as achievable through a political or and ethical means. This is not intended to accuse Butler of indecision. The political and ethical always include and exclude each other in their quest for such life.[13] It is within this ambivalent relation that her answer to the question lies. Livable and viable lives can be achieved through politics and ethics as long as the subject is one that maintains and sustains itself by the indices above and, moreover, is open to the world. Her ambivalence also maintains an opening to both the political and ethical discourse. Butler draws a distinction between politics and ethics. She is, nevertheless, not interested in what has been traditionally understood as institutional public politics (parliamentary, congressional, prime-ministerial or presidential) but rather takes her cue from both feminist and queer theory, Foucault and to a lesser extent Agamben (1998). She is interested in politics which have been traditionally understood not as public but as private concerns. Feminists, as we know, demonstrated that private issues – issues relating to the home, or to the private lives of individuals – are always political in the sense that their exclusion from the public realm is a political exclusion. The feminist and queer struggle engaged with reinstating the political significance in this. Agamben (1998), in his historical and philosophical analysis of power, reminds us that the political power of the sovereign always relied on the exclusion of zoe (private) from politics (public). Like Foucault, he argues that bio-political life, the governmentality of material bodies bereft of what we traditionally understand as humanity, is the constellation of today's political life. Butler's quest for a livable life navigates through this particular articulation of the political. *Antigone's Claim* (2000a) as I explain below is the very articulation of this.

Ethical ambivalence

> I don't know whether air that is not exhaled comes close to becoming 'bad air', but certainly the ethical bearing in this instance degrades the biological condition of life. Given that the Levinasian subject also rehearses an

> 'insomniac vigilance' in relation to the Other, it may still be necessary to continue to call for 'good air' and to find a place for the value of self-preservation, if one wants, for instance, to breathe and to sleep.
>
> (Butler, 2000c: 27)

Judith Butler, in her essay 'Ethical ambivalence', states her concerns with the so-called ethical turn in the social sciences and humanities. The essay, which focuses specifically on the work of Nietzsche and Levinas, sets out to demonstrate the similarities between the two philosophers. Nietzsche's subject is one that is self-creating, it is one that wills power, by putting aside or forgetting the primary violence that brought it into being. Levinas's subject comes into being through violence that from the start causes a split in the subject. The violence occurs when the Other makes a demand, on the 'I'. That demand not only asks for the attention of the 'I' but also *for* the 'I', the ego. This demand constitutes the relationship between the subject and ethics. In acting responsibly and therefore ethically towards the Other's demand, the 'I' forgets the violence of the split. Both Levinas and Nietzsche, Butler writes, share an understanding of the subject that 'bears no grudges, assumes responsibility without ressentiment' (Butler, 2000c: 25). But she goes on to demonstrate the paradoxes in their thought leading to the impossibility of their ethics. Nietzsche's *Genealogy of Morals* (1998) calls for the destruction of values and the abandonment of slave morality, but at the same time writes resentfully of the Jews whom he closely identifies with such morality. Levinas, in *Otherwise than Being* (1998), salvages the Jew from the resentment that Nietzsche depicts by dedicating the book to those that have been assassinated by the National Socialists, setting the Jew as the emblematic victim (Butler, 2000c: 25). In this way, Levinas shows no resentment towards the Jew. However, simultaneously, his warning against Zionist persecution and the citations from Pascal and Ezekiel at the start of the same book depict the Jew as the persecutor (Butler, 2000c: 26), exposing the infiltration of resentment into ethics. Ethical discourse, in providing a responsible subject, both sidelines and represses the politics that it is critiquing. This repression enters the text, philosophy and our world more generally through the example or citation. This re-entry, which is not really a re-entry at all, for it has always been there, demonstrates that the answer for a livable life lies within the parameters of the ambivalence between the political and ethical sphere (as both terms have been described earlier in the chapter). When she writes

> The subject who might seek to become righteous according to the ways of such a God will be one who is not only accused and persecuted from the start, but one who is also accusing and persecuting. In this view, there is no innocence, only the navigations of ambivalence, since it seems to be impossible to be persecuted without at once being or becoming the persecutor as well. What remains to be considered is how this scene of

> ethical inversion nevertheless leads to a responsibility that is constantly confounded by self-preservation and its attendant aggression.
>
> (Butler, 2000c: 26)

...she explicitly alludes to the necessity of taking seriously this ambivalent position that we find ourselves in, wanting to preserve ourselves and others but also the impossibility of doing away with the violence – not the primary violence that Levinas's and Nietzsche seem to suggest that we forget – but rather this secondary but not negligible violence that we find ourselves enacting unconsciously, perhaps, when we battle for preservation. When she draws on the metaphors of air, respiration, aspiration and sleep in the essay, she takes this point further. She warns us against an ethical discourse that forgets to account for the materiality of life, that gives itself unconditionally to conscience, animating in this respect the above metaphorical figures and reminding us that zoe not bios is the human condition. Butler navigates her quest for a livable, viable life by maintaining two type of ambivalence, between the political and ethical and between materiality and agency (or conscience). What is paramount for such a life is a different conceptualisation of the subject, one that is the effect of language and practices, that struggles or resists its coming into being and manages to remain open to what will face it in the future. *Antigone's Claim* (2000a) exposes how such a subject is able to reconfigure the parameters of political livability. *Giving an Account of Oneself* (2003) demonstrates how it opens up the space for an ethical and responsible life. It is to these texts that I now turn.

Let's begin with *Giving an Account of Oneself* (2003). This book was published after the attack on the twin towers in New York by alleged al-Qaeda terrorists and, since the lectures were given in the aftermath of these attacks, we must read Butler's philosophical account of ethical responsibility within this context. When she writes in the first chapter of the book,

> It may be that the question of ethics emerges precisely at the limits of the schemes of intelligibility, the site where we ask ourselves what it might mean to continue in a dialogue where no common ground can be assumed, where one is, as it were, at the limits of what one knows and still under the demand to offer and receive recognition.
>
> (2003: 18)

She alludes to the necessity of thinking the parameters of livable and viable lives within the very conditions of their impossibility, where no common ground or foundation can be assumed. These words can be contextualised in different ways. They could refer to 'unresolvable' fallings out between friends, lovers, colleagues and the Palestinian–Israeli conflict, the animosity that India and Pakistan hold for each other, and so forth. But it would be nevertheless misleading to think that the above is prescriptive. Rather, it is a description of the way in which the subject constitutes itself and its relation to the world.

Butler sets out to 'revise recognition as an ethical project' (2003: 35). The concept of recognition, as we have seen from the analysis of the *Phenomenology of Spirit* (2004), produces a subject through its externality; it *needs* the Other – whether this Other takes the form of an individual, language, the state, or community – simply to exist and be alive. Additionally, we have seen that the subject's desire for autonomy gives in to the desire to stay alive. She finds the concept of recognition useful because it produces the subject as the outcome of the agonistic relationship between the subject and its social and cultural spheres. This is where her account of ethics, the subject and responsibility begin in this particular book. The 'I' (subject) as she writes, 'has no story of its own that is not at once a story of a relation – or asset of relations to – a set of norms' (2003: 12). This 'I' then, by the sheer nature that it exists within a social realm, is never in possession of its 'I' or its being. The 'I' in this respect is an essence. For Butler, the 'I' is also never outside the conditions of its emergence. Her discourse of the subject does not rely upon the dichotomy that we have seen that figures in the works of Hegel, Nietzsche and Heidegger. For this, she explicitly relies on Foucault (2003: 16, 18). But, this does not mean that the 'I' does not acquire or possess agency or any ethical grounds. On the contrary, it means that this provokes the 'I' to *deliberate*[14] upon the conditions of its sociability and through this to evaluate its surrounding values (2003: 12–13). Before proceeding, we can observe that, for Butler, ethics emerges as the space for critical evaluation of social and cultural norms and that the 'I' can achieve this through *deliberation* upon the conditions that make its life unlivable.

Despite all this, the concept of recognition is not unproblematic. Even if one sticks with reinterpretations of recognition that constitute the subject as an ecstatic subject, 'that the I repeatedly finds itself outside itself, and that it cannot put an end to this repeated upsurge of its own exteriority' (Butler, 2003: 22), there is still the problem that Levinas alerts us to, namely that the Hegelian reflective subject constantly searches to find the same in the Other. Butler resolves this through the trope of desire, the desire to sustain one's life, as opposed to the desire for autonomy (2003: 34). So she writes:

> As a result, it would be important to consider that any theory of recognition would have to give an account of the desire for recognition, and recognize that desire sets the limits and the conditions for the operation of recognition itself. Indeed, a certain desire to persist, we might say, following Spinoza, underwrites recognition, such that forms of recognition or, indeed, forms of judgement which seek to relinquish or destroy the desire to persist, the desire for life itself, undercut the very conditions of recognition itself.
>
> (Butler, 2003: 35)

The quote transmits the double move that takes place within the Hegelian text vis-à-vis the concept of recognition (the failure of recognition) which enables Butler to make an important move in relation to the production of this ethical subject. If the desire to live underwrites the desire for a unified identity, then the subject that emerges out of this relationship through the norms that constitute it is one that is always going to be agnostic of itself or, to put it otherwise, it will always rely on the Other, on the non-identical, to constitute it and to enable the answer to the question 'Who are you?'(2003). It is this *move* that addresses the Levinasian problematisation of the reflexive subject. Butler points out that the 'I' is never really an 'I', but rather a 'you', somebody that has already been addressed to account for themself through language, when he or she is being named (see chapter 2). In respect of this, she writes:

> If I give an account, and give it to you, then my narrative depends upon a structure of address. But if I can address you, it must be that I was first addressed, brought into the structure of address as a possibility of language before I was able to find my own way to make use of it. This follows not only from the fact that language first belongs to the Other, and that I acquire it through a complicated form of mimesis, but also because the very possibility of linguistic agency is derived from the situation in which one finds oneself addressed by a language one never chose.
>
> (Butler, 2003: 40)

And since one never chooses the language in which one is addressed, nor can one ever possess the origin of this address, one will always be unknown to oneself. Butler goes a step further in her account of language. She gestures that the term language should not be limited to vocalisation by language, but also to those moments where the 'I' was 'touched, moved, fed, changed, put to sleep, spoken to and spoken around' (2003: 48), those signs that form the subject but, like the language that it finds itself in, the subject *cannot* retrieve or return to. Her reliance upon this is used once more to demonstrate that the subject will and does not truly know itself, and consequentially one can't reduce the Other to sameness. The Other remains singular and non-identical to the 'I'. The 'I' which comes into being, as we have seen, through the Other can never account fully and coherently of him/herself. It is rather eternally interrupted.

But if, as she writes, the subject is not responsible for his/her coming into being, if the subject is indisposed and injured by this coming into being, how can this subject be responsible for its actions? In saying that the subject is dispossessed, incoherent, unknowable does not mean that it can't be responsible. As she writes, 'to take responsibility for oneself is to avow the limits of any self-understanding, and to establish this limit not only as a condition for the subject, but as a predicament of the human community itself' (2003: 55). One might ask, if one disavows self-understanding, conscience *per se*, one surely can't be responsible for what one has never done, for injuries that were given by the Other? We may say that if I get punched without provocation – since to be constituted by the Other means precisely that one got a punch in the quest for self-identity – it might mean that the only way to respond is to punch back, to give the Other a black eye, to cause the Other's nose to bleed, even to kill the Other.

But let's think again about how Butler understands our coming into being. Our coming into being is always produced via the normative, via language (both in its material and figural sense), *but* we are unable to retrieve our origin, the very space and temporality of our origination and, thus, our very first injury. As we are unable to return to the original injury, then if we retaliate by punching the Other it means that we can't get back our original face. On the contrary, if we proceed to punch the Other, what will be reflected is that we really can't reach this origin. The norms that bring us into being therefore carry within them an element of unintelligibility, of unknowingness that ricochets into the formation of the subject. If the 'I' can never know itself, is not conscious of itself as Hegel and Nietzsche want us to think, then the subject can never be at the foundations of ethics, but is 'a problem for ethics' (2003: 65). Here, she is in agreement with both Foucault and Adorno. The 'I' is always inhuman, it is not, self-consciousness. The 'I' can only 'humanise' itself, be responsible to itself, by *deliberating* upon the fact that it is unknowing, inhuman. This is also the 'truth', in the parrhesiatic mode, that one needs to risk (and let's not forget that this risk and truth is a truth that is inextricably linked to power), if one is to act responsibly, ethically and have a livable and viable life. As she concludes,

> If we can be said to make ourselves...and if new modes of subjectivity become for us a possibility then they are not arbitrarily made by an individual with especially creative capacities. They are produced when the limiting conditions by which we are made prove to be malleable and replicable, where a certain self is risked in its intelligibility and recognizability in a bid to expose and account for the inhuman ways in which 'the human' continues to be done and undone. In a way, this happens when we come up against the limits of any epistemological horizon, and realize that the question is not simply whether I can or will know you, but whether 'you' qualify in the scheme of the human within which I operate. Ethics requires that we must risk ourselves precisely there, at the moment of our unknowingness, when what conditions us and what lies before us diverge from one another, when our willingness to become undone constitutes our chance of becoming human, a becoming whose necessity knows no end.
>
> (Butler, 2003: 80)

Butler above explicitly suggests that our reactions, our ethical and responsible actions, undo the conditions that bring us into being, and in that respect they are political. The quest for self-government, and in this respect the quest for communal government, is neither an ethical stance nor a political journey but rather simultaneously both, making the origin of either the ethical or the political more and more indistinguishable.

In *Antigone's Claim* (2000), this is more apparent. Butler reinterprets Sophocles' tragic play *Antigone* (1984). *Antigone* (1984) has been at the centre of discussion over the years by classicists (Steiner, 1986), philosophers (Derrida, 1986; Hegel, 1975, 1988, 1996, 2004; Heidegger, 1977; Irigaray, 1985, 1993a,b), political theorists (Benhabib, 1992; Hartouni, 1986), visual arts theorists (Phelan, 1997), psychoanalysts (Lacan, 1992), and legal theorists (Douzinas and Warrington, 1994). The dominant interpretation of *Antigone* portrays her as an exemplary ethical figure, her actions defying legal and political power. In *Antigone's Claim*, Butler sets out to see to what extent *Antigone* can be read differently. At the backdrop of this lies Butler's uneasiness with feminists who 'seek the backing and authority of the state to implement feminist policy aims' (2000a: 1). Antigone becomes a journey through which she is to discover whether and to what extent the ethical domain can provide feminism with a different horizon for achieving the material aims, concerns and issues that it publicises. As I will explain in the forthcoming chapters, Butler sees the legal arena and the state as being unable to recognise the needs, desires and the agency of subjects.

For those unfamiliar with Sophocles' *Antigone* (1984), a few words about the plot of the play will enable you to understand why Antigone has become a celebrated ethical figure. Antigone is the daughter of the exiled King of Thebes, Oedipus. Oedipus, soon after his birth was exposed in the wilderness to die by his parents, King Laius and Queen Jocasta of Thebes. This parental act was triggered by the sayings of an oracle which professed that Oedipus would kill his father. Alas, Oedipus was saved and adopted by another king and queen, and lived a princely life. Part of the story, which is pertinent to us since it is interlinked with that of his daughter, has the young Oedipus longing to find more about his origins and consulting the soothsayers. The oracle proclaims that he is not the biological son of his parents but advises him against finding his real parents for he will end up killing his father. Oedipus disobeys the oracle and sets out on a journey of parental discovery. At the crossroads of Thebes, he encounters King Laius. They argue as to who has the right of passage over the crossroad and during the argument Oedipus kills Laius. He then solves the riddle that the sphinx used to bar strangers from entering Thebes. The Thebans, delighted by his achievement, reward him by offering the widowed Queen Jocasta as his wife. Oedipus ends up marrying his own mother who subsequently gives birth to Antigone, Ismene, Polyneices and Eteocles. When a plague besieges the kingdom of Thebes, Oedipus finds out that he is the cause of it through his marriage to Jocasta. Jocasta kills herself and Oedipus blinds himself and leaves Thebes. Jocasta's brother, Creon, becomes the regent to the throne. But soon after, Eteocles, the younger son of Oedipus, usurps the throne. Polyneices with a group of soldiers rebels against his brother and the city in a quest to take back the throne which by the rules of primogeniture rightly belonged to him. The two brothers end up killing each other. Creon then becomes king and pronounces an edict which bars Thebans from burying Polyneices and his army, as they were considered traitors. Antigone defies the edict and buries her brother. When Creon discovers from the guards that it was Antigone who buried him, he calls upon her to account for her conduct. Instead of confessing to her act, as Butler reminds us, Antigone refuses to deny that it was she who did the deed (Butler, 2000a: 7). This point, as I explain below, is significant in Butler's reinterpretation of the tragedy. I mention it here so you are aware of how Antigone accounts for her act. Creon angrily (despite the pleas of his son Haemon, who was to marry Antigone) orders that she is to be buried alive. Tirresias, the blind prophet, informs Creon that the gods are unhappy with his decision and as a result will send another plague upon Thebes. Creon rushes to save Antigone but arrives too late. Antigone has taken her own life. The play ends with Haemon taking his own life, unable to cope with the death of his bride to be, and Euridice, Creon's own wife, also committing suicide.

Kings were vested with legal and executive powers. As sovereigns, they were able to promulgate edicts, declare wars, grant pardons to those that pleaded for them, and ultimately make laws. With this in mind, it becomes rather obvious why interpreters of this play read the figure of Antigone as the paradigmatic ethical figure. Antigone is the one who defies the laws of the state, embodied by the sovereign Creon.[15] In defying the laws of the state, by both burying her brother and killing herself, she demonstrates that she is not a criminal, but rather is obedient to divine laws (gods, kinship, customary burial rites). In doing so, Antigone is said to convert her act into an ethical act. Antigone explains her acts in her own way:

> I'd never have taken this ordeal upon myself, never defied our people's will. What law, you ask, do I satisfy with what I say? A husband dead, there might have been another. A child by another too, if I had lost the first. But mother and father both lost in the halls of Death, no brother could ever spring to light again.
>
> (Sophocles, 1984: 105)

What this statement reveals is that burying her brother, an act of defiance of law but also an act that risks her life, was done in honour or celebration of the particularity of her brother. Her brother, unlike a child or a husband, is irreplaceable, especially since both her parents are dead. She stresses that she would not have acted the same in other circumstances, turning her act into a singular act. Ethical subjects – subjects that act responsibly, as we have seen from the discussions of the subject – are the ones that celebrate the singularity of the other, without reducing the other to the universal and the laws that govern this universality. It is not difficult to see how Antigone is made into an ethical heroine, given this.

Butler, like a detective, searches for clues within the tragedy and amongst Hegel's, Lacan's and Irigaray's interpretations of the play. She tries to find out whether one can make such a claim regarding Antigone. She discovers that, despite their theoretical differences, Hegel, Lacan and Irigaray share a common view regarding Antigone. For them, she is 'not a political figure, one whose defiant speech has political implications, but rather... one who articulates a pre-political opposition to politics representing kinship as the sphere that conditions the possibility of politics without ever entering into it' (Butler, 2000a: 3). Their common interpretation positions ethics in the sphere of the private. The idea of kinship, that Antigone is said to hold above any public law, is what precisely disables her to enter the public or political sphere, but at the same time puts her at the boundaries of the public. More precisely, Lacan, as Butler writes, has Antigone,

> border the spheres of the imaginary and the symbolic where she is understood, in fact, to figure the inauguration of the symbolic, the sphere of laws and norms that govern the accession to speech and speakability. This regulation takes place through the instantiation of certain relations within the field of symbolic norms.

Hence, 'kinship is rarefied as enabling linguistic structure, a presupposition of symbolic intelligibility, and thus removed from the domain of the social' (Butler, 2000a: 3). And for Hegel, equally but differently, 'kinship is precisely a relation of "blood" rather that one of norms. That is, kinship is not yet entered into the social, where the social is inaugurated through a violent supersession of kinship' (Butler, 2000a: 3). The feminist philosopher Irigaray also holds a proximate position. Butler explains:

> For Irigaray, the insurrectionary power of Antigone is the power of that which remains outside the political; Antigone represents kinship and, indeed the power of 'blood' relations, which Irigaray doesn't mean in a precisely literal sense. For Irigaray, blood designates something of bodily specificity and graphicness that fully abstract principles of political equality not only fail to grasp but most rigorously exclude and even annihilate. ... Antigone thus signifies for Irigaray the transition from the rule of law based on maternity, a rule of law based in Kinship, to a rule based on paternity.
>
> (Butler, 2000a: 3–4)

More generally for all three thinkers, the ethical domain stands at the cast of the juridico-political domain, without ever being reduced to it. Antigone's attachment to the law's of kinship, despite her public denunciation of the civic laws, produce her action as a private and therefore an ethical one. In this tautological (and it is tautological, because it sets from the start the ethical as the private and thus reads through it the actions of Antigone) and circular understanding of the play there is no blurring of the boundaries between the ethical, legal and political. Butler nevertheless is able to provide us with a different reading of both Antigone and of the relation between the ethical, legal and political. Her reading demonstrates that all these spheres are not necessarily separate from each other but rather exclusively inclusive of each other.

As we have seen, Butler's subject is one that comes into being through norms and language that pre-exist it. Though, let's not forget that the subject becomes agentic through its resistance to these norms. This very constellation of the subject puts the subject within the sphere of the public. Language or norms are public. For Butler, in this sense there is no pre-political or private, our coming into the world establishes us as public and therefore political figures (Butler, 2000a: 46–47). Butler, demonstrates this most strongly when she talks about Antigone's refusal to deny that she buried her brother. Butler informs us that Green's translation of the play has Antigone confessing to the deed. Nevertheless, the Greek words have her deny that she buried her brother. Let's cast our eyes for a second over the meaning that Butler gives to this:

> 'Yes, I confess it', or 'I say I did it' – thus she answers a question that is posed to her from another authority, and thus she concedes the authority that this other has over her. 'I will not deny my deed' – 'I do not deny', I will not be forced into denial, I will refuse to be forced into a denial by the other's language, and what I will not deny is my deed – a deed that becomes possessive, a grammatical possession that makes sense only within the context of the scene in which a forced confession is refused by her. In other words, to claim 'I will not deny my deed' is to refuse to perform a denial, but it is not precisely to claim the act. 'Yes, I did it', is to claim the act, but it is also to commit another deed in the very claiming, the act of publishing one's deed, a new criminal venture that redoubles and takes the place of the old.
>
> (Butler, 2000a: 8)

In not denying that she buried Polyneices, we are told that Antigone usurps sovereignty of her actions. She resists the very terms in which Creon wants her to address his question, a resistance that makes Creon and his messengers call her manly (2000a: 8–9). This resistance gives Antigone agency, for as we know from Chapter 2, it is at the moment whereby the subject resists the norms that bring it into being, the modes of address cause agency to emerge. But Butler questions the extent to which Antigone's usurpation of sovereignty is one that falls within the parameters of masculine sovereignty (2000a: 9). As we have already noted, Antigone cites the laws of kinship as authorisation for her act, but at the same time, she transgresses these laws, because she tells us that she would not have done this for *anybody* else. So in transgressing the laws of kinship, she mirrors the act of her brother Polyneices who himself transgressed them by running an army against his brother Eteocles. In denying her deed, she uses language to usurp authority, but despite the fact that she does not confirm Creon's mode of address, she mirrors his sovereignty and therefore is called manly. In becoming manly, she makes Creon unmanly. This is used by Butler to demonstrate that there is no stabilisation of gender in the play or, more generally, there is rather a flowing temporality of genders, making it difficult to talk of sovereignty as masculine.

But there is another caveat in Butler's interpretation. We have seen so far that a temporal conception of the subject emerges, and we have also seen that the subject is the outcome of language and deeds. But it is the language of denial that demonstrates that Antigone embodies the very laws that she is opposing, this very language of denial brings into being her transgression but simultaneously establishes the law, for it is only through its language that she can become authoritative. As we are reminded most eloquently in the chapter on 'Promiscuous obedience', Antigone, in a most paradoxical manner, also obeys the law of her own father. Oedipus, in Sophocles' other play, *Oedipus at Colonus*, curses his children to an unlivable life in the name of death. In killing herself, she obeys the curse of her father, but in doing so she displaces her love of her father's law, on to her brother, for it is for him that she dies: 'She obeys his demand, but promiscuously, for he is clearly not the only dead man she loves, indeed, not the ultimate one' (Butler, 2000a: 60).

Indeed, Antigone might, as Butler demonstrates, come into being as an inhuman, dead subject. The curse of her father has already put her in that space of an unlivable life, but, nevertheless, if she had followed the laws of Creon, she would have continued being a dead woman walking. Her resistance to confessing the 'crime', her burial of her brother, her transgression of the laws of kinship but, simultaneously, her obedience and embodiment of the law can be seen as a series of performative acts that recite not only that Antigone is already a public figure, but also that the idea of kinship on which the reinterpretation of the play by Lacan, Hegel and Irigaray relied is based upon the scandal of kinship (Butler, 2000a: 58). The prohibition of incest, which is the lesson of *Oedipus Rex*, can't sustain itself on its own. And to this effect, Butler writes: 'To the extent that the incest taboo contains its infraction within itself, it does not simply prohibit incest but rather sustains and cultivates incest as a necessary spectre of social dissolution, a spectre without which social bonds cannot emerge' (2000a: 66–7). If indeed this is the case, if *Antigone* does gesture to the spectre of promiscuity within the normative parameters of the incest taboo, then, for Butler, there emerges the possibility of redrawing both legitimate and illegitimate norms of kinship (2000a: 67). *Antigone* therefore is read as opening us up to the possibility a more livable and viable life, one where different types of kinship can be lived (homosexual kinship) and the grieving of lives that have been foreclosed by the private understanding of kinship could be allowed a public space (people with HIV). Let's not forget that Antigone thought that her life was worthless if she was unable to provide her brother with the appropriate burial rites. Antigone, who comes into being through the norms that she does not possess, through a language that is not her own, a human walking towards death, offers, as Butler writes, a catachrestic reading of the human, in the sense that she has been stolen of her humanity. However, in re-appropriating and risking the truth, she turns her inhumanity, her zoe into a possibility for the future.

Her act of denial is read as a political and legal act and this inevitably allows us once more to observe that the limits of the ethical, the question of the subject as the foundation of ethics, is really a problem *for* ethics. But still, the question of a livable and viable life, material subjects, is one that oscillates between the spheres of the ethical, political and legal.

When Heidegger criticises metaphysical philosophers for forgetting, in their attempt to find what it means to be human and their preoccupation with the meaning of human, he points out that the human is thrown into the world, is ek-static and through ek-stasy moves towards a future of death. Butler, in merging the issue of method (performativity) with the question of life, comes closer to demonstrating the Heideggerian quest for the essence of being. The human is thrown into the world, it comes into the world through language norms that are represented as culturally intelligible, but at the same time this human is always inhuman, it always resists or deliberates these norms that bring it into being. The human is mere materiality, in the truly Heideggerian sense of labour (Heidegger, 2004: 243), but this laborious (resisting or deliberating) self-making, is also agentic, it has, in other words conscience – although Butler's conscience is an unknowing one (it does not pre-exist the subject), it is one that comes into being at the moment of materiality, resistance or deliberation, it is always ecstatic and it is constituted by the Other. It is in this sense that Butler's writing about being is not *about* being, but is a story that is told by the being itself in the process of its own making. It is also in this sense that her subject is not already reflexive and can't reduce the Other to itself, for it is always in the process of making. If we are to have livable and viable lives, then zoe is at the centre of them, offering for Butler both the conditions of our existence but also its consequences, in the sense of its unknowing future. Ironically, if we can be certain of anything it is that, if we are to rethink how we can have livable and viable lives, despite how different and irreconcilable each life is to each other, we need to think of the subject within the parameters that Butler proposes: a subject that *deliberates* before it acts in the face of absolute difference and moves towards the Other *despite* this difference.

Notes

1 Literature in other words becomes that space where we question the possibility of being able to decide to what extent the textual characters are moral or immoral, creating therefore an aura of ambivalence and indecision.
2 See Chapter 5 for a more extensive elaboration of contemporary continental philosophy and politics.
3 In *Giving an Account of Oneself* (2005) Butler discusses extensively Levinasian ethics. This analysis and critique did not appear in the (2003) version of the book which I consulted in writing this chapter. Here she demonstrates that Levinas's claim that ethics is pre-ontological can't sustain its claim once we pay attention to his example to the Jew as the persecuted. At this instance the pre-ontological and the ontological get confused (2005: 94).
4 For further discussion on this point about the ecstatic subject of Hegel, see Nathan Roteinstreich, 'On the ecstatic sources of the concept of alienation' in *Review of Metaphysics*, 1963; Jean-Luc Nancy, *Hegel: The Restlessness of the Negative* (2002) and Catherine Malabou, *The Future of Hegel: Plasticity, Temporality and Dialectic* (2005).
5 For a critical evaluation of this see Alain Badiou, *Manifesto for Philosophy* (1999) and Gilles Deleuze's 'The image of thought' in *Difference & Repetition* (1994).
6 As Kojeve (1980: 183) observes, Hegel's philosophical method is *not* dialectical, but phenomenological. In other words, he describes the process of reaching concrete reality (dialectics) but does *not* engage in dialectics. Before being wholly tautological here, it is both necessary and appropriate to explain a little bit further what a dialectical method entails and how Hegel overcomes it. Most philosophical writings

from Plato onwards engaged with a dialectical or dialogical method in order to arrive at the truth about the world, humans, animals, objects, art, politics, etc. The Platonic dialogues on love, for example, contained in the *Symposium* (2005), begin by asserting that we have only one concept of love. This position, the initial thesis, is revealed through contested dialogue and, as in the case of the *Symposium*'s inebriated multiple opposing opinions about love (anti-thesis), is shown as being mythical. There are many opinions about love and a compilation of all of them can produce an objective or rather a more objective truth. Truth therefore becomes a synthetic process. The synthetic truth turns out to be a compilation of one-sided explorations into philosophical or scientific truth. In this way, the truth as One-Whole is produced. The production of the truth as One-Whole also 'captures' the overcoming of all these three stages of the dialectical process (thesis, anti-thesis, synthesis). As Kojeve puts it: 'they are overcome or annulled with respect to whatever is fragmentary, relative, partial, or one-sided in them – that is, with respect to what makes them false when one of them is taken not for an opinion, but as the truth' (1980: 180). At the same time, the One-Whole preserves what each of these opinions represents as an aspect or perspective on the total and, lastly, it moves them to a 'superior level of knowledge and of reality, and therefore of truth' (Kojeve, 1980: 180–181). The philosopher becomes the one who enables the production of this synthetic truth, that is neither singular nor plural, but rather both at the same time. Hegel, instead of participating in the philosophical cog of the production of truth, merely describes it and is able to do so because he has the experience of it. In this respect, one could say that the experience of the history of philosophy's claim to truth enables Hegel to describe the absolute truth without having to engage in its method. Experience, as we are told in the 'Preface' of the *Phenomenology of Spirit* (2004), does not refer to scientific experience, understood as an experience by which the subject that does the observation is totally detached and independent from the object that is being observed. Hegel, on the contrary, understands experience as the very relation or antagonism between the subject and object. Experience is what reveals concrete reality or the truth. And in turn, this reality that is concrete is both revealed in discourse and discourse reveals a reality (Kojeve, 1980: 179). I am persisting with an extensive elaboration of this here because it links back to Hegel's *overcoming* of the dialectical method. It is this particular conceptualisation of experience that allows Hegel to disengage from the dialectical method. Since he can experience the One-Whole as both an outcome of discourse and as what comes within discourse, he is already part of this dialectical process and therefore superfluous to its enactment.

7 See Kojeve (1980) and Hyppolite (2000).

8 Taylor talks about this as the historical and ontological dialectics (1999: 131–134).

9 Butler additionally uses this quote to suggest that Hegel engages in the perversion of grammar to produce the subject as restless.

10 See Kojeve (1980: 13). Kojeve suggests that the desire for recognition signifies the overcoming of one's attachment to its animal state of being and a movement towards one's own truth. Let's not forget that Hegel in the 'Preface' of the *Phenomenology of Spirit* explicitly points out that man is burdened by the senses and, if man is to reach truth, then we must get rid of our sensual attachments (Hegel, 2004: 4–5).

11 Amongst others see Heidegger (1962, 1969, 1985, 1988).

12 Foucault (1988, 1990, 1992)

13 See Agamben (1998: 8) on the notion of inclusive exclusion. See also Fitzpatrick's (2001) analysis of law and inclusive exclusion.

14 For an account of deliberation and democracy, see also Derrida (2005).

15 Douzinas and Warrington (1994: 25–92) provide us with a rich and useful reading of the different types of laws that are contested in the tragedy.

Chapter 4

Double law

> The right to punish, therefore, is an aspect of the sovereign's right to make war on his enemies: to punish belongs to 'that absolute power of life and death which Roman law calls *merum imperium*, a right by virtue of which the prince sees that his law is respected by ordering the punishment of crime' (Muyart de Vouglans, xxxiv). But punishment is also a way of exacting retribution that is both personal and public, since the physico-political force of the sovereign is in a sense present in the law.
>
> (Foucault, 1991a: 48)

> The juridical structures of language and politics constitute the contemporary field of power; hence, there is no position outside this field, but only a critical genealogy of its own legitimating practices. As such, the critical point of departure is the historical present, as Marx put it. And the task is to formulate within this constituted frame a critique of the categories of identity that contemporary juridical structures engender, naturalize, and immobilize.
>
> (Butler, 1990: 5)

'I am not interested in the rule of law *per se*, however, but rather in the place of law in the articulation of an international conception of rights and obligations that limit and condition claims of state sovereignty' (2004a: 98), Butler writes towards the end of 'Indefinite detention', one of her essays in *Precarious Life: The Powers of Mourning and Violence* (2004a). Indeed, she is not interested in the *rule of law*, and to be precise she *never* has been. 'Indefinite detention' is her more recent and explicit engagement with law, but despite law making multiple appearances in this piece, the essay is, as the subtitle of the book points out, interested in the concepts of life, power and violence. Now, as the book was written as a response, a polemic response I would suggest, to the US and UK reactions to the 9/11 attacks on New York's twin towers and the Pentagon, by alleged al-Qaeda and Taliban inspired terrorists, it is obvious why Butler is taking up these concepts.

The consequences are well known; in addition to the painful loss of thousands of people working in these buildings, in addition to the destruction of property, psychological and physical traumas, financial losses, global empathy with the victims of the attacks and those who launched them, we also inherited a new geopolitical situation, a 'war on terror' and, everything that goes with it. As the attacks were perceived as attacks on US security or, as the US president George W Bush put it on the national day of remembrance on 14 September 2001, '[w]ar has been waged against us by stealth and deceit and murder'.[1] And, as this was perceived by the executive as a war against the nation, 'a nation [that] is peaceful, but fierce when stirred to anger' (ibid.), as George W Bush put it, the nation would retaliate because the conflict had begun without warrant and would end, as once more he remarks, 'at an hour, of our choosing' (ibid.). And, indeed, as a result, a series of counterattacks were launched and are still being conducted by the United States and its allies, predominant among them the United Kingdom, against Afghanistan and Iraq, two countries thought to shelter terrorists or pose a threat to global security. The war in Afghanistan saw the arrest and detention of al-Qaeda and Taliban 'militant' men and their indefinite detention at Quantanamo Bay, Cuba. So when Butler thinks about life, violence and power in the aforementioned book, she does so against the backdrop of these specific events and the way they have mobilised or transformed understandings of power, life and violence. Law figures in her discussion in relation to these concepts.

Now, most of us would have probably thought that in such circumstances western liberal democracies would rely on the law to make sure that a war, even if it is a 'war on terror', would take place within their constitutional framework. As we learnt and still learn in our constitutional law classes, law and its institutional apparatuses (judges, courts, etc.) ensure that the separation of powers is not overstepped or abused. In other words, law is supposed to secure us from any executive abuse. Legal protection from abuse of executive power can, of course, be suspended. But the suspension takes place if extraordinary circumstances have figured, that is, in cases of war, political terrorism or general strikes. At the same time, there is a normal precondition that the general powers given to government to deal with such emergencies will in principle be found in Acts of parliament, in the case of the United Kingdom. While, The Defence of the Realm Acts 1914–15 and the Emergency Powers (Defence) Acts 1939–40 gave the executive in the United Kingdom authority to administer every aspect of life during the two world wars, the courts were not banned from evaluating challenges to abuses of power that were brought forward to them – although they were very reluctant to do so.[2]

Whether emergency powers belong to a juridical or executive sphere has been a sore point of discussion for some time, and not only amongst constitutional lawyers, political theorists and philosophers. Agamben, in the first part of his book *State of Exception* (2005a: 1–31) describes some of these debates which to reiterate are centred around the question of whether the decree of a state of exception belongs to the juridical or executive sphere.

When Butler writes in the quote above that she is interested 'in the place of law in...state sovereignty' (2004a: 98) today, we might be excused for thinking that the sentence betrays a certain understanding of the role of law in general, that Butler sees the law as a kind of police person to the executive. She after all wants to know how law articulates its relationship to state authority, rights and international treaties and freedoms. But – as the chapter on 'Indefinite detention' and her earlier work, as I explain below, suggests – she is in no way interested in promoting 'the rule of law *per se*'. She after all is fully aware of the fantasy of the rule of law (2004a: 98), the use of law for political means and, especially, the use of law as an instrument of government. What are we to understand from the sentence quoted above? It raises precisely two issues, which for her are inextricably linked. The first is existential, the second political. So when she raises the issue of the place of law, she is asking foremost about its place in relation to the question of life. Can it, in other words, promote and sustain a mode of life that is livable and viable? If yes, how? What political issue is raised in relation to the power of law? What kind of power is law now endowed with? And once more, how can this power (and if it is a power, what type of power does law have?) be used politically so it could enable the sustainability of life?

So when in 'Indefinite detention', Butler discusses the decree of 'state of emergency' declared by the US administration during the aftermath of 9/11 which saw the beginning of two wars and the indefinite detention of so-called al-Qaeda and Taliban 'militants', she is not by any means relinquishing the old debate about jurisdictional issues relating to decrees of exception, but rather she is trying to find out how such decrees relate to law, our existence and politics. She is not alone in this. Agamben, who even prior to the 9/11 attacks engaged with the decree of 'state of exception' in his *Homo Sacer: Sovereign Power and Bare Life* (1998), clearly writes in *State of Exception* (2005a) (the follow-up to *Homo Sacer*), '[t]he essential task of a theory of the state of exception is not simply to clarify whether it has a juridical nature or not, but to define the meaning, place, and modes of its relation to the law' (2005a: 51). To retain the discussion to jurisdictional problems debases the effects of the 'state of exception' on life and our political potential. Or to put it in slightly more positive terms, it restricts the discussion to technical issues that obscure its operational effects and the understanding we draw from it about the meaning of law, life and politics. So the particular task of the philosopher, Butler in our case, is to untangle, undo, deconstruct if you want, the position of law in this situation and the meaning of this position.

Butler, as I explain in this chapter, sees law's influence on the political or existential terrain as diminishing. The law has lost any capacity to exert any influence or restraints on these spheres. We can even say that the law is becoming impotent. It has become *once more* an instrument for the proliferation of sovereign power.[3] Now, again, this sounds paradoxical from somebody who admits to being aware of the limits of the rule of law and its politicisation. Again, we will be forgiven if we read through this construction of the current position of law a desire to return to a certain meaning of law that is well situated within a liberal discourse – precisely the type of meaning ingrained in those who understand law as the institution that protects us from the abuse of executive or legislative powers, by policing the boundaries of these jurisdictions. This conclusion would be slightly misguided. In order to understand Butler's frustration with the current place of law, we have to go back to her understanding of subject formation. As we have seen from earlier chapters, Butler's subject is not independent of the conditions that bring it to life (linguistic, legal, political, social, material) but, simultaneously, it attains an *agentic* position. As we have seen, this possibility emerges at the very moment in which it resists these conditions of its formation. Resistance, as I have explained in Chapter 1 of this book, does not dismantle the whole socio-symbolic strata or the conditions that enable subject formation, but what it *does* is gesture towards different aspirations of life and the possibility of their materialisation. So when she repeatedly writes in 'Indefinite detention' that the law has become an instrument of governmentality, when she suggests the necessity of prosecuting detainees through established criminal courts and not through *ad hoc* administrative established tribunals, what she is getting at and arguing for, is not some type of romantic return to a rule of law, but for law to retain its hold on to the one thing that perhaps distinguishes it from other institutions, its agonist spirit that is translated through the modality of trialing. Only then can it have a role to play in this 'new', if it is a new, status quo. And only then can it 'contribute' to the viability and vitalisation of life. To put it otherwise, in crude Hegelianism, if the law is the slave here and its object is 'life' and 'life' is what the executive wants to secure from it, then law's agonism that is centred around its desire for autonomy (desire not to be an instrument for the executive) should be focused upon its desire for survival, its agonism for life. Then and only then could it perhaps contribute to the production of viable and livable lives. But this might require law to perform a different task. Law would, as I explain later in this chapter, need to take up the task of the translator – to translate and rather than interpret our irreconcilable differences when we make demands for life *per se*.

Before I begin analysing Butler's understanding of these relationships and the possibilities or impossibilities that they produce in relation to the subject and life, I will introduce Agamben's analysis of the state of exception. This intervention is useful not only because I consider that Agamben and Butler share similar commitments to the possibility of a viable life, not only because Agamben provided us with an access to the operation of sovereign governmentality even before 9/11, but simply because his ideas have influenced Butler's own analysis of the operation of power when a decree of a state of exception is activated.

This chapter will proceed initially to engage with Butler's own understanding of the type of power which she has seen emerging in the United States since the 9/11 attacks. 'Indefinite detention' provides us with a succinct account of the relationship between law, politics and power that is present in her other work, namely *Undoing Gender* (2004b), *Excitable Speech* (1997b), *Bodies that Matter* (1993) and *Gender Trouble* (1990).

This approach might appear slightly idiosyncratic (approaching her ideas from the perspective of her most recent publication to explain her earlier contribution) and at odds with the method that I have used so far in analysing her work (following a genealogical approach). But I can justify it on the grounds of the conclusions that Butler's 'Indefinite detention' chapter is making. In it, she appears to suggest that the juridical order lost any effect that it might have had in creating life, a conclusion that she did not hold earlier in relation to law. You may recall that in *Excitable Speech* she explicitly forewarns us of the limits of law. She argued for an avoidance of any form of censorship of hate speech. When the state and the judiciary 'legislate' against injurious speech by outlawing it in the name of our security and recognition of our equality rights, they structurally and effectively preclude us from answering back to such injuries. Having the possibility of being able to answer back renews vitality and viability. But, moreover, the effects of the institutionalisation of this banning are none other than the limitation of our lives by concretising the idea that only law and state institutions, such as the executive, can hold the monopoly on the use and regulation of violence. In other words, by banning injurious speech, law bans the very possibility of the creation life, the resistance to the linguistic practice of interpellation. This is precisely the limit of law that she points to in *Excitable Speech*.

But law is by no means perceived as ineffectual or impotent. On the contrary, in doing so it might limit the sustainability of life (as explained in an earlier chapter) while at the same time sustaining law's own life, and demonstrating that it can preserve its life by controlling violence that strikes at the heart of either its principles (equality, tolerance, etc.) or institutions. The limits of law, in *Excitable Speech*, do not refer to its capacity but rather to the effects that it has upon life. However, in 'Indefinite detention', Butler speaks of a crippled law, an impotent law. But, as quoted above, she also searches for a new role of law when the state of exception is declared. This of course at first blush is a very paradoxical position to have. While in her earlier work she problematises law, here she calls unequivocally *for* law, or for a new role for law. How can we address this paradox? Even when law effectively restricts the structures of our livability, it still produces space for creativity within its limits. For example, rap and reggae musicians, despite attempted regulation of hate speech both in the United States and United Kingdom, continue to produce music that is homophobic and gynophobic and in this way allow a cultural evaluation of whether their speech is injurious or not either by prompting a refusal to buy the music or attend concerts (a neo-liberal resistance alignment), or causing a counter-discourse that resists and answers back to the injurious speech in various public arenas. 'Injured' groups and individuals still have the opportunity to offer an alternative narrative to the one that the injurious speech provides, a narrative that sustains their survival, but is by no means a reinvigoration of life. Survival becomes the rule. And survival is possible through the limits of law because law does not have a monopoly on the narrative of public life. The narratives of those that perpetrate such speech or are affected by it are still recorded, still present and, more importantly, still able to signify that there is another public, a counter-public, than the one advertised by the state and its institutions, challenging in this way the meanings of public, state and law.

But with an impotent law, a decaying law, what we see taking place is something else. Law does not use force to sustain its survival, but rather is being *used* by the sovereign as a technique of governmentality: a life-support machine to the executive, a killing machine to those deemed a threat to the executive. This is, as we will see, the current role of the law when a state of emergency is being declared. The effect of this is totalising in every meaning of the word. It totalises narratives, it precludes those that are deemed a threat from providing us with a counter-narrative, it precludes the possibility of a legitimate trial – one of the possible but albeit restrictive ways through which a counter-narrative can be recorded and at least sustain survival – and above all it gives licence to kill, as happened in the United Kingdom on 22 July 2005, when plain-clothes police officers shot and killed an unarmed Brazilian man whom they had followed from an address that was under surveillance. The man was never asked to stop, he picked up the free newspaper available at the tube station, used his Oyster card to pass the ticket barrier and dashed to catch the train that was about to set off from Stockwell station in London. While sitting in the train carriage, he was restrained and then shot dead by police officers. The officers were operating under s 3 of the 1967 criminal law which states that: 'A person may use such force as is reasonable in the prevention of crime.' The police have been given the power to shoot and kill if they anticipate that a person could threaten the lives of people around them or the lives of police officers in the vicinity, after the two terrorist attacks in London that took place on 7 and 21 July respectively. The law is literally used here to kill. And the Brazilian man who lay dead on the floor of the station was a material body, but he was also a narrative, a story that has been discarded in the name of security, democracy, moderation and to quote the UK Prime Minister Tony Blair, 'our way of life'. The difference therefore between a limited law and an impotent one is the very fine line between survival and death.

As we have seen, a limited law can be contested either within its own institution, such as the institution of the trial, or even more it can itself be put on trial, in other spaces, for example, in music or alternative media or other public forums. The counter-narratives, that I refer to above as media whereby the totalitarianism of the so-called official public institutions or spaces are encountered and resisted, operate as trials, ensuring our sustained survival. Survival, of course, is not an aspirational state of life for one to have, but perhaps it is better than an executive death. And to return to Butler and her paradoxical reprisal with law, and her quest for a place for law, it is one that as I would explain, becomes necessary when even survival is not a choice.

The second section of this chapter will consider how this understanding of law is reflected in Butler's other work and, moreover, how it relates to disciplinary power, a modality of power that in her earlier work she used to criticise juridical power and law. But now, I turn to the work of Giorgio Agamben and his analysis of state of exception.

Legal suspensions and the question of violence

> To show law in its nonrelation to life and life in its nonrelation to law means to open a space between them for human action, which once claimed for itself the name of 'politics'.
>
> (Agamben, 2005a: 88)

The *State of Exception* (2005a) offers a rich tracing of both the history of the use of state of emergency decrees and an in-depth analysis of past and contemporary critical reflections that surround it. I am not concerned here with recounting this. What follows is an account of the core of his argument. For Agamben, a critical evaluation of this concept is of importance, but its pertinence does not lie with those discussions that try to either claim the term as a juridical concept or as an extra-juridical concept (2005a: 51), as I already indicated, but rather its potency lies with understanding both the effects and meaning of the ambiguity of its operation as a mechanism that is both within and without law. Put otherwise, what becomes important for us to understand is how it relates to the law. If we focus mainly on the jurisdiction of the concept, our discussion is restricted on technicalities and our attention is diverted from the substance of what happens when a state of emergency decree is activated. A relational analysis opens up the possibility, as I touched upon above, of understanding the effects that it has on life. But before focusing on the core of his argument, it is pertinent to contextualise, albeit crudely, the parameters of his thesis.

Agamben, in *Homo Sacer* (1998) – the first of his three books dwelling on sovereign-governmentality, the other two are *Remnants of Auschwitz* (1999a) and *State of Exception* (2005a) – shows that the origins of the political lie not with the inclusion of life in city matters but rather with the ban or exclusion of certain lives from it. He argues that the decision as to what type of life is to be excluded lies in the hands, or rather in the mouth, of the sovereign. This proposition puts the sovereign at the centre of political power and makes sovereign power the locus of politics. But, as we shall see, Agamben's sovereign is not Hobbes's sovereign who is 'personified' in the figure of the Leviathan, contractually bound to both represent and secure its subjects (Agamben, 1998: 109). Agamben's sovereign, unlike Hobbes's Leviathan, bans (and does not represent) life (or certain lives) from the polis. Now, as you can see, Agamben returns political power, constitutional power, to the figure of the sovereign but turns the tables to alert us to its exclusionary dimension. Contrary to Foucault, who argued that in modernity we can view the 'downfall' of sovereign executive powers and the emergence of two different modalities of power, disciplinary and bio-power (an overall decentralisation and dispersal of power which for the first time puts life at the centre of politics) (Foucault, 1990: 143), Agamben's thesis proposes that, in modernity we view what was always already there (and he demonstrates it by drawing upon a variety of texts from Roman law and medieval political theory), that bare life or zoe[4] was always included in the city, albeit in a paradoxical way, by exclusion. As he explains, his position emerged from an aporia that he encountered in Foucault's later work. Foucault evaluated a series of techniques (e.g. surveillance and governmentality) used to put life at the centre of political activity and consequentially to produce identities, subjects and statistics. His analysis revealed that power was neither centralised, nor for that matter possessed by the sovereign, but rather it was dispersed amongst individuals and institutions. Agamben points out, though, that the later Foucault appears to suggest that the modern western state was able to integrate 'techniques of subjective individualization with procedures of objective totalization' (5–6) without offering an explanation as to how this occurs. Agamben takes this as his point of departure and suggests that these two technologies, the technologies of the self and institutional techniques find their meeting point in the figure and practices of the sovereign. And to this effect, he writes 'that the inclusion of bare life in the political realm constitutes the original – if concealed – nucleus of sovereign power. *It can even be said that the production of a bio-political body is the original activity of sovereign power*' (6), stating explicitly that bio-politics (the government of life) is inextricably linked to sovereign power.

Agamben utilises the declaration of a decree of 'a state of exception', traditionally used by the sovereign in cases of emergency, as an example of the link and coincidence of sovereign and governmental power, as the moment at which certain lives are produced as bare lives (lives that are not sacrificial) included from the polis and its everydayness by simply being excluded. When the sovereign declares such a decree, and this is the core of his argument, the law is suspended. Consequently, this action takes place outside the law, but simultaneously the decision to suspend the law brings the sovereign within the law because it is the sovereign who forms the decision for the constitution to be suspended. As he writes, '[t]he sovereign decision of the exception is the originary juridico-political structure on the basis of which what is included in the juridical order and what is excluded from it acquire their meaning' (18, 19). As it is the sovereign who decides upon this and since such a decision is based on alternating circumstances, as a consequence, what is and is not law and who is and is not a legal subject is constantly mobile. To put it otherwise, the state of exception is precisely the threshold of the sovereign decision. On the basis of this, you can see that the discussion as to the jurisdiction of the state of exception reveals itself to be even more futile. Or to be more precise, we should address the 'state of exception' within this paradoxical 'schema' of being inclusive and exclusive to the legal order. Agamben draws his understanding of the operation of the 'state of exception', the production of the sovereign as the one who decides upon when a 'state of emergency' should be declared, amongst other sources, from Carl Schmitt.

Schmitt's theory of the sovereign, developed in two books, *Constitutional Theory* and *Political Theology*, explains that when the sovereign declares a state of exception the law is suspended. But as Agamben explains, quoting from Schmitt's *Political Theology*, despite the fact that the decision to declare a state of exception is extra-juridical, an executive decision, in this situation, according to

Schmitt, both the norm and the decision retain their juridical essence (2005b: 289). How is this possible? Well the declaration of the state of exception 'creates the normal situation in which the law can be in force' (2005b: 289). If you want to think of this in figural terms, then imagine the sovereign having this big mouth that when it decides that there is such a status quo, when disorder threatens order, simultaneously makes the status quo the norm, that is, says that this is the norm now, this is why I need to suspend the law, and thus returns it within the juridical sphere. As Bredekamp writes,

> [t]he concept of the state of exception expresses Schmitt's conviction that democracy loses its foundation when different factions pursue their divergent interests to the point where a splintered political system is no longer able to guarantee the security of law. Under these circumstances, an extra societal force, the sovereign, must suspend the law in order to save them.
>
> (1999: 252)

And we might add with Agamben that precisely at this point it returns law back to itself (2005b: 289). So it is in this sense and through these circumstances that for the moment we may say, with Agamben and Schmitt, that the sovereign is 'he who decides upon the state of exception'. But Agamben goes on to argue that the 'state of exception', and along with it the sovereign decision, has now become the rule (1998: 12) or, put otherwise, is not anymore a decision that is taken up in exceptional circumstances. How does he arrive at this conclusion?

To understand this, we must turn to Walter Benjamin, whom Agamben deploys to not only explain and expose the differences that Schmitt and Benjamin have, or to unveil their correspondence and textual covert references to each other's work, but most of all to point out how the exception becomes the rule and the effects that this brings about. I will elaborate on the importance of Benjamin in Agamben's understanding of the relationship, or rather irrelationship, between law and life below, an issue that is inextricably linked to this debate, but first let me explain by virtue of a brief introduction, Benjamin's position.

Benjamin, in *The German Tragic Drama*, engages with the figure of the sovereign. In his analysis of baroque German tragic drama, as Bredekamp points out, Benjamin 'shows rulers who are seemingly able to govern the state of exception and, ideally, to exclude it' (1999: 260). Moreover, Bredekamp continues, '[t]he symbol of the epoch is neither the clarity and permanence of the laws nor the moment of the sovereign's decision, but rather the "inability to decide"... and the torsion of hesitation' (1999: 260). To put it bluntly, for Benjamin there is no potent authority in counter-Reformation Germany (Agamben, 2005a: 55–56). Weber (1992: 5–18) explains with even more clarity how Benjamin arrives at this position but his explanation must take us once more back to Schmitt.

As we have seen, Schmitt's sovereign is the one who decides the 'state of exception' and declares the suspension of the law, but also by doing so brings an extraneous and anomic situation back into the realm of law. And Weber suggests that if such a decision, the decision to suspend the law 'can never be predicated or determined in advance' as it is determined by external factors, unexpected threats to law, then it cannot be an absolute decision. In other words, it can be precisely an exceptional suspension of the law (Weber, 1992: 10). To put it differently, Schmitt sees the suspension of the law as a reaction (and therefore unexpected) to an extraordinary state of the world (a world whose normality of time is threatened) and the suspension of the law is necessary in order to bring the world back to normality. What becomes important in the Schmittian position is that the state of exception should be itself deactivated once the norm is re-established.

But Benjamin as Weber explains 'describes the sovereign in the very terms that Schmitt rejects: the sovereign is charged with the task of "excluding" the state of exception' (1992: 12). As we have seen through Bredekamp, Benjamin's understanding of the sovereign is embedded in his thesis of the baroque sovereign, one who is unable to make decisions, and cannot alone decide on the state of exception. When Weber writes that Benjamin's sovereign excludes the state of exception, he means precisely that: the sovereign's inability to make a decision excludes the state of exception from the realm of sovereign jurisdiction. Thus, the state of exception is pushed into a vacant space, an anomic space (Weber, 1992: 14). But so far, it has not become evident how this becomes the rule. To understand this Weber, alongside Hamacher (2002), proposes that we have to understand Benjamin's thought not only in abstraction but also as enveloped with historical sensibility.

Again, a comparison between Schmitt and Benjamin will clarify this. For Schmitt, the sovereign is not a mere abstract political concept, but rather a historical concept. (Weber, 1992: 11). Political sovereignty is depicted as being evolved from theology. Schmitt draws a structural comparison between the sovereign and God. This comparison, between the sovereign and God, reduces the postulation into one of analogic identification. Instead of lamenting upon the differences between these conceptions, Schmitt's structure accentuates their sameness. Their sameness is related via their nexus to transcendence. God is transcended through the world, the sovereign through the state (Weber, 1992: 11–12).

For Benjamin, on the other hand, what transcends the state is that which is exterior to it (anomie or the state of exception), exteriorised once more. Now, does this reflect? The baroque sovereign reflects that there is an exteriorisation of the state of exception, an inability to bring it inside, within the norm and this simultaneously captures the exteriorisation of transcendence. If you prefer, what gets exteriorised is precisely the belief that there is something that goes beyond the material world (Weber, 1992: 12). In doing so, the 'state of exception' is no longer something that dwells outside the sovereign but instead dwells with him and, more importantly, is 'an internal part of the state and of the world, of the state of the world' (Weber, 1992: 12). Accordingly, although this desire of the baroque sovereign to transcend transcendence is also what prompts its malfunction, it unveils the ruler as being like any other creature on earth, 'left entirely to its own devices, without any other place to go, the state of exception has become the rule' (Weber, 1992: 14). So when the ruler is left to its own devices, incapable of deciding, then the 'state of exception' operates outside the realm of the norm, within an empty and anomic space, and it is in this sense that the 'state of exception' itself becomes the norm.

So far we have seen this discussion concerning the 'state of exception' as being represented as a reaction by Benjamin to Schmitt's *Political Theology*. Agamben, though, argues that we should actually read the 'encounter', if one can call it that, as one that originates with Benjamin's 'Critique of violence' and not with Benjamin's critique of *Political Theology* (Agamben, 2005a: 55–56, 2005b: 288–289). Agamben's proposition expiates, as we shall see, his analysis of norm and life. I would though like to suggest, that reading the *German Tragic Drama*, and the 'Critique of violence' alongside each other enables us to get a stronger hold on Benjamin's complexity of thought. Nevertheless, it is important to note that Schmitt responded to Benjamin's criticisms in *The German Tragic Drama* in his *Leviathan* in 1937, in which he covertly criticised Benjamin for ignoring the symbolisation of the Leviathan (Bredekamp, 1999: 261). With this, he critiques Benjamin's failure to grasp the fact that disorder feeds the figure of the Leviathan and, consequentially, enables the state of exception to be inaugurated by him (Bredekamp, 1999: 262). I am not going to pursue this line of inquiry here but, for constitutional law theorists interested in this debate, perhaps it is worth considering the minute differences between these two theorists via the figure of the Leviathan. I have mentioned all the above so as to indicate Agamben's sources of influence that have prompted him to claim that the 'state of exception has become the rule'. Below follows an examination of Agamben's exegesis of the irrelation of law and life, through his analysis of the declaration of a decree of a state of exception, I consequently engage with the battle between Schmitt and Benjamin.

Since I am introducing Agamben's conceptualisations of the way the 'state of exception' operates as a way of connecting it to Butler's exegesis and quest for a place for law in our geopolitical situation, it is pertinent to remind you that both these authors invested in forming an understanding of the relationship between law and life. What is the importance of this? As we have seen so far, the sovereign decision to declare a 'state of exception' does not only have command or control over which acts are legal or illegal, but at the same time has the power inclusively to exclude from the 'city', to ban certain lives to its borders, to produce their death, to the extent that those that perpetrate any offence against them will not be subjected to the tribulations of a punishment. In order to understand this occurrence, we must somehow return to a place where we can critically evaluate precisely the operational grounds of the state of exception, namely law and life. It is to this that I turn below.

So what happens to life when the 'state of emergency' becomes the rule? Agamben's analysis of the term 'force of law' addresses this issue directly.

Agamben begins his exegisis by returning us to the Roman and medieval uses of the term. We are informed that the term 'force of law'[5] in Roman and medieval law refers to the capacity of law 'to command, to forbid, to allow, to punish' (2005a: 37). In Roman law, it emerges that there was no apparent distinction between law and the 'force of law'. Nevertheless, modern law draws a distinction between law declared by legislative assemblies and the 'force of law' at the aftermath of the French Revolution of 1789. As he writes:

> modern doctrine distinguishes between the *efficacy* of the law – which rests absolutely with every valid legislative act and consists in the production of legal effects – and the *force of law*, which is instead a relative concept that expresses the position of the law or of acts comparable to it with respect to other acts of the juridical order that are endowed with a force superior to the law (as in the constitution) or inferior to it (such as decrees and regulations issued by the executive) (Quadri 1979: 10).
>
> (Agamben, 2005a: 37–38)

Agamben observes nevertheless that the *syntagma* (linguistic units made up of words or phrases that are arranged sequentially) of the term 'force of law' in both Roman and modern law is identical. The term 'force of law' refers to decrees like the state of exception, and not to norms or law. In drawing upon the modern distinction, we can note, as he writes, that it expresses a paradoxical relationship between the norm or law and its applicability. The term 'force of law' 'defines a "state of law" in which, on the one hand, the norm is in force [*vige*] but is not applied (it has no "force") [*fonza*] and on the other, acts that do not have the value [*valore*] of law acquire its "force"' (38–39). The norm or law, in this case becomes independent of its application, the 'state of exception' independent of the norm. The beauty of this paradox though lies in what it exposes: it unveils that the connection between the norm and its application does not rely upon a linear cause and effect or logic (39, 40). In other words, we have a situation that, while we have laws, they are not applied but suspended and what gets applied is a decision (a sovereign decision) that has no legal value but relies on a fictitious nexus to law to gain its force. The 'force of law' we can say gains its power or effectiveness because it operates upon this presupposition, namely a linear link between law and its applicability. It is precisely this conception that gives law its 'mystical' aura (39). The 'force of law', we can say is a performative act, speech act and act, in general, whereby what is cited, the law or the norm as the foundation of the act, is purely fantasmatic or, to put it within his language, it does not follow the logic of cause and effect. It is important to note here that for Agamben the sovereign pre-exists the utterance of a state of exception.

This is one of the differences between Butler and Agamben. For Butler, as we shall see, it is precisely the utterance of a state of exception that creates a sovereign governmental power. I will follow the effects of this difference in my analysis of her work.

But, returning to Agamben, this presupposition, the linear link between norm and applicability, enables the sovereign constantly to redraw the boundaries between what is legal and illegal. If this is correct, Agamben shows that the state of exception, brings to the surface something very important, namely that there is no linear connection between law and its applicability, but rather a fictitious or mythical belief of the existence of such a connection. This revelation or demystification demonstrates something even more sinister, that there is no coincidence between law and life. Let me explain this further.

As we have seen, the 'force of law' identifies the phenomenon that law is not linearly and logically connected to its applicability. This allows Agamben to infer that law and life or facticity are *not* linearly connected. The law, or the norm, is revealed as detached from life. Any claim to such connections is therefore unfounded, given that law is exposed as a closed system whose very survival relies on this nexus. So when he writes that:

> [t]his means that in order to apply a norm it is ultimately necessary to suspend its application, to produce an exception. In every case, the state of exception marks a threshold at which logic and praxis blur with each other and a pure violence without logos claims to realize an enunciation without any real reference.
>
> (40)

He means that the sovereign relies upon this fictional nexus to usurp his 'authority' when faced with a threatening situation, but this reliance or act is without any reference. This also raises another interesting point, namely, that 'in extreme situations "force of law" floats as an indeterminate element that can be claimed both by the state authority (which acts as a commissarial dictatorship) and by a revolutionary organization (which acts as a sovereign dictatorship)' (38–39). Here, he alerts us to the fact that the sovereign is not the only one who, in our history, was able to usurp this fictitious nexus between law and its applicability. Revolutionaries also usurp this force of law and, in doing so, they also act like sovereign dictators. As there is no normative foundation to the 'state of emergency', or because it functions within a space of anomie, then anyone can claim to be acting in its name. But there is a difference between the sovereign declaring a 'state of exception' and the revolutionary acting in its name. When the sovereign declares a state of exception, what we see taking place is what Schmitt described, namely that the sovereign suspends the law but at the same time brings this suspension within the realm of the norm. When the revolutionary operates the state of exception, it deposes the law, or withdraws from the law. What Agamben reactivates here is that there are two dialectically opposed 'forces of law' that expose differently but simultaneously this disconnection between law and its applicability.

This enables Agamben to demonstrate a subsequent effect (an effect that is of interest to us here), namely that the norm is not connected to life. In either case, whether we are relating the decree of a state of exception to the sovereign or the revolutionary, what is revealed is a disconnection between life and the norm. The fiction shows us that the Schmittian sovereign, for example, needs to suspend the law in order to relate it to life, whereas the revolutionary deposes it in order to connect to the particularity of its life circumstances. To drive the point home, he raises the problematic vis-à-vis the Kantian notion of judgment. He argues against the Kantian theory of judgment which postulates that the particular (application) is subsumed in the general (rule), if this were the case and there was a causative link between the norm and its applicability then the trial as a juridical practice would have been rendered obsolete (39–40). The trial is the practice that puts the norm in contest with life, with the life situation that is before it. Listen to what he says,

> [i]n the case of the juridical norm, reference to the concrete case entails a 'trial' that always involves a plurality of subjects and ultimately culminates in the pronunciation of a sentence, that is, an enunciation whose operative reference to reality is guaranteed by the institutional powers.
>
> (39–40)

If it is, then the case that law and life don't coincide when a decree of the state of exception, a decree that has the 'force of law', is declared, and if the juridical 'trial'[6] is the institution that exposes this, would the introduction of the practice of 'trial' make the connection between the norm and life possible? At a purely abstract theoretical level, the answer to this might appear to be 'yes'. But at the level of the concrete, which in Agamben's case is historical situationism, the times we are living in, it has to be 'no'.

Why is this the case then? Agamben correctly points out that retrieving the moment whereby the norm or law relates to life is not possible (86–88). His reasons are captured in the following sentence: 'From the real state of exception in which we live, it is not possible to return to the state of law [*station di diritto*], for at issue now are the very concepts of "state" and "law"' (87). In one dense sentence, Agamben captures two important problematics with returning to the state of law: the first is the impossibility of returning to an original state of law for, as explained through the analysis of the 'force of law' and norm, if there is no cause and effect connection between them but rather just the presumption of a nexus, then there is no 'original' norm on which the state of exception is based on. The call for a return to such an origin would be as fictitious as the origin itself. Foucault (1980: 139–164) and Butler in various ways and different contexts have demonstrated the fantasmatic character of the 'origin' and its effects. As we have seen, Butler explains how the fantasy of the origin naturalises and stabilises genders, with consequently the foreclosing of the possibility of genders that do not assimilate to the fantasy to be denigrated to abject subjects. I have also indicated in the previous chapter that Butler's critique of the 'origin' holds true for other subject formations, a point followed up later in this chapter in relation to detainees in Quantanamo. Nevertheless, as we know, Butler's 'abject' subject (the foreclosed subject) resists interpellation and through the resistance acquires its agency. And this also means that, in doing so, it exposes the fantasy of the 'origin' that is at the core of not only the juridical order but more generally of metaphysical philosophy. For Foucault, the grand historical narrative and its claims to truth coming from the nexus of cause and effects that is understood to constitute historical events forecloses or subjugates knowledge that is incidental, popular and bodily (1980: 139–164) that ultimately exposes the ungroundedness of origin claims. For Agamben, as we can sée from the above quotation, the problem of a return is impossible to resolve because of the phantom character of state law. Consequently, a plea to such a return, and this is the second problematic that the sentence reveals, will incidentally throw us into an uncritical assessment of the state and law, two concepts that require urgent reconsideration.

Why then are the concepts of state and law (the practice of the trial is part of them) problematic today? At one level, a call for a return to state law fails to observe that when a state of emergency is declared precisely what is being activated *is* state law, law that does not only rely upon a fictitious nexus between law and its applicability, but moreover law that is an instrument of sovereign governmentality. For Agamben, though, it is not the fiction of the non-coincidence of law and its applicability, or law and life, that is problematic but rather that the problem arises because this fiction coincides with a single person (2005a: 86). When it does this, the sovereign dictator for example, what disappears is the revolutionary or divine aspect of the 'force of law', that aspect that unravels the fiction (2005a: 86). In such situations, the 'juridico-political system transforms itself into a death machine'[7] (2005a: 85). So now, with this in mind, we can see why the trial cannot enable the unconcealment of the non-relation between norm and life. In such situations, what happens is that the trial itself becomes an instrument of governmental sovereignty. For Agamben, what remains pertinent is constantly and persistently to make sure that we expose the non-relation between law and life that the decree of state of exception unravels. This may open a space for human action, for politics to be activated (2005a: 88). Agamben ends the book by hoping for a kind of politics that would sever the coincidence of law and violence and bring about the Benjaminian notion of pure violence.

I will return to the notion of pure violence shortly but, for explanatory purposes, it suffices to say that the notion refers to lawless violence or violence without ends. How is pure violence possible then? The possibility of politics or human action emerges precisely because the 'force of law' is a plastic concept or a floating signifier. Since its function or applicability is not based on any logic or cause and effect link, then it could be used by anyone. Agamben points out that revolutionaries can and have used the 'force of law'. Nevertheless, their use of the 'force of law' was not used to sustain and apply the law, but rather to depose it. It is precisely this deposition of the law that demonstrates the non-link between law and life, nomos and anomie, that within Agamben's framework could be given the name 'pure politics', politics without ends, but purely in existence for itself (2005a: 38–39). If you like, the only possibility of 'escaping' the death machine that is the condition of contemporary life is to stop returning anomie to norm, life to law.

How is this really possible, how does the plasticity of the term 'force of law' enable this and what can we understand by the term plastic? The term plasticity draws our attention to Catherine Malabou's work. In *The Future of Hegel* (2005), she offers an extensive explanation of the term. The substantive plasticity enters into the English, French (*plasticité*) and German (*plastizitatät*) languages in the eighteenth century and they all derive from the Greek verb πλάσσειν (*plassein*), which means to form (Malabou, 2005: 8). She goes on to explain, in a more theoretical passage that '[p]lastic…designates those things that lend themselves to being formed while resisting deformation' (Malabou, 2005: 9).

Agamben, as I have explained above, understands the 'force of law' to be a floating signifier. As such, it can be adopted in different situations and by diverse groups without losing its form and, specifically here, without losing its force of the norm but simultaneously not being the norm (Agamben, 2005a: 38–39). If we apply this to Malabou's understanding of plasticity, we may suggest that the term can be used in different ways without losing its form and that this precisely unravels the disconnection between norm and life. So when the revolutionary and the state use it, as already indicated, its functions are very different. For example, when the state uses it, it functions as a means of 'protecting' the state (through the suspension of the law) from external or internal insecurities, but in the hands of the revolutionary it is used to depose the law. It is not that the 'force of law' is split thus enabling these different effects to occur, but it is rather its plastic form that enables them to happen.

We may visualise the 'force of law' as nuclear power, which in the form of a bomb can destroy life but in the form of energy holds within it the possibility of sustaining life. The term is thus able to reformulate itself but, at the same time, resists this reformulation by not losing its 'essence'. This shows the non-relation between the norm and life, as well as law's mythical foundations. Malabou goes on to inform us that the malleability of plastic allows it to 'take on different shapes and properties according to the functions intended' (9), and at the same time 'it draws itself to extremes' (9). By this, she means that plastic concepts can either crystallise or destroy forms, such as life. It is the function that the form is put to that becomes problematic rather than the form itself. So if we continue to use the example of nuclear power, as long as nuclear is utilised by both the scientist and the sovereign then its destructive and creative characters are dialectically opposed to each other, exposing its potential danger. But the moment it becomes the sole instrument of the state and the scientist becomes one of the state's agents, it can turn into a death machine. This analogy, if related to the concept of the 'force of law', allows us to observe that it is the use of the 'force of law' that could render it violent and destructive and not the intrinsic qualities found in the concept itself. So when Agamben writes that the problem with the 'force of law' arises when it is contained in the hands of a single person, he brings to our attention three things: (a) that the 'force of law' is not inherently destructive, though it could be; (b) the possibility that this plastic term has the ability to destroy life; and (c) that this possibility is more imminent when the 'force of law' is placed in the hands of one person. At the same time though, as I have shown above, the term does not lose its 'essence' and this shows the disconnection between the norm and its applicability.

Today, this is no more evident that in the United States. The government through the declaration of a state of emergency holds in indefinite detention individuals captured in Afghanistan and Iraq without offering them 'legitimate' trials either military or criminal. Given our contemporary status quo, we can unhesitatingly say that the norm is either impotent or in decay. But as I have explained previously, the 'force of law' can be considered a plastic concept, because it is not connected to the law it does not have to be monopolised by the state. History has shown that it is activated by revolutionaries who effectively use it to depose the law in an attempt to initiate a new status quo. To put it unsubtly, the 'force of law' is a term whose fictional attachment to the norm opens our eyes to its political potentiality. Agamben's urge for political action is embedded in this. In relation to this he writes:

> But if it is possible to attempt to halt the machine, to show its central fiction, this is because between violence and law, between life and norm, there is no substantial articulation. Alongside the movement that seeks to keep them in relation to all costs, there is a countermovement that, working in an inverse direction in law and in life, always seeks to loosen what has been artificially and violently linked. That is to say, in the field of tension of our culture, two opposite forces act, one that institutes and makes, and one that deactivates and deposes. The state of exception is both the point of their maximum tension and – as it coincides with the rule – that which threatens today to render them indiscernible. To live in a state of exception means to experience both of these possibilities and yet, by always separating these two forces, ceaselessly to try to interrupt the working of the machine that is leading the West toward a global civil war.
>
> (Agamben, 2005a: 87)

If there is a future for the world, it is clear that he foresees it emerging from the possibilities that this plastic concept, the 'force of law', gives to us and that the future lies precisely in the deposition of law and political activation. Agamben here is close to the ideas of Benjamin and more specifically to Benjamin's concept of pure violence. Let us for a second glance at Benjamin's essay and draw our parallels between these two thinkers.

Benjamin wrote the 'Critique of violence' (2004) in 1921 concerning the political events in Germany after the First World War and the growth of German nationalism. Additionally, Hanssen brings to our attention the fact that Benjamin was in contact from 1919 with Hugo Ball and Ernst Block, who

> [not] only did they confront him with the 'question of political activity' in the wake of the Bolshevik Revolution, the collapse of the German empire,

> and the short-lived 1919 Munich Soviet republic, but they introduced him to the work of George Sorel.
>
> (Hanssen, 2005: 16)

Against the backdrop of both political events, contacts and Sorel's influential *Reflections of the Revolution* (1961), Benjamin wrote the 'Critique of violence', an essay that without any shadow of doubt provides us with an immense insight into the relationship between violence, law, life and justice. It is, nevertheless important to point out that the essay is also saturated with Benjamin's wider concerns, those of language. Benjamin's unique and multiple writings have at their centre concerns relating to the notion of 'pure language' that he was developing (Agamben, 1999b: 48–61; Bullock and Jennings, 2004: 505; Hamacher, 2000: 108–136). As Bullock and Jennings point out in the chronological diagram in the 2004 edition of Benjamin's *Selected Writing: Volume 1, 1913–1926* which they edited, the 'Critique of violence' integrated his ideas on 'pure language' with politics (2004: 505). We can quickly and crudely describe 'pure language', as language bereft of both immediacy and signification. This language is language of pure means but no ends (Agamben, 1999b: 52), or language that speaks for itself.[8] The connection between language and politics is elaborated below in relation to Benjamin's essay 'Critique of violence'.

The essay concerns itself with producing a critique of violence and, as Benjamin writes, 'expounding its relation to law and justice' (2004: 236). For Benjamin, violence is inherent in law and his remarks at the start of the essay make it clear that a cause becomes violent when it enters into a relationship with morality (236). And law is, for Benjamin, a moral system (236). He goes on to demonstrate that law is inherently violent by explicating how violence and law relate to means and ends. Law operates through ends and means. As the essay explains, both natural and positive law operate this system of ends and means. Natural law understands violence as a natural phenomenon and finds it absolutely justifiable to use violent means for an end (236–237). Natural law in its various formulations or positions understands law as being founded upon 'objective moral principles which depend upon the nature of the universe and which can be discovered by reason' (Freeman, 1994: 80). Violence therefore would be used in preserving these types of natural and moral principles. Hobbes, for example, writes in the *Leviathan* (1972) that in the state of nature man was agonistic to other men in order to achieve his preservation. Violence is inevitably used in order to sustain man. It is considered as a 'justifiable' means to an end. When man realises that he by himself can't achieve his self-preservation he enters into a social contract. As is well known (in relation to Hobbes's *Leviathan*), when man 'signs' up to the social contract he gives up his individuality and obeys the law and the sovereign in order to preserve his life. Consequently, man's so-called natural right to use violence is transferred onto the sovereign who can now use violence against subjects who contest the newly 'signed' security. Violence, therefore, within the parameters of natural law is used as a means to an end, where the end becomes self-preservation. Positive law, on the other hand, understands violence as the outcome of history[9] and, therefore, the use of violence becomes a relation to ends rather than to means.

Precisely what does Benjamin mean by this? If positive law could be loosely understood as laws that are set by human beings to govern human beings, and this would be Austin's understanding of positive law (Coterrel, 1989: 52–82), then justice becomes the end of law and law the means whereby it can preserve it. While, as Benjamin points out, positivists might fail to explain the criteria for justice, on the other hand, they distinguish between sanctioned and unsanctioned violence, which consequently leads them to the distinction between justice and injustice (238). A workers' strike will be considered as sanctioned violence because it takes within it the parameters of the law, or more specifically within the parameters of the conditions law sets for a strike (239). A general strike, though, is considered as an abuse of the right of strike, an unsanctioned type of violence that forces the state to decree a state of emergency in order to contain it and therefore preserve the legal order (240). In either case (natural or positive law), as Benjamin suggests, the threat of violence is being represented as originating or coming from outside the law, as coming from the people (239). Put differently, law refrains from representing itself as violent, though it resorts to violence when it needs to protect itself or its objectives such as that of justice. The resort to the concepts of 'means' and 'ends' are used to justify legal actions. But, as Benjamin correctly observes, law's resort to violence takes place when law is threatened with destruction. But if this is the case, then law cannot claim that its end, justice that is, is being endangered. If this is indeed the case, then we are left to conclude that violence or rather law as violence *becomes* the law.

This (law's relations to its end) leads to law's decay and becomes even more apparent in Benjamin's description of law's two types of violence: 'law making' and 'law preserving' violence. Law, as he argues, depends on the practice of positing, on putting things into place, such as laws or legislation. But such positing, he concurrently explains, can't function without violence. Law's violence becomes apparent, visible each time law turns into a preserving force. But it is important to note that, for Benjamin, violence is not an external factor that occasionally threatens law but rather is a constant condition of its existence. When Benjamin turns his eyes to private law to consider to what extent it is a violent or non-violent law, he ends up suggesting that even this non-violent law, in terms of using non-legal means (courtesy, etc.), turns into a violent one when this non-legal means that private persons use to relate to each other become attached to 'conflicts relating to goods' (Benjamin, 2004: 244). So, we can say that law constantly redirects its energy, effort, processes and its 'essence', which is identified with positing to preserve 'law and order'. While this transformation tends to be represented as a public service, as one that caters for the public, we can inevitably and simultaneously see that what this *does* or brings about is precisely law's self-protection. When we hear phrases such us the police established 'law and order' at the end of a demonstration, what this means is that the police literally protected 'law and order'. As Hamacher writes,

> By turning from positing to preserving law, it must also turn against hostile forces of positing and thus indirectly against its own principle – the principle of positing itself. In order to remain what it is – violence of law imposition – law imposing violence must become law-preserving, must turn against its original positing character, and, in this collision with itself, must disintegrate.
>
> (Hamacher, 2000: 109)

But law turning into 'law preserving', violence ends up bringing about law's own decay, as law turns against its essential principle which, for Benjamin, is captured by the concept of law positing or law making violence.

Now, in order to understand the significance of this vis-à-vis the 'state of exception' and its exposure of the irrelation between norm and life, we need once more to turn to Benjamin's *The German Tragic Drama*. But, before doing so, it is important to note one more thing that, as Hamacher writes, in the aforementioned situation we can see the decay of law, but what we don't see is the disappearance of violence (Hamacher, 2000: 110). I will return to the significance of this in a second, but at the moment let us see how Benjamin's exposition of law's decay connects back to *The German Tragic Drama*. Like the baroque sovereign – who is represented as transcending transcendence, putting creation (positing) in its own hands and becoming incapable of making decisions, unable to posit an exception, like any other creature – here law's 'positing violence' puts law creation it its own hands, bereft of any attachment to any external authority, and now, instead of being able to make law, becomes unable to fulfil its biggest desire, that of creation, and instead spends its energy trying to protect itself from threat. In addition, Hamacher, as I have already noted, brings to our attention that 'the presence of violence – which at least latent in every juridical institution – complies with a dialectic that forces the disintegration not of the principle of violence itself and the power it institutes, but only of its respective forms' (2000: 110). If law's primary aim then is self-preservation and while achieving this brings about its own ruin because it ignores that its own existence is due to particularly unstable revolutionary forces, or, to put it in more abstract terms, it fails to recognise that it was not created *ex nihilo* but actually was created out of turbulence, then it consequently fails to destroy or exclude violence. Simultaneously, law's 'violence is one which serves that institution – if only to perpetuate it – and which, therefore, cannot be taken as a form of liberty, mediacy and justice' (2000: 111).

If indeed the relationship of law to justice is founded on a fictitious or uncorresponding (as already explained) relationship, then we may conclude that law cannot serve justice. But how can justice be served? The importance of Benjamin's essay does not merely sit with his description of 'law making' and 'law preserving' violence, but rather with the potentiality that this exposes. First, Benjamin showed us that the splitting of law and its violence (the movement from positing to preserving) reveals that the ends of positive law do not correspond to justice. This parallels Agamben's analysis of the law and 'force of law'. Agamben, as we have seen, explains that the relation between law and its application or norm and life is exposed by the state of exception as one of an irrelation, or, to put it another way, is one that relies precisely on a fictitious nexus between the two. This fiction functions as long as we can see that there is an irrelation between the two. But when the 'force of law' is stripped away from the possibility of deposition, precisely by acting as if it does not contain in itself either violence or threat, then it turns into a death machine. If the tension is sustained, then the possibility for human action can take place. However, it is important to observe that Agamben does not concur with the idea of the split to demonstrate that it is possible to have human action. It is not, in other words, because of law's split personality – law preserving and law making violence – that we can observe the non-connection between law and life that gives rise to human political action, but rather because the 'force of law', because it is understood as a floating signifier, can attach itself to different groups and function differently. Second, the split unravels the argument that law's use of violence is unjustified. And third, based on the later observations, that when violence is used by other groups, political parties, etc., in deposing the law, this violence takes the shape of pure violence (i.e. violence that is pure means).

Even so, I want to propose that the profoundness of Benjamin's critique of violence does not lie with a critique of the monopoly of violence (a monopoly that he sees being in the hands of either the executive or administration of law) but rather in observing that the law preserving violence enables us to see that there is no direct relation between law and life, as long as violence relates to means and ends. The only way in which violence could be productive is when it is pure, when it is, in other words, pure means and no ends. This is the only moment when violence manages to relate to life. And it manages to do so because it exposes the potential meanings that the term life brings about. It makes us think about the extent to which life means just mere existence, bare life in Agamben's terms, or something better. This point becomes even more apparent when, towards the end of the essay, Benjamin considers explanations given by revolutionaries when considering the use of violence. This is how he puts it:

> 'If I do not kill, I shall never establish the world domination of justice... that is the argument of the intelligent terrorist. ... We, however, profess that higher even than the happiness and justice of existence stands existence itself.' As certainly as this last proposition is false, indeed ignoble, it shows the necessity of seeking the reason for the commandment no longer in what the deed does to the victim, but in what it does to God and the doer. The proposition that existence stands higher than a just existence is false and ignominious, if existence is to mean nothing other than mere life – and it has this meaning in the argument referred to. It contains a mighty truth, however, if 'existence', or better, 'life' (words whose ambiguity is readily dispelled, like that of 'freedom', when they are used with reference to two

> distinct spheres), means the irreducible, total condition that is 'man'; if the proposition is intended to mean that the non-existence of man is something more terrible than the (admittedly sub-ordinate) not-yet-attained condition of the just man. The proposition quoted above owes its plausibility to this ambiguity. Man cannot, at any price, be said to coincide with the mere life in him, any more that it can be said to coincide with any other of his conditions and qualities, including even the uniqueness of his bodily person. However sacred man is (or however sacred that life in him which is identically present in earthly life, death, and afterlife), there is no sacredness in his condition, in his bodily life vulnerable to injury by his fellow men.
>
> (Benjamin, 2004: 250)

The extensive quote above utilises the explanation given by revolutionaries as to why the life of a sovereign is not sacred and at the same time is used by Benjamin to expose the tension that it produces in relation to the meaning of life. It draws our attention to the idea that when revolutionaries resort to violence, what Benjamin calls 'pure violence' (violence that it is not sanctioned by law, pure means), they destabilise our understanding of life, the concept of 'sanctity of life', preserved in the commandment, 'Thou shall not kill'. This destabilisation allows us to see that the sacredness of man, or life for that matter, is not that sacred, if the conditions of livability are sanctioned by the concept of the just man. In such cases, existence is devalued; it becomes bare life. Existence is devalued, because as we have seen, this existence always comes second to the preservation of law itself. To repeat what has been said above, positive law and its institutions (police, courts, etc.) use the objective of justice to justify their use of violence in, for example, the case of the general strike. The aim of law becomes ultimately one that caters first for its own preservation and then for the preservation of justice, and lastly to life. 'Pure violence', violence that is only located within the parameters of means and outside legality, can produce the possibility of livable life, precisely because it does not attach any ends to its actions, precisely because it works in the opposite direction to the 'split' that law's violence has produced. Benjamin produces a unique understanding of law, a law that does not consider or relate to life, or the conditions of making life more viable. Law and the sovereign appear to be precisely the entities that propose this function of the 'force of law' and turn it into a death machine. So if the revolutionaries show us anything, it is their desire for a better life, a life that is not reduced to bareness, a product of both sovereign and legal governmentality. But this would require, as Agamben has done, to put 'bare life' at the centre of this discussion, to explore, as Benjamin and Agamben do, the possibilities that human action can bring about in turning the debate and action away from sovereign law to pure politics.

It is at this point that both Agamben and Butler coincide with Benjamin's understanding of the law and its applicability. But it is also at this point that I suspect their positions divert. Like Benjamin, both of them are concerned with thinking about possible ways in which we can have more viable and livable lives. Agamben resorts to the potentiality or possibility that politics (and not law) could bring to *bare life* (material conditions of life) and, as we all know, in *Homo Sacer* (1998) Agamben argued convincingly that this is the condition of our lives. Judith Butler, on the other hand, without disputing the potentiality of pure politics, still holds some hope for law in vitalising life, as I will explain below. This hope comes primarily from considering the agonistic function of law symbolised by the practice of trial. Agamben, as I explain, does not ignore the practice of trial. But he appears to suggest that the practice of trial precisely disguises the disconnection between law and life, the very point that constantly needs to be undone. So because the law and its institutions are depicted as decaying or impotent, he focuses on the practice of sovereign decision-making when a decree of a state of emergency is declared. The sovereign, in its attempt in bringing the exception within the parameters of the law or the norm, actually exposes the myth that nothing transcends it, that the so-called authority that the sovereign uses to do so (suspend the law) is based on a non-relation between law and its applicability, and thus is the sovereign's self-creation, immanent in the sovereign as it is in any other creature. And it is in this sense that the decree that suspends the law becomes the norm and it is no longer, as Schmitt has it, a reaction to an extraordinary situation. But still this has devastating effects: constantly redrawing the boundaries between legality and illegality with consequential effects on life, or to be precise on certain lives. Certain lives are reduced to bare life, mere existence. But at the same time, their inclusion in the 'polis', as mere existence, and their exclusion as citizens show us that bare life is the 'original activity of sovereign power' (Agamben, 1998: 6), the essence of the political. And if or since this is the case, then our only way out is to engage with lawless violence, to expose that the sovereign operates on precisely these grounds. What Agamben writes is pertinent and true of our times, it instantly brings to mind the detention centre at Quantanamo Bay and Belmarsh Prison. It does not question whether a different modality of trial, a trial that does not return sentences of guilt and innocence, may bring the possibility of violence without ends; or to what extent limited trials, trials embedded within law's violence, can sustain our survivability. As Butler obliquely suggests, the practice of trying in a court of law provides the subject with the possibility of antagonising, resisting and answering back to the accusations which were brought against them. This is not only true of criminal or constitutional trials, but also of civil ones such as libel trials. The effects of a trial are to give the subject the possibility of telling their story, albeit within the confines of the law, its rules and procedures, to have their story recorded and to counter-attack, and to at least be given the possibility of survival rather than be put to death. On 22 July 2005, the police coldly killed the 27-year-old Brazilian electrician, Jean Charles de Menezes, at Stockwell tube station because he was acting suspiciously. As later became clear, this suspicion was based upon the fact that he left a residence under surveillance and he was dark-skinned. The police were looking for the perpetrators of the attempted bomb attacks in London on the previous day, but when they killed this man, they withdrew from him the possibilities of surviving, of telling his story in court or even of telling his story to the investigation officers. Executive powers under a state of emergency may literally turn into a death machine, a possibility that a trial would certainly reduce, or at least that is what Butler argues.

Law, sovereignty, governmentality and the question of life

The question of life, or more particularly the question of how our lives can continue resisting those conditions of restriction that are imposed upon us by state apparatuses (such as governmental officials and legislative limitations) so as to be able to have livable and viable conditions, is what connects Butler's thought with that of Agamben and Benjamin. As I indicated above, the last two are interested in the possibilities that pure politics can contribute to making life possible. But, Butler's journey into this question considers the possibilities that politics, law and, ethics may contribute to making a livable and viable life. While in an earlier chapter I have addressed the way in which an ethics of recognition can enable this, here I consider the role and place of law in the creation of possible lives.

To recap so far, Benjamin and Agamben, suggest that law, preoccupied with its own preservation, ends up contributing to the destruction of life. Butler, as we will see, offers mostly 'covertly' a different story. What follows is divided into two sections. The first section deals explicitly with Butler's thoughts on law in the aftermath of the 9/11 attacks on the twin towers of the World Trade Center in New York. The second part deals with her earlier work and her understanding of law and its limits.

Life indefinitely and the role of law

Two pages into 'Indefinite detention', Butler proposes the following regarding the US treatment of detainees in Cuba and the use of power:

> I would like to suggest that the current configuration of power, in relation both to the management of populations (the hallmark of governmentality) and the exercise of sovereignty in the acts that suspend and limit the jurisdiction of law itself, are reconfigured in terms of the new war prison.
>
> (Butler, 2004a: 53)

From the very start of the essay, we can observe that Butler separates modalities of power and law. Governmentality and sovereignty are read from the start as forces that act upon jurisdiction, the 'territory'[10] of law. At first blush, the proposition and its consequences create an aporia at least to those who are familiar with Foucault's modalities of power, the very modalities that Butler is invoking in this essay. In *Discipline and Punish* (1991a), Foucault appears not to differentiate between the sovereign and the law. But what is often missed by readers of Foucault is precisely this, that Foucault never equates the sovereign with the law, but rather vests the sovereign with the 'force of law'. Foucault recognises that there is a jurisdiction that is legal. This jurisdiction, through the instrument of the *trial*, decides upon the 'truth' of the alleged event, and through the instrument of punishment publicises the 'truth'. To this effect, Foucault writes, '[t]he body, several times tortured, provides the synthesis of the reality of the deeds and the truth of the investigation, of the documents of the case and the statements of the criminal, of the crime and the punishment' (1991a: 47). For Foucault, the juridical order entertains itself with the trying of the accused (1991a: 44–48). The king or prince, on the other hand, as the opening quotation of this chapter indicates, engages with another practice consequently aiming at a different effect. The sovereign is vested with the right of deciding over the life or death of the accused. In this sense, the sovereign is vested with power which comes in the guise of the 'force of law'. Consider his words:

> Besides its immediate victim, the crime attacks the sovereign: it attacks him personally, since the law represents the will of the sovereign; it attacks him physically since the force of law is the force of the prince. ... The intervention of the sovereign is not, therefore, an arbitration between two adversaries; it is much more, even, than an action to enforce the respect of the rights of the individual; it is a direct reply to the person who has offended him.
> (Foucault, 1991a: 47–48)

Foucault is very explicit here about the relation of the law to the sovereign. The law is the will of the sovereign, a position that he sustains later on in *Society Must be Defended* (2003) in which he once more states that the juridical system is in the service of the demands and benefit of royal power (2003: 25–27). Moreover, he explains that even when the juridical system is concerned with the limits of sovereign power it never ceased to be *about* royal power. Nevertheless, this proximity even nexus between the juridical order and the sovereign cannot allow us to conclude that the sovereign *is* the law. In establishing a juridical order whereby his power can be catered for, the king demonstrates that his interests reside in preserving himself and his territory or, as Foucault puts it in his essay on 'Governmentality', 'the end of sovereignty the exercise of sovereignty' (2002a: 210). The interests of the juridical order, on the other hand, are the interests of the sovereign, in preserving his power, its end though is exercise or practice of production of 'truth' no matter how fictitious this might be. When the sovereign therefore decides over the life or death of subjects, it is not the truth that is being reproduced but, on the contrary, what is being demonstrated is the sovereign's will, power backed by the 'force of law'.

It is this distinction, between sovereign power and legal jurisdiction that informs Butler's analysis of the contemporary political situation in the United States. However, as I have already noted, she invokes another modality of power: that of governmentality. Governmentality, Foucault writes, is a practice of government that we see emerging in the sixteenth century but that reaches its apex in the eighteenth century (2002a: 212). While sovereignty had as its end the preservation of the sovereign and his territoriality, government's end is the management of populations. Its emergence is linked with the coming into being of an administrative apparatus, the police, mercantilism and statistics. Foucault's reception of the concept of government comes from La Perrière's *Miroir Politique* and is defined 'as a right manner of disposing things so as to lead not to the form of the common good, as the jurists' text would have said, but to an end that is "convenient" for each of the things that are governed' (2002a: 212). By this, it means that a good governor, who above everything has to be patient (unlike the sovereign whose main characteristic is the right to kill or let live), will use tactics (even laws as tactics) to, for example, secure maximum security for their own population. This modality of power, as Foucault suggests, allows the state to survive (2002a: 221). There is much more we can say about this modality of power, but for the moment I will pause here, so as to return to Butler's use of power in the aforementioned essay.

When the US government issued a state of emergency after the 9/11 attacks in New York, Butler suggests that a new, synthetic modality of power emerges. The issue of the decree introduced not only the suspension of laws but also did away with the separation of powers that are considered to be the pillars of the US constitution. The essay explains how this was managed, is still sustained and the effects that it brought about. The current status quo manages itself through the re-emergence of a new type of sovereignty, a type of sovereignty that uses governmentality *as* technique.[11] While Foucault provides us with a chronological understanding of the emergence of sovereign and governmental power, Butler reminds us that Agamben argues that both sovereign and governmental power are contemporary and they have an inverse relation to the rule of law (Butler, 2004a: 60). As I attempted to explain above, Foucault's analysis of the ends of juridical, sovereign and governmental order stipulates that sovereign and governmental powers have an inverse relation to the rule of law. While of course there is an undisputed chronology in Foucault that relates to the emergence of these modalities of power, nevertheless, by returning to Agamben, Butler cites her agreement regarding the synchronicity of these powers and their effects. It is also, however, important to note that Foucault is relatively clear in *Society Must be Defended* (2003) that sovereign power, or disciplinary power, does not disappear once governmental power emerges but rather that 'society' is to a large extent being permeated by this new form of power. His words below, relating to sovereign and governmental power, are evidence of this:

> I wouldn't say exactly that sovereignty's old right – to take life or let live – was replaced, but it came to be complemented by a new right which does not erase the old right but which does penetrate it, permeate it. This is the right, or rather precisely the opposite right. It is the power to 'make' live and 'let' die. This right of sovereignty was the right to take life or let live. And then this new right is established: the right to make live and to let die.
>
> (Foucault, 2003: 241)

In forgetting, perhaps ignoring, this both Agamben and Butler move on to make another important point which, irrespective of this lapse, would still not hold untrue of Foucault. Agamben writes that sovereign and governmental powers' antithetical relation to the rule of law emerges at the moment when the norm is suspended or when the law is withdrawn. Law as Butler explains

> withdraws from the usual domain of its jurisdiction; this domain becomes opened to both governmentality (understood as an extra-legal field of policy, discourse, that may make law into a tactic) and sovereignty (understood as an extra-legal authority that may well institute and enforce law of its own making).
>
> (2004a: 60)

But Foucault also talks of the withdrawal or ineffectiveness of law when new powers emerge. For example, in *Society Must be Defended* he explains how disciplinary power operates and how it does not have as its reference point the law but rather the human sciences (2003). To this effect, he confirms that practices of normalisation are not endemic to law, but rather to policing, schooling, psychoanalysis and psychiatry, etc. Agamben, conflates the norm with the law and effectively makes the law the epitome of normalisation. But, despite all this, we can say that Butler's and to some extent Agamben's exposition of contemporary modalities of power provide us with an analysis of power based on today, one which Foucault could not have foreseen but towards which he would not perhaps have been gravely antithetical.

Butler builds Agamben's understanding of how sovereign power operates to propose her own version of sovereignty. Sovereignty, she writes, is

> produced at the moment of this withdrawal, and that we have to consider the act of suspending the law as a performative one which brings a contemporary configuration of sovereignty into being, or more precisely, reanimates a spectral sovereignty within the field of governmentality.
>
> (2004a: 61)

The above is a distinct understanding of sovereignty. Agamben has proposed that the sovereign declarative utterance of a state of emergency activates the suspension of the law and constitutes the new modality of sovereign governmentality. This proposition implies that the sovereign pre-exists the utterance. Additionally, it suggests that Agamben might have a particular understanding of who exactly this sovereign is. It could be the President of the United States, the Roman Emperor, etc. For Butler, on the other hand, it is precisely the utterance of the state of emergency, or extraordinary conditions, that forms this sovereign governmentality. There is, in other words, no sovereign before the declaration. Her reading does not allow the naturalisation of power, in the sense that there is an original holder of such power, nor does it consequently understand power in foundational and solidified terms, even if she proposes, as we shall see, that this type of power has the characteristics of a totalitarian regime. So one could say that she holds to the general 'structure' of power proposed by Foucault, power being multifaceted and in multiple places. Of course, her proposition creates multiple sites for sovereign governmentality but, simultaneously, she creates multiple sites for resistance. Butler proposes that the withdrawal from law shares the characteristics of a performative act, in the sense that it brings into being what is already there (that sovereign power is not founded upon law) but at the same time transplants this modality of power onto governmental practices, such as the practice of managing detainees, making decisions in military tribunals, etc. These governmental practices which would otherwise have been part of some legal apparatus, for example, prison codes of practice, laws of evidence, etc., now act as 'sovereign' satellites without any legal foundation and can make decisions over the right to life or death of these detainees (2004a: 94–95). Governmentality, which is generally associated with the practice of managing populations, is now revitalised as a practice where decisions over life and death can be taken.

This new coalition between governmental and sovereign power, as Butler suggests earlier in the same essay, has as its aim to augment and proliferate state power (2004a: 58). This is achieved in two ways: first by establishing military tribunals, whereby trials can come to 'independent' conclusions that nevertheless can be reversed by the executive; and second by detaining the prisoners in Quantanamo Bay indefinitely. The production and effects of these two practices of spreading sovereign power are extensively discussed. There is of course, as the essay covertly suggests, an interrelation between the two practices (establishment of military tribunals and indefinite detention). They are both the product of the same method, namely that of performativity. Second, each one of them presupposes the other for its operation. Let's take the use of performative speech acts first.

You remember that Butler argues that this new form of sovereign power comes into being at the moment when it withdraws the applicability of law. The withdrawal correlates to the performative act that brings this new type of power into being in the same way, through a series of performative speech acts that are not founded in law but use the 'force of law' to justify their actions. In relation to the establishment of military tribunals, Butler explains the operation of performative speech acts by citing the justification provided by a Department of Defense representative when asked by a reporter why they did not use the already existing military courts to try the detainees. The representative, in answering the journalist's question, justifies the establishment of these tribunals by saying that the circumstances needed another 'instrument' (2004a: 83). As Butler writes,

> the law is not that to which the state is subject nor that which distinguishes between lawful state action and unlawful, but is now expressly understood as an instrument, an instrumentality of power, one that can be applied and suspended at will.
>
> (2004a: 83)

At the moment of the utterance, the representative of the Department of Defense brings into being the coincidence of these two models of power. Law is withdrawn due to the necessity of the special circumstances that the state finds itself in and it is replaced by sovereign power that uses law as a technique of governmentality (withdrawal of law in order to achieve the best management of the detainees). There are further consequences or effects that this statement activates. By delegating the power to decide over the future of the detainees to a tribunal, power is transferred to the president of the United States to decide over the life of these detainees. While the tribunal can decide whether it could apply the death penalty, for example, the US president has the power to decide whether to overrule their decisions or not.

In the same channel of thought, her essay uses Haynes's (Defense General Council) response to a similar question by a journalist as to the future of the detainees. The journalist asked Haynes what would happen to the detainees if the military tribunal found them not guilty. He answers that, even if this were the case, detainees would not be released unless the state was satisfied as to whether they were dangerous or not (2004a: 74–75). Once more, we observe that through speech acts, the Defense General Council suspends the law or, more specifically here, the possible tribunal decision. The place of law is taken up by sovereign power that could at any point withdraw its applicability for the so-called better protection of US citizens. It is at the moment of legal withdrawal that we can see the efficacy of sovereign and governmental powers. Haynes's statement is also telling in other ways. As Butler observes, the detainees are not considered by the US administration to be common criminals but something more, dangerous individuals. Her observation invokes subtly Foucault's essay 'About the concept of the "dangerous individual" in nineteenth-century legal psychiatry' (Foucault, 2002b: 176–200).[12]

This alleged 'dangerousness of the detainees' is also integral to a series of answers given by Donald Rumsfeld regarding their indefinite detention. When Rumsfeld was asked why they (the US administration) are holding these detainees indefinitely he answered that if they were not restrained they would go out and kill (2004a: 73). He explicitly shows that it is the ends that justify their means but, even more, that these means are founded on legal grounds. In doing so, they stipulate that they are acting within the parameters of international and national law. In relation to their compatibility with international law, they cite the example of Britain, where 'European human rights courts... allowed the British authorities to detain Irish Catholic and Protestant militants for long periods of time, if they "were deemed dangerous, but not necessarily convicted of a crime" ' (2004a: 71). And in relation to domestic legislation, the US administration cites at present the restraining and hospitalisation of mentally ill people which takes place without the invocation of a criminal charge (2004a: 73). In both cases, however, there is a correlation between the detainees and the concept of the dangerous individual without the necessary explanation of how this dangerousness is evaluated. The invocation of the 'dangerous individual' allows the state once more to use law as a technique of sovereign power, continuing the suspension of the norm but at the same time making the exception to the norm the norm in itself (2004a: 67). As Butler suggests, the use of performative speech acts works in a way whereby the indefinite detention of the detainees along with the use of special military tribunals are justified, sustained and rendered coherent. The invocation of danger and the dangerous individual is a performative speech act that allows the administration to exercise indefinitely power that is extra-legal. The release of images of the detainees, both through television and photography, aims to strengthen the effect of this performative act. As she writes, 'there is a reduction of these human beings to animal status, where the animal is figured as out of control, in need of total restraint' (2004a: 78).

If we consider in their totality the effects of this series of performative acts, we can clearly see that they reduce the detainees to bare life, to subjects that are outside '*bios politicos*' (2004a: 67–68). While Butler is in agreement with Agamben on this point, she does not hesitate to problematise further this conclusion. As she correctly remarks, Agamben leaves unanswered the question as to why certain citizens and not others are reduced to bare life (2004a: 67–68). In her attempt to understand why this happens, she turns to the equivalence of the detainees with the mentally ill and the figure of the dangerous individual to provide a plausible understanding of who counts as bare life. 'Bare life', those who are dead but not sacrificed, according to her are those that are equated with danger, animality, incivility and madness. Those who have no volition or will, whose acts are deemed unintelligible and who are the very personification of inhumanity. There is a certain type of life, in other words, that is not deemed livable and viable and that is read as a threat to those lives that are worth something. Butler is correct in problematising the way in which the 'metonymic practice puts the catchphrase of uncivilised on the detainees' (2004a: 71–72). It is also important that she attempts to understand on what grounds and conditions some lives are deemed bare life.

There is, though, an unintended suggestion in her writing. When she problematises the correspondence of terrorist detainees and the mad, she appears to suggest that the mad are totally unintelligible, dangerous, etc., and the equivalence or correspondence of mad–terrorist is truly catachrestic. While of course I think that she is correct in evaluating this correspondence, what she additionally and unfortunately succeeds in doing is to construct the insane as unintelligible, unmotivated and uncivilised. Foucault alerted us to the clinicians' *invention* of insanity and, moreover, alerted us to precisely the construction of the insane as one based on instrumentalisation. In *Madness and Civilization* (1991b), for example, he suggests that the separation of madness from reason coincides with the birth of the psychiatrist and his specialised knowledge. The perception of insane acts as unintelligible, bereft of will and uncivilised, he subtly suggests is a mere construction.

If, indeed, we look more closely into the details of some late eighteenth and nineteenth century legal cases (Nicholson (see Macalpine and Hunter (1991: 311–313), Hadfield (1800), M'Naughtens (1843)), we can without any shadow of a doubt undo this precise construction of insanity that Butler is invoking.

The three cases that I parenthetically cite above provide us with a different understanding of the insane. They are all cases of insane individuals who attempted to kill figures of political significance. Nicholson attempted to assassinate King George III and was charged with treason. Hadfield similarly attempted to assassinate King George III and he was also charged with treason. McNaughtens assassinated Drummond, the Prime Minster's private secretary. MacNaughtens' actual target was the Prime Minister, Sir Robert Peel himself, but he mistook Drummond for the Prime Minister. MacNaughtens was charged with murder.[13] I have explained elsewhere how the acts of these individuals can be seen as practices by which they mimic the sovereign power that brings them into being, in an attempt to both resist it but also attain their own agency and survival. Perhaps their acts can even be read as acts of pure violence, in the Benjaminian sense, of unsanctioned violence. These individuals and their acts alert us to the intolerable conditions of their being. As I mentioned earlier, Benjamin suggests that the revolutionary does not hold that life is sacred when the conditions imposed by a legal system make life intolerable. Nicholson, Hadfield and MacNaughtens are doing the same thing. Through their acts they challenge the intolerability of their lives and at the same time project into the future a different potentiality of a livable life. But returning to Butler, I have no intention here of putting down Butler's position, but rather I am suggesting that perhaps there are ways in which one could use this precise metonymic practice to the advantage of those who are deemed 'bare life'. We can, for example, challenge in its totality the construction of the dangerous individual and its various configurations that has permeated both the legal and the political discourse.

Nevertheless, Butler's concern here is slightly different. As I mentioned at the start of this chapter, she is concerned not with law, but rather with power, and ultimately she is concerned with how we can have livable viable lives. Her observations so far demonstrate that this new form of power (sovereign-governmentality) produces unlivable and unviable lives. Butler forces us to think about whether it is possible, given the conditions that govern us, to produce livable and viable lives. Would law be such a space? While throughout the essay she seems to suggest that the detainees should be put through the process of a proper trial, within the parameters of the rules of evidence, towards the end of the essay she clarifies her position and contends that she is *not* interested in upholding the rule of law. We can interpret this to mean that she is not interested in rule-based trials if rule-based trials will be in the hands of sovereign-governmentality. This appears to be in tune with Agamben's position on trials. We might say that in Butler's case a rule-based trial will still produce the unbearable effects for detainees if the rules and the practice of trying them remain instruments of governmental sovereignty. Nevertheless, unlike Agamben who dismisses the role of law in curbing governmental sovereignty on the grounds that I have explained above, Butler is curious to see whether law can have a 'place... in the articulation of an international conception of rights and obligations that limit and conditions claims of state sovereignty' (2004a: 98).

She explains her awareness of the limitations of law by focusing on the limits of international law and the Geneva Convention. As she states, the convention provides protection only to the states that are signatories to it (2004a: 86). States that are described as being 'rogue', people that are displaced and stateless and citizens of emerging states, none of these can be protected by the convention. She is clearly aware that law is incompetent in providing the parameter for a livable and viable life. Still, throughout the essay, she stubbornly calls for the detainees to be tried through the criminal or military courts. Why does she do so? If we are to understand this paradoxical position that she holds, we must look not only to this essay but to her other work where she either explicitly or inexplicitly invokes the law. If we are to give a more meaningful understanding to her call to put detainees on trial than merely saying that Butler is a left legal liberal who upholds a faith in law, we need to understand the architecture of her thought.

In doing so, I want to take us back to *Excitable Speech* (1997b). In this book, Butler explicitly writes (as I explained in an earlier chapter) that the subject comes into being through language. When one is named at birth, she suggests that this demonstrates a proto-violence whereby the subject through speaking back and answering to the name given to her or him can gain a sense of agency. Of course, this process of injury goes on throughout one's life and one's ability to remain alive relies on this endless process of speaking back. We could say that the process of re-appropriating the naming is one of pure violence and therefore political. But the regulation of injurious language (hate speech, pornography, etc.) curtails the possibility for the subject of staying alive, being recognised and recognisable (1997b: 5). What is being invoked in *Excitable Speech* is the possibility of creating vitality through the modality of agonism, warring with the conditions that bring us into being. This agonism that she describes very much resembles the process of the trial. Her invocation of the trial[14] in 'Indefinite detention' is an invocation to sustain this agonistic spirit that law creates and gives rise to the possibility of providing the structures for the creation of livable and viable lives. If the model of such a life is one of putting on trial, then it becomes important for Butler to call for the model of the trial to be central to the possibility of the detainees having a livable and viable life. Unlike Agamben who, as I have explained, thinks that law has no connection to the production of life, Butler can see the role that law can play in this production. At the same time, like Agamben, she is aware that for this possibility to take place we need to transform the conditions in which we deal with political action whereby our understanding of what it means to be human needs to be considered. Human rights, she argues, have failed so far to wrestle with the meaning of the human. The trial as a model creates the space for such considerations to take place. But, at the same time, Butler points out that such a wrestling, such a trying of the term human, must remain open to what this term might possibly mean. As she writes,

> [t]o be human implies many things, one of which is that we are the kinds of beings who must live in a world where clashes of value do and will occur,

> and these clashes are a sign of what a human community is. How we handle those conflicts will also be a sign of our humanness, one that is, importantly, in the making.
>
> (2004a: 89)

And, as you can see, what becomes important for her is not only the concept of humanness but also the ways we will handle conflicting understandings of this, for it is our handling of such an issue that will produce our humanness. She suggests that law can play a role in this. But for such a transformation to take place, the main role must be given to the realm of the political for it will require some common impetus in handling this conflict.

Her reference to a 'we' above provides us with this possible line of inquiry. Benjamin also talked, in 'Critique of violence', of private ways of dealing with conflicting situations, such as courtesy and trust (2004: 244). Is Butler thinking of such a practice and its possibilities? The answer to this is both yes and no. Butler, as we will see (and perhaps as you might have guessed by now), does not reduce private actions to the sphere of the private, but rather sees private actions as being political or carrying within them a political impetus. So bearing this in mind, we may suggest that she sees some forms of action that are not opposed to Benjamin's as having significance by providing a platform for engaging with the meaning of humanness. For example, in *Giving an Account of Oneself* (2003), as discussed in Chapter 3, she raises the practice of deliberation as a necessary precondition for considering the possibility of an ethics of recognition. Deliberation is a practice that has legal, political and individual effects. Deliberation is a way of handling an issue. It postpones a quick and thoughtless reaction to differences in opinion, ideals or beliefs that confront us. It can, and this is how perhaps it connects to the issue of life, postpone an exaggerated reaction to a threatening situation that could bring more harm to life than good. But this suggestion comes from a rather covert approach to interpreting Butler's work. This does not mean that we should not consider this as a possible proposition from her, but rather that there is perhaps another more evident but parallel track of thought that can enable us to see how she imagines this process of considering the meaning of humanness and life taking shape. Butler poses this as a question. She wonders what type of power may be able to put a stop to the dehumanising effects of the current status quo (2004a: 98–99). Indeed, what type of power can provide such an opening? If our lives are totalised by a sovereign power that uses governmentality as its strategy for reterritorialising itself, then what type of power can put a stop to the production of this death machine? If law is impotent because it lost its possibility of allowing subjects to answer back, then what type of power can reverse this decay? Agamben calls for a pure violence, in the spirit of Benjamin. I suspect, by reflecting upon 'Indefinite detention' and Butler's other work, *Gender Trouble* and *Bodies that Matter*, that she will not invoke the modality of pure violence to address this question. Indeed, as she stated in a lecture that she gave on 30 October 2004 at Birkbeck College, she is searching for possible answers within philosophies of peace.

And, on 1 November 2004, in another paper at Tate Modern, she explained that she is committed to a type of violence that does not kill. So it is the requirement of violence that does not kill, but revitalises life that Butler cares for, and I suspect this is what she is looking for within various modalities of power. I want to suggest and explain below that this returns her to a combination of disciplinary and governmental power, whereby the very materiality of bodies and the conditions that they find themselves in can be re-addressed through practices of resistance. At least, these are the modalities of power and possibilities that she invokes in *Gender Trouble*, *Bodies that Matter* and *Excitable Speech*.

Disciplining law

> In appearance, the disciplines constitute nothing more than an infra-law. They seem to extend the general forms defined by law to the infinitesimal level of individual lives; or they appear as methods of training that enable individuals to become integrated into these general demands. They seem to constitute the same type of law on a different scale, thereby making it more meticulous and more indulgent. The disciplines should be regarded as a sort of counter-law. They have the precise role of introducing insuperable asymmetries and excluding reciprocities.
>
> (Foucault, 1991a: 222)

As early as 1990, in *Gender Trouble* (1990), Butler, being strongly influenced by the work of Foucault, contests that the juridical order could be the space where women can look for a better life. She writes:

> Foucault points out that juridical systems of power *produce* the subjects they subsequently come to represent. Juridical notions of power appear to regulate political life in purely negative terms – that is, through the limitation, prohibition, regulation, control and even 'protection' of individuals related to that political structure through the contingent and retractable operation of choice. But the subjects regulated by such structures are by virtue of being subjected to them, formed, defined, and reproduced in accordance with the requirements of those structures. If this analysis is right, then the juridical formation of language and politics that represents women as 'the subject' of feminism is itself a discursive formation and effect of a given version of representational politics. And the feminist subject turns out to be discursively constituted by the very political system that is supposed to facilitate its emancipation. This becomes politically problematic if that system can be shown to produce gendered subjects along a differential axis of domination or to produce subjects who are presumed to be masculine. In such cases, an uncritical appeal to such a system for the emancipation of 'women' will be clearly self-defeating.
>
> (Butler, 1990: 2)

Her earlier work, including *Bodies that Matter* (1993), dealt explicitly with the question of gender formation and effects and possibilities arising from her analysis. As we can see above, from the very start of *Gender Trouble* she sets out to *contest* the significance that law plays in gender formation, but moreover she sets out to challenge the notion that law can productively affect the lives of gendered subjects. Her specific quest, of course – in the book that gave her international recognition and respect as a philosopher of gender – was first to evaluate the discussion in feminist philosophy concerning gender and sexual politics which was widely associated at the time with French feminism. In *Gender Trouble*, Butler critiqued the premise of sexual difference that at the time was prominent but was additionally used to articulate gender demands and was promoted, and still is, by feminist philosophers such as Luce Irigaray. Butler explicated how non-normative sexual practices challenge the stability of gender formation that figures in the discourse of sexual differentiation, which regrettably promotes that there are only two genders, a masculine one and a feminine one. But a secondary effect of her writings was the opening up of philosophy to a wider and more pertinent understanding of subject formation, one that takes the concrete, non-normative sexual practices in her case, as competing, universalising claims, that question, challenge and promote different aspirations for livability to the ones already proposed. To understand this point we must turn to her discussion of universality.

Influenced by Hegel, she understands the relations of the universal and the concrete not as being distinct and mutually exclusive from each other but rather as being not only interdependent but also constitutive of each other. In 'Restaging the universal' (2000b), she argues that a formal universalism, one that purports to be established through a self-referential rationality and accordingly lays claims to human nature, reveals the impossibility of sustaining such a position. Hegel, she writes, critiques Kant's formal universalism, by identifying the universality of the concrete. If the universal is to correspond with every human, then what is revealed from this is that not every human would be identified with such universal claims. As she writes, 'if we can say that conceptions, states of consciousness, feeling, what is specific and living, also pertain to every person, we have apparently identified a universal feature which does not fit under the rubric of universality' (2000b: 17). This, she argues, produces a twofold universality, 'in the first instance it is abstract; in the second it is concrete' (17). Once this is established by Hegel, Butler goes on to argue in parallel fashion to that shown in the previous chapter on ethics, that

> not only is the thinking self fundamentally related to what it seeks to know, but the formal self loses its formalism once it is understood that the production and exclusion of the 'concrete' is a necessary precondition for the fabrication of the form. Conversely, the concrete cannot be 'had' on its own, and is equally vain to disavow the act of cognition that delivers the concrete to the human mind as an object of knowledge.
>
> (Butler, 2000b: 18)

Once the mutual co-dependence between the formal and concrete universality is established, Hegel goes on to link the question of universals to his theory of mutual recognition and the problematics arising from it (Butler, 2000b: 20). If you remember from the previous chapter, when two self-consciousnesses meet and recognise themselves as A = not B and B = not A, the initial response is to attempt to do away with each other. But as I explain using Butler's work, the desire for self-preservation prevents this from happening. In situations of a reign of terror, Hegel observes that the opposite happens. The faction that holds a claim to the universal and also claims that it represents the general will set out to annihilate any remnants of the concrete, those groups or individuals that lay a counterclaim to this formal universality. While a state of terror situation is the most dramatic of examples, when this happens it does not preclude the fact that this is more commonly the case with abstract universality (23).

But if this is the case, and if we follow the logic that suggests that formal and concrete universality are constitutive of each other, this means that formal universality vanishes without the concrete (23). Therefore, consequentially, '[abstract] universality itself vanishes as a concept which is said to include all such life: this vanished immediacy is the universal will itself' (23). Consider, for example, the shooting and killing by metropolitan police officers of the Brazilian electrician mentioned earlier in this chapter. The police were acting under the auspices of formal universality. They were using s 3 of the Criminal Justice Act 1967 authorising the use of force in the prevention of crime. They were also using a set of guidelines issued by the police as to how to approach a situation when the suspect is a terrorist. Both the formal law and formal norms of practice lay claims to be formulating a universal understanding of how a suspected criminal/terrorist might be acting and how we can universally delimit their movements for the sake, and this is the important point, of universal and general security. In this particular case, Menezes who was shot in the head by eight bullets was not a terrorist. The abstract and universal law and normative practice issued in the police guidelines, at this point acting in their generality, are undone by the very concreteness of this case. The annihilation of this man reveals precisely that universal security does not adhere to the needs of every individual, but instead in some instances works against them. We can say that formal universalism is the vanishing point. Since, formal universality disappears when it seeks to eliminate any traces of concreteness, it allows us to consider the possibility that concreteness *per se* does not only constitute formal universalism but, moreover, it also adheres to another universality, albeit a contesting one. Based on this analysis, Butler suggests that it is possible to think of the concrete which is more often referred to as the particular, as a competing universality that antagonises the claim to universal representation made by formal or abstract universality. This is what allows her to make the wider point in relation to the philosophical concerns relating to subject formations and universalism. As she goes on to suggest, the claims of women, gays, lesbians, transsexuals, people of colour – and generally groups whose practices are considered to lie outside the norm when they make demands for political and other transformations – should be made under the name of competing universality. Claims in the name of particularity tend to reinvigorate the formal universal to the extent that the formal universal will continue to territorialise such claims, for they will always be absorbed by it. A competing universal claim will need, through the formal universal, to translate its various demands. In this case, unconventional dimensions can be produced that will 'expose the limited and exclusionary features of the former one at the same time that they mobilise a new set of demands' (40). And as she explains later on:

> Thus the question for such movement will not be how to relate a particular claim to one that is universal; where the universal is figured as anterior to the particular, and where the presumption is that a logical incommensurability governs the relation between the two terms. It may be, rather, one of establishing practices of translation among competing notions of universality which, despite any apparent logical incompatibility, may nevertheless belong to an overlapping set of social and political aims.
>
> (Butler, 2000b: 168)

Gender Trouble sets out to do all this and at the same time, as I suggested at the start of this section, problematises some types of feminism that look to the juridical order for achieving representational and liberatory aspirations. In following Foucault, Butler points out too that law, or to be precise the juridical order, its institutions and language, both regulate and control subjects and to this respect any form of representation that law might offer is always already under its own jurisdiction and conditions. Subjects in this respect are produced by the juridical order as subjugated. The early Butler, we can say, is radically opposed to the juridical order. It is to this extent that, when she talks about the universal, she is clear that our understanding of the universal should not be limited by formality or, more specifically, by formal allusions to universal human rights, but should be understood as being constituted by concrete and substantive practices. The political significance of this lies in her refusal to promote an understanding of the subject that is static and without agency. If she adhered to an understanding of the subject as merely juridical, it would mean that subjects that engage in non-normative practices would always be considered as unintelligible. Moreover, such an understanding of the subject would ignore that intelligibility has its own historicity not attached to teleology. To put it in another way, the subject, whether gendered, sexual or racialised, is for her neither a mere observer of its formation nor does its formation rely solely upon juridical law.

In *Discipline and Punish* and *History of Sexuality, Vol. 1*, Foucault explains how the subject is produced through disciplinary power. As the introductory quote to this section points out, for Foucault, disciplinary power is law but a different type of law, an infra-law: a type of law that is ahead of the juridical, that permeates the social, cultural and political body, and precisely produces subjects through the exercise of a series of disciplinary practices, including those of surveillance. As Brown and Hartley (2002: 11) remind us, disciplinary power does not lie with the state but rather with culture and society. It is to this extent that, in the quote above, Foucault imagines disciplines fighting against the juridical order. This promotes an understanding that the norm, engendered by a series of practices, is not located with the law but rather in the social and cultural body, its various institutions and discursive practices. The law is no longer perceived as the sole producer of the norm. In *Gender Trouble*, Butler takes up disciplinary power and gender as being one of its processes to offer an understanding of how certain genders come to be understood as intelligible, and how others are foreclosed from the spectrum of intelligibility. Intelligible genders are the ones that can maintain a certain stability and continuity between gender, sexuality, sex and desire (1990: 18). Any sexual practices or desires that derogate, destabilise and break the above are prohibited. In *Gender Trouble*, she set out to show that there is nevertheless no ground behind practices that pronounce certain genders as intelligible, but rather that it is the very proclamation of this that constitutes intelligibility as such. Gender performativity became the very practice that exposes this. In doing so, Butler argues that the practice of gendering is a mere performative practice, that simply names what it calls into being. As I have already indicated elsewhere in the book, this practice, though, enables the subject to become agentic, to resist the very norm that formed it, through the disclosure of the norm's fantasmatic grounds. Resistance emerges out of this as a critical genealogy (1990: 5) of these legitimating practices, one that, let's not forget, is embedded in but not confined by them.

Disciplinary power is used as a weapon for disciplining juridical law. In the sense of encountering and countering law's claim to universality and demonstrating that its very existence relies on those foreclosures that it brings about. Disciplinary power is also used to show that the normative is not always coincidental to the law, or to put it otherwise, the normative is *not* the law. This means precisely that norms are not static, they can be transformed by the subjects that are to be formed by them. To be called a woman, for example, relies on a cultural understanding of what a woman 'is' that, in turn, is based on the differentiation between man and woman. But when a woman becomes a man through surgical reassignment, for example (and I am by no means suggesting, and nor is Butler herself, that this is an uncomplicated process without any practice of surveillance (medical and bureaucratic) being present), we can see that he both destabilises the normative understanding of what 'is' a woman (gender, sexuality, sex and desire), unconceals the very fantasmatic grounds of the norm and simultaneously shows that norms are not static. Similarly, but not within the concept of gender, when a young man runs away from the police who are shouting at him, what he is doing is resisting the interpellative call that somehow names him as a criminal. His running away enables us to see that the normative understanding of who is criminal is based precisely on discursive practices that produce the category of the criminal based on social and cultural so-called variants.

So to put it another way, disciplinary practices produce, as Foucault would have it, counter-disciplines that produce different narratives of the normative, allowing the subject's survival. This was not the case with Menezes, but our survivability as citizens of or visitors to the United Kingdom relies precisely in possibilities opening up, no matter how minimal they may be, that can allow us to undo any possible normative hegemony. Consider for example, Butler's own understanding of the norm from 'Competing universalities':

> [n]orms are not only embodied as Bourdieu has argued, but embodiment is itself a mode of interpretation, not always conscious, which subjects normativity to an iterable temporality. Norms are not static entities, but incorporated and interpreted features of existence that are sustained by the idealizations furnished by fantasy.
>
> (Butler, 2000b: 152)

The reinterpretation of the norm, through the praxis of resistance, allows one's survivability. Moreover, it reconfigures the plateau of intelligibility. In *Excitable Speech*, as we saw earlier, she called for the avoidance of any form of censorship that could do away with the constant reconfiguration and survival of subjects even if their calling into being is an injurious one. At the heart of Butler's understanding of how we can maintain, sustain and have livable and viable lives lies the structure of antagonism. When norms do not become the law, when in other words the state, and with it the sovereign, does not totalise the sphere of intelligibility, either by using the law as a governmental instrument, or disciplinary practices like surveillance to govern every aspect of our lives, then we can resist the cultural norms that bring us into being. Moreover, if we engage with this struggle as competing universalities then we can attain something more than our survival, our viability. But, and this is I think what explains Butler's recent quest for a different role for the juridical law, *when* the law and norms become one, or at least are presented as one so that the likes of George W Bush call upon our cultural survival on the basis of a hegemonic understanding of which law and practices are intelligible, then the possibility for survival as humans becomes delimited. A very small space for resistance remains. Every form of dissent is interpreted and considered not only unintelligible but moreover dangerous, a threat to national security and cohesion. Law, as I explained earlier, becomes for Butler the only vehicle for resistance and, specifically through the practice of the trial, the only force for dissent. But in order to do so it has to, as Benjamin and Agamben suggest, do away with its interest in its own preservation. For Agamben and Benjamin, as we have seen, this necessitates a deposition of law. But Butler, in this case, where a state of exception is declared, would insist on law, or more precisely on the practice of trying, associated with the law. This trailing, though, would have to shift its emphasis from being about law's own preservation to one where it will cater for life's own survivability. How could this become possible? As she suggests in 'Competing universalities', borrowing from Spivak's work,[15] the practice of translation may enable the agonism between competing universalities, competing concepts of the human. Such a practice will entail working with precisely the differences between competing notions without reducing the one into the other. Law perhaps can take up the task of the translator. But, nevertheless, the task of the translator would necessitate, despite any logical incompatibilities between competing universalities, that there might be some common grounds for 'social and political aims' (2000b: 167). So perhaps the law could become that space whereby the illogical incompatibilities – or at least the illogical incompatibilities between those that are said to perpetuate the global terrorism and those that fight it – could meet. And perhaps a translation of what it is to be human, without the confinements of justice, the ends of law, can become the means for such discussion, if human survival and vitality can still be entertained. For, as Butler writes, life is precarious (some lives more than others, a position shared also by Agamben and Benjamin), always an ambivalent concept, but as things now stand it risks losing its ambivalence if we continue to support the sovereign's contention that what it is to be human, and what life means are neutral terms.

I have invoked a double use and understanding of the law in Butler's work. On the one hand, she produces a critique of the juridical law and state law and, on the other, an evaluation of the possibilities of disciplinary power, of normative production and reinterpretation. At the same time, I have shown that within Butler's thought lies another law, the law of resistance and antagonism: a law that she claims can sustain our survivability and livability; that, if it is to agonise for life's survivability, might need to take up a different task, to become a translator if it is not to remain an instrument of sovereign governmentality. Its potential lies precisely in having unintelligibility as its horizon of possibility. It operates under the precondition that there is no intelligible universality, just competing meanings of life and humanness. In beginning this role of translation, within this precondition, law might then produce a threatening difference to the current totalising state of exception. This might be a small difference, an aberration, but it will perhaps, as Butler would want, serve as the 'ground' of a future non-violent law.

Notes

1 http://www.whitehouse.gov/news/releases/2001/09/20010914-2.html (accessed on 15 December 2006).

2 See *R v Halliday, ex parte Zadig* (1917) AC 260 and *Liversdidge v Anderson* (1942) AC 206.

3 If we take Foucault's writings on the three modalities of power (sovereign, disciplinary and bio-power) on board, we can say that up to the eighteenth century sovereign power was the most dominant modality of power. In modernity, we see the introduction of disciplinary and bio-power. As he makes clear (2003), none of these powers disappears from our times, what happens though is that different times are marked by a certain power. In the late nineteenth and twentieth centuries, for

example, we see the introduction and proliferation of governmental power. So when I say that Butler writes of the re-emergence of sovereign power, I allude to the re-intensification of this type of power in our times. The chapter follows a close analysis of these modalities.

4 In Greek there are two words designated to the word life. One is *zoe* (bare life) and the other is *bios*. Agamben considers the meaning that Aristotle applies in these words. The first, zoe, refers to life that is concerned with the sphere of the private (domestic issues relating to the home, etc.), while the second, bios, relates to the type of life that engages with questions that concern the struggle with the conditions of materiality, such as those of justice and ethics. Politics, according to Aristotle, is founded upon this precise distinction between zoe and bios, the private and the public sphere. Nevertheless, as his thesis goes, the precise distinction that founds his politics and along with it western metaphysics, is not sustainable anymore. We are living in times where life, and more particularly bare life, is politicised.

5 Derrida has offered a rereading of Walter Benjamin's 'Critique of violence' in his essay 'Force of law: the "mystical foundation of authority"' (1992b).

6 I want to suggest that Agamben does not use the word 'trial' here in a pure juridical manner, but rather it is the agonistic modality of law with itself , with its normative parameters that the term 'trial' signifies.

7 The English translation has in place of 'death machine' the words killing machine. The French and Italian versions retain the most accurate meaning in the words 'death machine' which I use here. My gratitude to Anton Schutz for bringing this to my attention.

8 For a more sophisticated analysis of Walter Benjamin's concept of pure language, see Agamben (1999b: 48–61); Duttmann (2000: 31–56); and Hamacher (1996: 294–236, 2000: 108–136).

9 Hamacher (2002) offers a sophisticated analysis of this. Accordingly, every law and every positing of law is subject to another more superior law. This more superior law is the historical change of which he writes. Historical transformation is both internally and structurally organised by an ambiguous relation towards 'means' and 'ends'. Since law, in its various configurations (statutory, case law, etc.), develops in accordance to this model of history, it cannot say that its end is justice. Law's reliance or dependence on history bars it from unquestionably stating that justice is its end, since it always exists ambiguously towards either ends or means. This analysis also enables us to see that despite the fact that law posits violence as something external to it, violence is structurally internal to it. It is based, if you prefer, on the phantasmatic presumption that it is law's ends that justify its means. For an even more elaborate analysis of Benjamin's understanding of the relation of history to guilt, see Hamacher (2002) 'Guilt history: Benjamin's sketch "capitalism as religion"'.

10 The word territory is put in inverted commas here because I wanted to bring to the attention of the reader that jurisdiction is no longer used only as a reference to spatial boundaries. On the contrary, jurisdiction refers to the custodian status of a detainee. For more in relation to a case of detainees in Quantanamo Bay and their *habeas corpus* challenges brought before the Supreme Court of the United States, see Motha (2005).

11 This position still holds true now even after the cases heard by the Supreme Court of the United States relating to grant of a writ of *habeas corpus* to certain detainees in Quantanamo bay. For further discussion on this see Motha (2005).

12 Foucault in this essay talks of the institutionalisation of individuals who committed crimes that were considered to be motiveless. The dangerous individual, who was in some respects insane, was the one whose crime was without motive or reason.

The dangerous individual was to be assessed via the concept of risk. When an individual cannot account, or take responsibility for one's act, judicial practice is rendered impotent.

13 For more on these cases see, amongst others, Loizidou (1997).

14 Giorgio Agamben argues, in *State of Exception* (2005a), that, in the case of juridical law, the concrete case always entails a 'trial' of which the end is to pronounce a sentence guaranteed by other institutions of the state (39–40). This observation suggests, that amongst other things, the operability of law necessitates the practice of trial, otherwise we can clearly see the decay of law. For the centrality of trial in philosophy, see Julia Chrysostally 'Setting the scene' in *The Implications of the Philosophical Critique of Subjectivity for Law with Special Reference to Legal Subjectivity and Sovereignty* (PhD thesis to be submitted to the Department of Government, University of Essex).

15 See Spivak (2003: 162) and Benjamin (2004: 253–263).

Chapter 5

The melancholic drag queen and its political potential

> To claim that politics requires a stable subject is to claim that there can be no political opposition to that claim. Indeed that claim implies that a critique of the subject cannot be a politically informed critique but, rather, an act which puts into jeopardy politics as such. To require the subject to stabilise means to foreclose the domain of the political, and that foreclosure, installed analytically as an essential feature of the political, enforces the boundaries of the domain of the political in such a way that enforcement is protected from political scrutiny. The act which unilaterally establishes the domain of the political functions, then, as an authoritarian ruse by which political contest over the status of the subject is summarily silenced.
>
> (Butler, 1992: 4)

This chapter focuses on Butler's articulation of the political. In doing so, I take as a precondition that Butler's work does engage with and articulate the political. She convincingly argued in 'Merely cultural' (1998: 33–44) against the left Marxist attack on post-structuralist cultural politics as being merely cultural or, to put it in more concrete and effective terms, 'destructive, relativistic and politically paralyzing' (Butler, 1998: 34) and unable to account for economic and social inequality being embedded with the presumption that there is a stable distinction 'between material and cultural life' (Butler, 1998: 36). Moreover, the effects of such accusations are worrying. They appear to denigrate the private sphere, or suggest that the demands of new social movements are apolitical (Butler, 1998). But as I have said, I will not engage with this debate. Instead, I intend to examine the structure, practices and sensibilities that produce Butler's conception of the political.

I begin the chapter not with Butler's account of the political but, rather, with an account of how the political has been articulated and debated within philosophy. This works as a comparative index through which we can formulate a clearer explanation of her political and its differences. I start by offering an account of the political via the work of Nancy, Arendt, Agamben and Foucault. I then proceed to analyse Butler's conceptualisation of the body, which as I argue is both the 'essence' and the ground of her political. Finally, through her practice of resistance, I explain that Butler's political structure is based upon an agonistic type of politics. When she criticises in her writing those who understand cultural politics as being merely cultural, arguing that

> [t]he only possible unity will not be the synthesis of a set of conflicts, but will be a *mode of sustaining conflict in politically productive ways*, practice of contestation that demands that these movements articulate their goals under the pressure of each other without therefore exactly becoming each other.
>
> (1998)

She shows that the political can avoid succumbing to death or the totalitarianism of unity if it remains open to contestation. But this reveals that agonism is the only viable political practice. As we shall see, Butler's agonism is not only reserved for political action, but it is the very core of her political philosophy.

The political

> It is this double exigency – recognition of the closure of the political and practical deprivation of philosophy as regards itself and its own authority – which leads us to think in terms of re-treating the political. This phrase is taken here at least in two senses: first, withdrawing the political in the sense of its being the 'well-known' and in the sense of the obviousness (the blinding obviousness) of politics, the 'everything is political' which can be used to qualify our enclosure in the closure of the political; but also as re-tracing of the political, re-marking it, by raising the question in a new way which, for us, is to raise it as the question of its essence.
>
> (Lacoue-Labarthe and Nancy, 1997: 112)

In December 1980, Lacoue-Labarthe and Nancy, two prominent French philosophers, set up the Centre for Philosophical Research on the Political at the Ecole Normale Superieure in Paris. The centre was inaugurated with a three-day colloquium on the political. The primary aim of the event was to discuss the essence of the political. This was also to be the overall aim of the centre. The co-directors envisaged 'the questioning of the political itself as to the political or, more exactly, the questioning of the philosophical itself about the political' (Lacoue-Labarthe and Nancy, 1997: 108). The density of this sentence captures precisely the difficulty of the task that they were aspiring to achieve at the actual colloquium and moreover in the life of the centre. Their overarching aim, though, was to show how the philosophical and the political belong to each other.

There was nothing new about their particular aspiration. Arendt (1990), as indicated in Chapter 3, has discussed this issue. She explained that, since the trial and execution of Socrates, philosophy has sustained an apprehensive distancing and distaste towards the political. And, in addition, she offered an erudite analysis of why this became the case, on how philosophy has since used this to represent itself as a discipline that operates through reflection and that distinguishes itself from politics, which was depicted by philosophy as operating on pure opinion. But, as I have explained, Arendt demonstrates how the philosophical and the political belong to each other. Therefore, the question of whether they are inseparable, the core of Nancy's and Lacoue-Labarthe's quest in the 1980s, restages a very old philosophical debate, one that the parameters of this book do not allow me to take up. In this context, then, I will take it as given that these two concepts belong together. However, Nancy's and Lacoue-Labarthe's work still offers a valuable interrogation of the political which I will cover later in this chapter.

Before doing so, I will draw upon Arendt's conceptualisation of the political for two reasons: (a) Arendt is one of the twentieth-century philosophers who explicitly engaged with the question of the political in philosophy; and (b) her understanding of the political has exerted an enormous influence upon philosophy. As you will see below, we can even trace Butler's understanding of the political in terms of resistance in Arendt's thought. Though, as will become apparent in the course of this chapter, there are some important differences amongst these two philosophers.

As Kaplan points out, for Arendt the political was best understood as a space 'of self-making in which diverse individuals and groups interact to create themselves and to shape their common world' (1997: 151). In *The Human Condition* (1998), she explained how the polis, the centre point of this political[1] – this space where our differences meet, contest with each other and shape a common world – excludes and should exclude activities that attend to the necessities of life. On the other hand, Arendt did suggest, drawing on the operations of the Greek polis, that those that attend to the necessities of life, either voluntarily or involuntarily (slaves, women) enable those who participate in conversations and argumentations as to the creation of a common good to become political citizens. As has been suggested, the private sphere, or the sphere of the production of necessities, is for Arendt a constituent feature of the political (Honic, 1992: 221; Isaac, 1992: 230; Kaplan, 1997: 151). Still, she considered necessities to be restraining, conducive to an unfree life, a life more characteristic of animals than humans. The private sphere, according to Arendt, is unable to give form to human uniqueness. How does she come to this conclusion? The polis is the space where beings come together to discuss, dissent and decide about their commonwealth and the main characteristic of this process is the fact that it takes place *because* of speech and action, what she considered to be unique to each person (Arendt, 1998: 176; Honic, 1992: 218). Arendt holds to this differentiation between public/private (Honic, 1992: 219) because she considers that each individual's uniqueness, a quality common to everybody but different from person to person, can only surface in the political and therefore public sphere. The home, or the private, is considered to be a space that is common to all, soundless, without distinction. Kaplan, drawing on Arendt's correspondence with Jaspers and her reflections on the 'Jewish question', argues that at least at a textual level there is a conflation in Arendt's work between the private and public (1997: 156–158). But, despite this, it is undoubtedly evident that Arendt wants to keep the two divided. In *The Human Condition*, for example, in analysing the political conditions of modernity, she writes with concern about the saturation of the political by the social. She writes that labour, work and similar considerations predominate modern life, with the effect that the sphere of contest and decision-making is *delegated* to individuals who act as experts, who face *no* dissent in taking decisions and consequentially can be seen as acting despotically. Arendt saw the political as a sphere of agonism where opinions are contested and, therefore, only if contestation, action and speech could remain alive could we retain an open political.

We can see so far that Arendt raises two important points about the political: two points that Lacoue-Labarthe and Nancy engage with directly either in disagreement or agreement: (a) that the political 'is always rooted in the world of men and of man made things which it never leaves or altogether transcends' (Arendt, 1998: 22) and; (b) that the social and its bodily necessities hinder the political. Honic captures these two points when quoting Arendt when she writes that in Arendtian politics 'not life but the world is at stake' (1992: 221). Indeed, for Arendt, it is not life *per se* that is included in the polis, not at least the life that Aristotle calls zoe, but rather the world, and the political takes place, happens, when we come together to decide, discuss and dissent upon what is to be common to all of us.

Like Arendt, Lacoue-Labarthe and Nancy are interested in pointing out (Lacoue-Labarthe and Nancy, 1997: 126) that the political and the philosophical are co-existent and, similarly, they are concerned with the totalitarianism of the political permeating every aspect of life. The phrase 'everything is political', all too familiar to us now, is used by them to drive home this point. If the social, psychological, aesthetic, etc. world has been invaded and taken over by the political, then, as they argue, we can say that the world is dominated by the totalitarianism of the political. Effectively, what this means is that the political can no longer be distinguished from other spectrums of life or inquiry. If, like Arendt, they propose that the philosophical and the political belong to each other, then this totalitarianism of the political signifies at the same time the completion of the philosophical. If their account is accurate, then we may conclude that the philosophical and the political are in imminent danger of becoming redundant or ineffective in the world, in the sense of being capable of a critical, productive and fruitful assessment of global, local and other transformations. The risk that a totalitarian philosophical–political regime faces is not dissimilar to Arendt's assessment of the prevalence of the social over the political. When this is the case, the political system ceases to be able to form knowledge, sensibilities and decisions based on external and descending factors; it becomes totalised for it has saturated every corner of life. Or at least, this is how they described the relationship between the world and the political in the 1980s. Having this in mind, Lacoue-Labarthe and Nancy set out to 'retreat' the political from its current state of affairs. How did they foresee this happening? And moreover what did this 'retreat' mean precisely? Here is what they say:

> first, withdrawing the political in the sense of its being the 'well-known' and in the sense of the obviousness (the blinding obviousness) of politics, the 'everything is political' which can be used to qualify our enclosure in the closure of the political; but also as re-tracing of the political, re-marking it, by raising the question 'in a new way' which, for us, is to raise it as the question of its essence.
>
> (Lacoue-Labarthe and Nancy, 1997: 113)

Playing with the double meaning of the French word retreat, which means both to withdraw and to retrace, they argue that 'everything is political' or, what they coin *la politique*, needs to be retreated, so that the essence of the political, what they call *le politique*, can be retraced. This retracing will not engage with empirical or factual components since precisely the problem with the political is its facticity, the fact that it is 'everywhere'. What do they mean by this precisely? If the retracing of the political engages primarily and prima facie with facticity, for example, with reconfiguring new institutions in which political goals and aspirations might materialise, this will not do away with the totalitarianism of the political, it would rather reinforce it. So in order to retrace the political, what they propose to do is to question the political philosophically, so as to arrive not at a different institution of politics, but rather 'the political institution of Western-thought' (1997: 110).

Moreover, this will require them to retrace the essence of the political, *lepolitique*. The retreat of the political (in both senses) has been inspired by Heidegger's critique of technology and metaphysics. Heidegger, as Critchley writes in 'Overcoming methaphysics', argued that technological advancements and, moreover, the domination of the technological in modern life will lead to the totalitarianism of the political, a 'homogenization of all areas of human life' (Critchley, 1993: 204). And the human being will inevitably be reduced to the figure of the worker (1993: 204–205). It is not necessary to dwell on the details of the trajectory that Lacoue-Labarthe and Nancy draw here,[2] but suffice to say that, like Heidegger, they see that the only solution to the totalitarianism of the political is to think essentially. Heidegger thought that the solution might come from working with the parameters of the possible 'which', as Critchley writes, 'the activity of the technological will is always attempting to exceed and push towards the impossible' (1999: 205) an activity that requires us to think the technological essentially. Lacoue-Labarthe and Nancy think of *le politique* similarly, within the limits that its remnants can demonstrate, and therefore essentially.

In addition, their prognosis of the political, if we can call it so, operates as a critique of deconstruction. They argue that deconstruction has engaged with the first meaning of the word retreat. Deconstruction has been able to address the limits of the political but has not retraced the political, which is paramount to our production of a non-totalitarian world, or at least a world that will try and avoid the totalitarianism of the political. They point out that while deconstruction has addressed politico-philosophical concepts, such as those of democracy or law, by pointing out their limits, it has nevertheless failed to address the question of the political which, as the two aforementioned philosophers, would have it addresses the 'political institution of Western-thought' or its essence. Deconstruction at its best, they would argue, signposts the symptoms, for example, of our democratic deficit, may enrich the ways of thinking about them, by posing questions that reveal this deficit, but deliberates in addressing the question of the political as being the institution of western thought.[3] According to deconstruction then, to be responsible, ethically and politically, we ought to postpone making a decision or a judgment (Critchley, 1999: 190–200). If we return this proposition to the question of democracy, then deconstruction will enable us to see that democracy is something that will come – the questioning of the limits of liberal democracy will guide us to it – only, at the same time, it will want us to defer any judgment as to how this democracy is to be. Or, to put it differently, democracy as a feature of the political *is* a vanishing point. Lacoue-Labarthe and Nancy find this proposition unsatisfactory. The constant and persistent interrogation of democracy, for example, or of *la politique* at a more general level, does not do away with the problems that the saturation or totalitarianism of the political has created. At best, we can say it postpones the problem, managing it through the act of deliberation, without addressing the essence of it.

Nancy, in his 1995 essay 'Being singular plural' (1997), offers a more graphical and explanatory exposition of *le politique*, the essence of the political. He chooses the fall of socialism in the then Eastern European countries to propose that what we experience there is what has already been present in modernity, the retreat of a community that is constituted either through the church or a sovereign figure and its transformation to one that is glued together by a 'we', a 'we' that makes and binds itself. This devolved 'we', as he terms it, that can be best comprehended as a 'being-with', *is* the ontological question of our times that necessitates a political accreditation. And since there is no single figure that this 'we' can identify with, what we have in its place is a plethora of disparate indices such as those of race, gender, class, etc., indices that cannot, according to Nancy, offer us a unified political unity, one that can be symbolised. This first part of his analysis is what we have described as the deconstruction of the political. He unpeels the levels of *la politique* (the concrete and factual) to identify what lies underneath it and, as we have seen, he discovers that what jells it together is a 'we' or 'being-with' which is no longer founded upon a figure.

The second part of his analysis, the part that addresses the essence of the political or *le politique*, comes in the form of a question. This question is directed towards the meaning of the self-made 'we' or 'being-with'. It is important to note that Nancy and Lacoue-Labarthe are not by any means suggesting that *le politique*, is created out of nothing. On the contrary, it is the outcome of the unpeeling or unconcealment of facticity, of everyday experience. How does he question philosophically this 'being-with'? How does he give meaning to something that can't be identified with a figure? His retracing of the 'being-with' is produced via the term *comparution*. *Comparution* means either making an appearance in a court of law or being-with. *Comparution* provides us with a different insight to 'being' than those so far revealed by philosophy. So far, critical engagements with metaphysical philosophy have addressed the question of appearance, the first meaning of *comparution* that Nancy undertakes to explain in his essay. Metaphysical philosophy understands the question of being, by having resource to the 'there', in other words, what is present. The question of being relies precisely on appearance, on the 'being there' of an entity such as a stone or the human. Put otherwise, metaphysics presupposes that an entity is what presents itself. Following, to some extent, the Heideggerian critique of metaphysics, Nancy provides us with a different perspective of appearance. While Heidegger has elaborated upon the question of what it means to be a being by addressing the ways in which entities appear to us intelligible and suggesting that an entity is a happening (being 'being'), a single event that 'begins' when one is thrown into the world, Nancy moves this thought differently to suggest, as Critchley puts it, that 'being is simply the being that it is not the presupposition of that existence…existence always exists in the plural, it is the being-in-common of many' (1999: 244). Being is, for Nancy, a 'being-with', without a single origin but rather of multiple non-original ones (Nancy, 1997: 83). Accordingly, 'being-with' is a happening that is impossible to be symbolised. It can't be a thing, like a flag that can stand in for a nation. A happening brings being, with the world *not* just merely in the world. Think of one's birth, for example. Birth throws one into the world, but at the same time it puts one *with* the world, it tunes one into the sounds of the hospital, the nurses and so forth. *Comparution* 'symbolises' (in the etymological sense of the word of gluing together what is broken) the socialilty of being, and to repeat once more what I said, when one appears in the world, one appears with *it* (1997: 37–38). The 'being-with', for Nancy, *is* an ontology. An ontology that is founded upon nothing, or, put otherwise, its foundations lie precisely in human making. And, even more, 'is an ontology of bodies' (Nancy, 1997: 84). Consider his words for a second:

> The ontology of being-with is an ontology of bodies, of every body, whether they be inanimate, animate, sentient, speaking, thinking, having weight, and so on. Above all else, 'body' really means what is outside, insofar as it is outside, next to, against, nearby, with a(n) (other) body from body to body, in disposition. Not only does a body go from one 'self' to an 'other', it is as itself from the very first; it goes from itself to itself; whether made of stone, wood, plastic, or flesh, a body is the sharing of and the departure from self, the departure toward self, the nearby-to-self without which the 'self' would not even be 'on its own'.
>
> (Nancy, 1997: 84)

Despite his denial of a figure that can symbolise this body-to-body 'community' which he suggests is the problem of the polis (1997: 23), we can very easily imagine it. If one was to risk arguing with Nancy against his ideas by proposing a series of images that might capture this, then one could imagine that this body-to-body image could be represented by the disparate bodies of protestors with disparate interests who come together over time to walk, play music and parade their dissent, or, to use one of Nancy's own images, bodies that touch each other with their mutual weight (Nancy, 1994: 28).

Let's think a little bit more of this image of bodies touching each other with their weight. These bodies are bodies that neither disintegrate into each other nor do they consolidate into one. Interestingly, these bodies are 'something' external and in addition 'something' that extends itself, that move backwards and forwards, without being ever one or belonging to one, but they are always singular–plural. There is an exteriority of Nancy's 'body' that is even exterior to language (1997: 84). 'Language is the incorporeal. . . . Either as an audible voice or a visible mark, saying is corporeal, but what is said is incorporeal.' (1997: 84) he writes, reversing the supremacy of meaning (said) over the vocality of the utterance (saying). Performative speech theory, as we have seen, invokes the same reversal with the only difference that it states that it is the utterance that undoes the truth in meaning. Nancy does not only suggest that it is the utterance that undoes meaning, but he pushes this proposition a step further to suggest that it is the very vocality of the utterance that undoes meaning. The utterance relies supremely upon its vocality: 'Being "is [not] only a word," but rather that Being is all that is and that goes into making a word: being-with in every regard' (1997: 86). The labour that goes into making a word, the labour of the voice in uttering a phrase, like 'I declare', is what appears to undo the truth of meaning. In doing so, Nancy desires to retrace *le politique* and, moreover, suggests the potentiality of having a form of mediation without mediators (law, sovereign, language, Christ) (1997: 94–95). Nancy puts the body at the centre of political practice, ethics and philosophy. As he suggests, this body social is the essence of the 'political institution of western thought'. In Nancy's polis, to be a body signifies being with others and the world and 'Being-with cannot be added on to being-there; instead, to-be-there is to be-with, and to be-with makes sense by itself, with nothing more' (1997: 98).

His polis, if it is a polis at all, reminds us of Arendt's polis and the political, with the exception of some essential differences. For Nancy, this polis is made of a plurality of self-making bodies that extend to the world and the world extends back to them, bodies that are both singular but at the same time plural, without losing the distinction of their singularity. Arendt's political is also the effect of a plurality of people coming together in the world, acting and deciding. But, as we have already seen, she excludes the labouring body from this political. Instead, embodiment is an anathema, a restraint to the political. Accordingly, the polis is best served by maintaining a differentiation between the public and the private.[4] In holding on to this differentiation, Arendt does not only uphold the classical distinction between the pre-political and the political but, consequently, produces an understanding of 'being' that is never quite immersed in the world, but rather is always nearby, before the polis and the political, a 'being-in' but *not* a 'being-with' the world. Nancy's 'being' in contrast is never *before* the world but, rather, is a 'being-with' the world. Following Nancy then, our decisions, or questions as to our political future (e.g. questions surrounding immigration, terrorism, wealth or poverty), need to be understood not as external to us, as standing before us awaiting our action, but rather – and this is the crunch of his ontology – that we are already with them, part of them, implicated in them. Here, I think is where the potential of his political 'manifesto' lies.

While Nancy includes both public and private life in the polis and Arendt focuses primarily on public life, Agamben (as we have seen in the previous chapter) argues that the political is constituted through the inclusive-exclusion of life (zoe) from the political. Agamben explains how western philosophical and political thought is at the moment totalised by sovereign–governmentality which consequentially produces this inclusive–exclusive bare life. The *polis* is not for him the exemplary space for the political but rather the camp. A move towards a 'better-life' will necessitate a critical evaluation or an undoing of this. As he writes, 'A political life, that is, a life directed toward the idea of happiness and cohesive with a form-of-life, is thinkable only starting from the emancipation from such a division, with the irrevocable exodus from any sovereignty' (2000: 8.8). For this to be achieved (as I explained in the previous chapter), we need to depose law, engage with pure politics, or politics without ends. The political, if we can call it so, is a space of contestation whereby what takes place is lawless violence. Foucault also showed through his studies on madness, crime, etc., that 'we have indirectly constituted ourselves through the exclusion of some others: criminals, mad people, and so on' (Foucault, 2002c: 404), but, unlike Agamben, he demonstrated that these exclusions which shaped modernity are not the product of sovereign decision-making. Who is to be institutionalised in a mental hospital and how they are to be treated were decisions vested in so-called expert institutions and specific practices. The prison, the clinic, the school, the laboratory promote and produce a kind of life whose constitution necessitates the exclusion of the abnormal, but all this is the product of disciplinary power. While Agamben's 'included-excluded' life (as we saw in Chapter 4) is one that can be killed but not sacrificed, Foucault's is one that is normalised. We may say that any killing takes place metonymically, in disciplining the body so as to produce an unruly will. At the level of bio-power, Foucault asserts that regimes of government take the place of sovereign power and operate at the level of managing populations as a means of producing and making life. Of course, decisions are taken when populations are managed but, as he would have it, these are decisions that have as their focus the making of life rather than taking life. I also pointed out in Chapter 4 that Foucault's bio-power also lets lives die (2003: 241) but we might want to pay attention to the passive contribution of power to this. This indicates that this type of power does not by any means take one's life – kill one – but rather allows one to die. Bio-power operates not only at the level of institutional government but also at a very individual level: the exercise of proper nutritional practices, generally understood as practices that care for the self are also engaged in the making of life (Foucault, 1988). Of course, it is important to notice that Foucault never anticipated or suggested that any modality of power, including bio-power, is one that delivers the subject to freedom. Agamben exploits a seeming contradiction in Foucault's work, namely that there is no explanation as to how the state's and the individual's use of bio-power coincide, to argue that the original power of the sovereign is the production of the bio-political body (Agamben, 1998: 6). Notably, Agamben's deconstruction of the political establishes the political as a relationship between the juridical and the political. While Foucault establishes a political that despite its restrictions is still enabled to make life through the various modalities of power that he describes, Agamben would only have this as being possible if 'pure politics' or 'pure violence' are instigated if, in other words, politics get severed from a discourse and practices that have ends as their focus.

By introducing these different invocations of the political, I want to propose that there exists at least a three-pronged articulation of the political in contemporary western thought. Those like Nancy put a multiple, dispossessed and material body at its centre and, similarly, those like Arendt understand the political as a coming together of a disembodied multiplicity in making something new. We also have philosophers like Agamben who argue that the political is staged upon the inclusive–exclusion of life from the polis and, as a consequence, the potential of the political lies in engaging with violence without ends, precisely the inverse of the type of violence that excludes 'bare life'. Foucault's political, though, is inextricably linked to his tripartite models of power (sovereign–disciplinary–bio-power). In modernity, he observes that the displacement of sovereign power and the accentuation of the other two powers is activated with the consequential effect that power is dispersed across different spatial terrains. The polis, therefore, ceases to *be* the epicentre of the political, but life, nevertheless, continues to be at the centre of government. One could say that, for Foucault, the polis ceases to exist as a figure of the political and what takes its place are disparate locations from where the political is being produced. Institutions and bodies become locations of the political (Foucault, 1991a: 375–376).

Despite the fact that all these critical thinkers differ in their understanding of the political, we sense a common desire. Their writings expose their desire to *think* of a better way of life. I write here 'a better' because none of them would want to produce a critique of the political that invokes the good life, that would precisely return the political to a closure, and totalitarianism. I need not explain how the index of a good life promotes a closure of the political. Arendt, Nancy and Agamben argue that a better life can be achieved through a configuration of political that exposes the inadequacies and limitations of the foundations of western modernity. Through the remnants of a deconstruction of the political, we can see what can be possible, we can see a better way of being, a way that (as they have it) must remain open to challenge and dissent since our contemporary configurations of the political move towards totalitarianism.

Foucault is the only one amongst them who suggests that what seemingly appears to be a totalitarian configuration of the political is just an appearance. Power is dispersed and, consequently, the totalitarian figuration of the political is also dispersed (Foucault, 1991a: 375–376). In offering this figuration of the political, he produces different locations of resistance and subject production. Or, to put it differently, even within the status quo of 'everything is political', there is still the possibility of a productive formation of life, one that is both enabled by power but that at the same time counters the very limits of the power that brings life into being. In some respects, Foucault's articulation of a proliferated and decentred political addresses directly the issue of recuperating *le politique* without resorting to a 'new' ontology, an ontology that risks precisely the possibility of closing up the political by returning it to an articulation of the body that becomes intelligible only if it gains its meaning outside linguistic intelligibility.

The 'originality' of the sonorous material body in Nancy, I argue, perhaps undoes the prevalence of a constructionist body, associated with certain philosophical and theoretical strands prevalent in western thought in the 1980s. But, at the same time, it precludes the possibility of understanding the body in its genealogical emergence, in the very facticity that brings it into being, which simultaneously deconstructs normative restrictions that might be imposed on life. The 'being-with' might be dispossessed in the sense that this body is never my body, but rather a body that the 'we' is always in the process of making (a point that would not be antithetical to Foucault), but nevertheless simultaneously this 'being-with', despite its multiplicity of origins (which one could translate as a multiplicity of time/spaces of production), is always historically contingent.

Nancy fails to address the specificity, contingency and effects bodies have and are exposed to once they are thrown into the world. While, in other words, he attests to the diachronic character of the body, he fails to address the relation between the diachronic and the synchronic, a necessary requirement of analysis, if we are to understand or even get a sense of how our existing lives relate to the political. It is not life *per se* that becomes important to consider as the question for the political, but rather lives, in their facticity, in their materiality and temporality. 'Being-with', if we are to stick with Nancy's language, cannot address the violence incurred by bodies – gendered, sexualised, racialised, ageing or insane bodies – unless it addresses the specific conditions of their emergence. Bodies might touch each other with their mutual weights, as he puts it, but how they touch and, even more, how that touch is articulated within the sphere of intelligibility is the paramount question, or even problem, of the polis. To put it otherwise, if there is a problem or question of philosophy and the political, it is the question of 'who are you?' (Butler, 2003); the question of 'how do you come to be the body that you are?'

As we shall see, Judith Butler builds upon Foucault's configuration of the political to activate her own understanding of the political. Like Nancy, she centres her analysis on bodies, but her bodies in their very materiality are neither exterior to the power that produces them nor passive to it. Her bodies are neither figural nor material but rather they are both. However, beyond everything her bodies are contingent and, I would argue, it is their very contingency, their possibility of re-emerging into the world anew that resists any possibility of an accusation of configuring the political in alignment to totalitarianism.

What follows is an analysis of Butler's political. I begin by addressing her understanding of the body and, specifically, the gendered body in relation to the political and I continue by explicating how her political is embedded in the practice of resistance. In addressing the above, I follow her work from a variety of sources. My analysis of the body emerges out of a reading of *Gender Trouble* (1990, 1999), *Bodies that Matter* (1993), *Undoing Gender* (2004b), as well as essays such as 'Contingent foundations: feminism and the question of postmodernism' (1992) and 'How can I deny...?' (2001). As for her understanding of the political, as I have already indicated, it is an understanding that is intrinsically linked to the question of the body. In addressing the body, I engage in tracing the trajectory of Butler's political. A political that is, as I have shown previously in the book, always related antagonistically to the other dimensions of life, namely life's ethical and juridical spectrums.

Bodies figural and material

> Thus, the constructive dimension of language is overridden in favor of one that assumes that language remains anterior to the object it represents. Of course, the theory of construction immediately raises the fear of a complete linguisticism, i.e. that the object is nothing but the language by which it is construed. But this kind of linguistic reduction must be resisted. The second problem with the claim that language represents power relations which, in turn, back or support linguistic practice, is that we fail to understand the way that power works through discourse, especially discourses that naturalize and occlude power itself. Again, this is not to claim that power is nothing but discourse, but it is to claim that the one cannot be thought without the other... But to focus on linguistic practice here and non-linguistic practice there, and to claim that both are important is still not to focus on the relation between them. It is that relation that I think we still do not know how to think.
>
> (Butler, 2000d: 9)

In 'How can I deny...' (2001), Butler engages explicitly with the relationship between language and the material body. In doing so, she takes an unusual route – different to the one that we have grown accustomed to her following when she talks about the body. Instead of directly talking about gendered bodies and engaging with feminist, queer and post-structuralist accounts and critiques of the body, she focuses her attention on Descartes' 'First meditation: about the things we may doubt' (1968: 95–101). Her overall account, of course, is directed towards feminist and queer discourses as her objective in the essay is to settle some criticisms levied against feminist thought that argues that there are no stable differences between the sexes and reduces everything to language (2001: 254).

The 'First meditation' is where Descartes sets out to demonstrate that the senses (or rather certain sensual experiences) cannot ground truthful or scientific knowledge. Instead, he sets out to demonstrate that doubt enables the possibility of the formation of true knowledge or, as Felman puts it, 'doubt strikes first the senses as a foundation of knowledge' (Felman, 1975: 209). The meditation begins with Descartes describing where he is and what he does. From the very start, he is detailed and visual in his descriptions: 'I am here, sitting by the fire, wearing a dressing-gown, with this paper in my hands, and other things of this nature' (1968: 96).[5] As Winders points out, this detailed description lures the reader to follow Descartes' thought (1999: 122), perhaps it even acts as a prop, transporting the reader who is elsewhere to the scene of the meditation. Whatever the case, Descartes does not fall short of entertaining the possibility that he might be delusionary – like the mad – impotent of producing true-knowledge, and to this effect he writes:

> And how could I deny that these hands and this body belong to me, unless perhaps I were to assimilate myself to those insane persons whose minds are so troubled and clouded by the black vapours of the bile that they constantly assert that they are kings, when they are very poor; that they are wearing gold and purple, when they are quite naked; or who imagine that they are pitchers or that they have a body of glass. But these are madmen, and I would not be less extravagant if I were to follow their example.
>
> (Descartes, 1968: 96)

He swiftly disavows the possibility of being mad, calling such consideration an extravagance and moves on to consider other sense-related stages, such as sleeping, and their relation to knowledge formation:

> However, I must here consider that I am a man, and consequently that I am in the habit of sleeping and of representing to myself in my dreams those same things, or sometimes even less likely things, which insane people do when they are awake. How many times have I dreamt at night that I was in this place, dressed, by the fire, although I was quite naked in my bed? It certainly seems to me at the moment that I am not looking at this paper with my eyes closed; that this head that I shake is not asleep; that I hold out this hand intentionally and deliberately, and that I am aware of it. What happens in sleep does not seem as clear and distinct as all this. But in thinking about it carefully, I recall having often been deceived in sleep by similar illusions, and, reflecting on this circumstance more closely, I see so clearly that there are no conclusive signs by means of which one can distinguish clearly between being awake and being asleep, that I am quite astonished by it; and my astonishment is such that it is almost capable of persuading me that I am asleep now.
>
> (Descartes, 1968: 96–97)

After reflecting on the blurring of the states of sleeping and being awake, he invites us to meditate on the relationship that sleep has to knowledge:

> Let us suppose, then, that we are now asleep, and that all these particulars, namely, that we open our eyes, move our heads, hold out our hands, such like actions, are only false illusions: and let us think that perhaps our hands and all our body are not as well as we see them. Nevertheless, we must at least admit that the things which appear to us in sleep are, as it were, pictures and paintings which can only be formed in the likeness of something real and true.
>
> (Descartes, 1968: 97–98)

Once he completes his meditation on sleep, he concludes that dreams, despite being fictitious, nevertheless resource themselves from real materials, such as colour or images that exist in reality. As Foucault suggests, this creates a differentiation between madness and dreams which eventually allows Descartes categorically to conclude that madness cannot be the source of true knowledge (Foucault, 2000: 391–417). This exclusion is even more apparent if compared with his entertainment of the idea of being mad. As Foucault astutely remarks, Descartes does not proceed to doubt this proposition. Since doubt is at the centre of the exercise, this omission operates to exclude madness from the realm of knowledge formation while, as we can observe from his entertainment of dreaming, doubt plays a pivotal role (Foucault, 2000: 393).

Butler – unlike Foucault (2000: 393–417) and Derrida (2001: 36–76) who univocally focus their exegeses on how Descartes treats madness and dreaming – moves the discussion in a different direction. She focuses upon the treatment of the body within the meditation. She proposes that the text reveals that Descartes' mistrust of the body exposes a certain tension. On the one hand, he doubts the body and, on the other, 'the very language through which he calls the body into question ends up reasserting the body as a condition of his own writing. Thus, the body that comes into question as an "object" that may be doubted surfaces in the text as a figural precondition of his writing' (2001: 258). This, she argues, destabilises the distinction between the material and the figural that his text intends to create. It is important to note here that Butler does not exclusively focus on the mind (soul)/body distinction that we so often see at the centre of discussions around this text, but instead she questions the way he uses language in order to doubt that the body is a capable source for the formation of knowledge. Or to be more precise, Butler reminds us that in order to doubt the body Descartes uses language. This reminds us, as Foucault did, that the meditation is a practice or exercise, that, as Derrida did, the meditation is a text, but also that it is both of these things – a text and an exercise. But Butler does not focus only on the meditation as an exercise but also upon the exercise that goes into producing the text and its effects (namely the exclusion of the body as a source of knowledge), that is writing. And, in strengthening this claim, she adds that, despite the fact that Descartes' meditation is introspective, he omits to say what took place before the writing of the meditation, allowing her to offer the following remark, 'the writing appears as contemporaneous with his introspection, implying, contrary to his explicit claims, that meditation is not an unmediated relation at all, but that must take place through language' (2001: 259). In deconstructing the text, she exposes the ambiguity that resides in the meditation regarding the body. Here, it is also pertinent to bear in mind her method of reading. Butler, as I have already pointed in Chapter 2, works from the effects of a process to question the process itself and, additionally, to point out to the political potentiality the limits of the process. This is exactly what she does here. At first, she observes that she has before her a meditation, an exercise or a practice that aims through deep thinking or emptying of the mind to arrive at some conclusion about something. Second, she observes that this exercise comes to her in the form of a text. And, finally, she is alerted to the fact that the text was produced through another exercise, that of writing. Putting all this together she is able to work from the resulting product to the ways in which this product comes to relate to the body.

As I implied at the very start of this section, Butler focuses on this particular text of Descartes so as to settle accusations levied against certain types of theory, including her own, that are most commonly interpreted as denying either sexual difference or materiality. In this particular essay, she addresses the relationship between materiality and language. However, in relation to these accusations, she shows that paradoxically they simulate Descartes' denial of the body. Here is how she comes to this conclusion. Descartes and 'his ability to doubt the body' she writes, 'appears to prefigure the skeptical stance toward bodily reality that is often associated with contemporary constructionist positions' (2001: 258). Drawing similarities between Descartes and constructionist theory appears rather peculiar and odd at first, but, on second blush, this similarity is not so unusual. Descartes, while using language to doubt the body, either ignores or never pays any attention to the ways in which language acts; in other words, he appears to comprehend language as a mere passive vessel in which his intentions travel. But, moreover, if we undertake an analysis of the ways in which language is used in the text, as Butler does, we can see that the method (doubt) used and his language do not necessarily correspond with one another. This point will be explained further below. Constructionists, on the other hand, pay attention to language, for example, they will not hesitate to suggest that the body is a linguistic invention (2001: 255), but in doing so they avoid asking questions such as 'in what way?' and 'to what extent?' (2001: 255) and effectively end up saying that the body 'is not made by language, but of language' (2001: 256). Like Descartes, constructionists fail to pay attention to the ways language acts, to ask the important questions such as 'to what extent this is possible?' and 'how does it happen?'. By ignoring the difference between being made by something *and* of something, as she critiques, they literalise 'the tropological functioning of language' (2001: 256) and inevitably end up establishing a kind of linguistic totalitarianism. So by deconstructing Descartes, Butler hopes to demonstrate, contrary to him, that language acts and that its very action returns to the text the body as a figuration. At the same time, she is demonstrating that the figuration cannot wholeheartedly capture the materiality of the body. On the contrary, what she shows (as I suggested earlier and we will see more of very soon) is a relationship between the figural and the material. Butler, as the introductory quotation of this section suggests, believes that this relationship between the figural and the material has not been adequately thought out, or that we haven't yet thought beyond the exposition of this relationship.

I have already explained how philosophers like Nancy relate to the materiality of life and construe that the linguistic is superseded by the material. What remains underanalysed, however, is how language labours and what effects that brings. Of course, Nancy takes further Heidegger's proposition that beings' dwelling *is* language to say that language is always in proximity to being, but 'unlike Heidegger' instead of investing his philosophical trajectory in questioning the meaning of this proximity, Nancy decides to argue what appears to be the effect of Heidegger's position, namely that materiality is supreme. In doing so, he appears to exclude the relationship that we have with language, the effects that come about when we are named, and when we resist certain naming. I highlight this because I want to point out not only that what remains politically important is the non-exclusion of either language or materiality, but, more pertinently (and this is Butler's point), that the exclusion of the one over the other hides in it the ways in which subjects are rendered unintelligible. What should be sustained is an open-ended and, therefore, inconclusive movement between the two. Then we can first demonstrate that what is rendered as unintelligible always pertains at the foundation of intelligibility (it is not something that we are to strive to achieve but rather is something that happens), but, moreover, we can expose the inadequacy of what is understood as a normative and universal realm. As the previous chapter has elaborated, Butler suggests that counter-universal claims, made by gay and lesbians, or people of colour, immigrants, etc., should question and put their demands in such a way as to demonstrate that their positions are universal, that they are, in other words, intelligible. By stating that one form of body is superior to another, say the figural over the material or vice versa, what we have is exclusion of the one over the other, an exclusion of certain forms of intelligibility over others, without in any respect reflecting on either of the two fundamental questions that such an exclusion brings about, namely: on what grounds do we produce these exclusions and how do they affect our understanding of the political sphere?

However, I now want to return to Butler's analysis of Descartes 'First meditations' so we can see in more detail how Descartes' doubt of the body returns the body in the text to its figural form and haunts his very intentions, namely to establish reason as the very foundation of all knowledge. As she suggests, he ameliorates the very possibility of thinking about the body's indubitability by leaving behind any previous knowledge and sensibilities that he might have gathered throughout his life. What might appear as an innocent and justifiable act, nevertheless aims at establishing a narrative coherence to his method. By excluding any previous knowledge and sensibilities from the method, Descartes wants to wipe from his hard-drive any reference to his own biography or history, to produce inevitably a meditative 'I' that is free of the cares of the premeditative 'I', to cast off his own material existence from his method (Butler, 2001: 259). But as Butler goes on to show, this splitting does not produce the narrative coherence anticipated. Consider, for example, as she does Descartes' description of the surroundings where the meditation take place, 'although we know them through the medium of the senses, for example, that I am here, sitting by the fire, wearing a dressing-gown, with this paper in my hand' (1968: 96). This sentence produces a paradox. Descartes does not deny here that the senses produce knowledge (Butler, 2001: 260). The senses occasionally are represented as being able to produce truthful knowledge. Butler finds this both intriguing and ambivalent. In the above sentence, we observe, as she does, that these senses produce a 'here', a spatial/temporal location that can be doubted, in the sense that his 'here' is not the here that we are located in: '[c]learly it is not here; the "here" works as an indexical that refers only by remaining indifferent to its occasion' (2001: 261). In other words, despite the fact that he invokes a 'here', to ground undoubtedly the space that we find him, but as this 'here' is a 'deictic' one (2001: 260), that is it refers to an extra-linguistic context, Descartes introduces an ambiguity, one that precisely opens up a way to interpret this 'here' as being *any* here. This is what I take Butler to mean when she writes that this 'here' remains indifferent to its occasion or happening, in other words, where it takes place. One of course can suggest that the fact that the 'here' can open itself to interpretation precisely demonstrates Descartes' point, that the senses are a doubtful source of knowledge. But, for Butler, the important point lies not so much with the doubtability of the senses or the body, but rather with the way what is to be doubted returns to support the doubt. What is important for her is that we can see in this that language acts in ways that are not necessarily intended by the writer.

This draws our attention even more acutely to the limits of the two facets of Descartes' thought. The first facet is obviously the philosophical facet. As we have seen from the very start, he proposes that the 'I' of the meditation is one that rids itself of any biographical-memorial thoughts. But here, he is precisely invoking a biographical 'I'. The second facet alludes to his narrative. Here, we can see with Butler, that the 'I' exceeds the spatial/temporal dimension that it tries to ground itself in (2001: 61). The 'here' gains a dimension outside the parameters that Descartes intends. What are then the effect of all this? Butler uses the moment at which the method used by Descartes fails to correspond with his narrative that follows to indicate that Descartes' attempt to create a separation between the materiality of his body, his memory or biography, returns to haunt him through both the material body and figural 'I' in at least two senses: (a) the figural 'I' returns in the narration; and (b) the material body returns through the invocation of the reader of the text. So the exclusion of either the figural or the material cannot be sustained

In the same train of thought, she highlights that throughout the text Descartes first invites us to imagine the body and then proceeds to doubt it. This invitation prima facie aims to establish that the mind is the producer of truth. But, simultaneously, it intends to demonstrate that the only intelligible subjects are the ones that can doubt the body and its ability to form truthful knowledge. But, what is even more paradoxical, is that this method relies heavily on imagination to sustain it. Imagination is often understood to be the product of the senses. In Descartes' imagination, as Butler indicates, it is the product of the cognitive realm. How does Descartes then try to establish this? Descartes asserts that his imagination does not come from things that he does not know or does not have any prior knowledge of. His imagination, in other words, is not perceived as being capable of *inventing* things. Butler proceeds to the etymology of the word 'invent', used by Descartes to negate a sense-based root of imagination. We are told that the word has its roots in the Latin term *effingo* and it means both to 'form an image' and to 'make a fact'. Now, what Descartes does is to use one of the meanings of invention to contrast it with imagination. He uses the meaning of invention that describes it as forming an image and cuts out from his explanation the meaning relating to the formation of a fact (2001: 264–265). However, this does not sustain his position that imagination is a fact-making process. When we are invited to suppose or imagine that he is asleep, for example, he creates a paradox: he wants us to imagine as *not* a fact, what at the same time arises from a fact. This equivocation between what is imagined as not a fact and being made from a fact is made, as Butler proposes, on semantic rather than conceptual grounds (2001: 265). The idea of imagination that he invokes here does not belong to the ideas they are based upon but rather on the meaning of words. In this case, it is the privileging of the meaning of the word invention as image-making that allows him to ground imagination as fact-making. But this attempt to use the body as being separate or apart from the mind registers a return of the body in the text as a figural term (2001: 266). The return of the figure in the text captures an interesting relationship between the material and the figural. As Butler writes, every time Descartes tries to suppose the body so as to doubt it, the body returns as a figuration (2001: 267). Each time this happens what we see is not the supremacy of the figuration over the material body, or, to put it another way, we cannot say from this that the figure can capture the body in its totality, but rather we can observe something more interesting taking place:

> The act by which the body is supposed is precisely the act that posits and suspends the ontological status of the body, an act that does not create or form the body unilaterally (and thereby not an act in the service of linguisticism or linguistic monism), but that posits and figures, one for which positing and figuring are not finally distinguishable.
>
> (Butler, 2001: 267–268)

The positing returns the body as a spectrality, a linguistic trope, but, simultaneously, it reveals the inconsumability of the one into the other (2001: 268). This inconsumability reveals not only that the figural and the material are inextricably linked or related to each other, but, moreover, and this is the crunch of her argument, each time we exclude the one from the other, this exclusion leads to the totalitarian political: one that by the force of exclusion establishes itself as a practice that is grounded naturally and, therefore, rationally. The spectral or figural body brings to the fore our formation into subjects which is grounded upon some pre-existing history or biography: who we become, precedes our coming into being, but the material body is there to remind us that, despite this dispossession, despite the fact that we don't possess our own coming into being, we always find ourselves resisting this dispossession, always sighing that our livability does not always correspond with the normative assumptions that the figural promotes. But we would not have been able to address this without the attachment to the figural. When we contest our material and cultural conditions, what we address at the same time is the figural presumptions that brought us to this struggle in the first place.

It is precisely this relationship, the relationship between the figural and the material, that Butler's work on gender formation articulates. Her political project has been one whereby she unveils at the very local level, at the level of gender formation, this relationship between the material and the figural and its political potential. Lately, her work has turned towards a critique of the formation of a wider range of subjects and identities – such as the 'detainees' in Quantanamo Bay, the Palestinians, the Israeli state – but I would argue that what remains integral to her thought is the centrality of the body in analysing conflicting political situations. The political potentiality of any subject, its survival and more particularly its ability to reinvent its life and make itself intelligible, relies precisely on invoking this doubling of the body.

As I have explained above, various critiques of the political appear to engage with the materiality of the body – in doing so forgetting the ways in which language acts upon the body, ignoring the biographical, or imagining that some bodies are purely passive towards the powers that bring them into being, being submitted to an uncontested regime of sovereign-governmental power (Agamben) – without adequately explaining how some bodies escape this totality of power. Butler's 'bodies' contest the primacy of the material by pointing out the complexities which emerge when practices, such as writing, introspection (meditation), surgery and a plethora of others, begin to articulate the body, but without concurrently posing a supremacy of the figure. This doubling of bodies that she promotes is not a philosophical sophistry, but merely a demonstration of Butler's intellectual ability to unravel the ambiguities and ambivalences within philosophy. It is, on the contrary, a political impasse to think of this doubling and to think of what it does. I want to suggest that there is an implicit idea in 'How can I deny…?', namely that by thinking about the doubling of the body and its endless moves, we could make intelligible (a) the ways in which power operates and (b) bodies that were cast as unintelligible.

If we were to go back a step and take another glance at the start of Butler's analysis of Descartes' 'First meditation', we can now see even more clearly how we can read what I have just suggested above. We are aware by now that, in order to perform this meditation, he unloads his mind from any previous fixtures. As Butler suggests, this requires him to sever memory and dismember his body in order to proceed. But, towards the end of the meditation, he invokes his memory when he considers the infallibility of God. He particularly asks himself to remember that any opinions that doubt this are unreliable and fallible (1968: 99–100). The meditation becomes something that will enable him to rewrite the memory of these opinions (1968: 99–100). We not only have here a situation where that memory, that 'inner discourse of the body' (Goodrich, 1990: 34) returns to haunt the text, but we find in the methodological approach that the very one who required the meditative or reading subject to dismember itself in order to be able to doubt the reality of the body and sensual world, to be suddenly projecting a different goal. As Butler observes, the

> [m]editation now appears as a particular kind of action, one that claims, must be repeated, and that has as its goal the forcible imprinting . . . of this same thought on the memory, an imprinting that is apparently forceful as God's engraving is profound: indeed, both convey a certain formative violence, a rupture of surface, as the effect of writing.
>
> (2001: 267)

What then does she mean by this? While initially the meditation was set up as a process whereby the method of doubt would be used to establish what is the truthful source of knowledge, now it appears that the repetitive character of the meditation has as its primary aim to rewrite a certain memory, the memory of those that doubt the will and infallibility of God. Since this practice requires a rewriting of memory, this practice simultaneously and paradoxically necessitates the engagement of memory: Descartes needs to remember and to remember he needs to write this memory, to include what he has already repudiated (the body) into writing. What this shows is that the meditation cannot be effective unless it engages force. In this case, this force is parallel to the way in which God inscribes his will on Descartes. In order for Descartes to demonstrate that he is a rational being, he needs to inscribe on his memory the ridding of his old memory from his hard-drive, in the same way that God inscribes his will. But this rational subject does not come to him unmediated. It is the outcome of a rewriting of the body, of unwriting the body, which forcefully returns, both spectrally and materially, in written language. If the method of the meditation is contradicted in practice then, what one cannot help concluding, is that the formation of subjectivity cannot be founded naturally, by will of the God or a Sovereign figure (whether this is the Sovereign *per se* or the law), nor is it a natural consequence of a cause, but it is rather a practice (meditation, writing) that requires discipline, the discipline of repeating what is considered to be already there (God, in the case of Descartes) in order to undo the violence that constitutes a differentiation and therefore an exclusion. But what we have also seen is that this performative act leaks through a body, a body that is both material and figural. A body that through its re-inscription into the text enables a wilful (agentic) subject to come into being. Butler's reading of Descartes' text allows us to see how integral is the body to the formation of subjects, but, as already indicated, the body that she proposes or reveals is a body that is both material and figural. Moreover, she shows that this body is not naturally given, but rather it comes into being through practices and this allows us to see the fantasmatic character of the belief of a natural-foundational given subject to be found either in the will of God or by the mind. Descartes forces the body in and out of the 'First meditation', and in forcing it in and out, we can see both the power that enable this to be done (God) and the resistances this produces (the body). The political significance of this is enormous. Butler, like Foucault, is able to propose that the production of subjectivity is an ongoing process that, despite attempts to produce normative subjects, is always going to meet resistance.

Resistance

> to a certain extent sexuality establishes us as outside of ourselves; we are motivated by an elsewhere whose full meaning and purpose we cannot definitively establish. This is only because sexuality is one way cultural meanings are carried, through both the operation of norms and the peripheral modes of their undoing.
>
> (Butler, 2004b: 15)

When she writes, in *Gender Trouble* (1990), referring to representational and French Feminism that 'the task is to formulate within this constituted frame a critique of the categories of identity that contemporary juridical structures engender, naturalize, and immobilize' (1990: 5), Butler precisely demonstrates the first part of her critique: that the rational subject is not the natural outcome of the mind, but is founded upon a forceful exclusion of the body, a practice that at the same time reveals to us that the body is at the foundations of subject or identity formation and, moreover, that any subject formation takes place within the parameters of movement, dispossession and contestation. The book itself sets out to be critical of feminism that 'restricts the meaning of gender' (1999a: vii–viii). Indeed, the book undertakes to show how gender is not a fixed category, nor can it be said to be founded upon sexual difference. French feminism (Butler engages in particular with the work of Luce Irigaray) suggests that women's oppression arises out of the linguistic and cultural construction of sexual difference. Women have been traditionally and historically understood as non-rational beings, as *res extensa*, who acted in the service of men. French feminism, by flagging this and using the concept of 'sexual difference' to reveal how this operates within language, undertook precisely to rewrite woman in the polis in ways that would mean she was no longer a representation of man, but rather was represented in herself. Though Irigaray never argued that a total emancipation of woman would be possible, she did suggest that the invocation of a new feminine language would work to at least subvert phallocentricism. However, in doing so, French feminism has enabled a particular figuration of woman, one that is constituted through heterosexual practices. Butler set out to question this figuration through invoking sexual practices that are not considered to be normative (1999a: xi). For example, in *Gender Trouble* (1990, 1999a) and *Bodies that Matter* (1993), she uses the homosexual body in drag and transsexual bodies to question the construction of two genders, feminine and masculine, that were made explicit by French feminist theories of sexual difference. In critiquing French feminism, she opens up the possibility of thinking of gender not as something stable but rather as something undone through a variety of practices. Her aim, as she put it in the tenth anniversary preface of *Gender Trouble*, was 'to open up the field of possibility for gender without dictating which kinds of possibilities ought to be realised' (1999a: viii). At a political level, her concern was simple, she wanted to propose a theory of gender that would not exclude or consider as unintelligible gendered subjects that were not the product of a discourse of sexual differentiation. She wanted to make a point that non-heterosexual subjects are subjects that mattered, are intelligible, ought to be recognised and have livable and viable lives in the polis. At one level, she challenged a prominent discourse that understood the subject as fixed and unitary. At another, through the practice of gender performativity, a deconstructive practice, she pointed out how resistance brings into effect foreclosed intelligible genders and reiterates and recites more potentialities of livable and viable lives. This last point, as I have suggested in previous chapters, rearticulates the norm.

I want to turn once more to the allegory of the melancholic drag queen that Butler invokes in order to clarify how and where she sees this taking place. The melancholic drag queen recites that what lies at the very foundations of heterosexual hegemony is the disavowal of same sex love. Put differently, heterosexuality is formed by the disavowal of homosexuality. Homosexuality is integral to the formation of heterosexuality. However, the melancholy of the drag queen allegorises the fact that our culture does not contain within it conventions that allow this loss to be mourned.

These two observations bring us to three very important revelations. First, that heterosexuality cannot be founded without homosexuality, without disavowing same sex love; second, that if homosexuality is at the foundations of the formation of heterosexuality, then we cannot disavow its intelligibility; and, third, that exclusion of homosexuality from the realm of intelligibility is fantasmatic, it comes into being through convention rather than through a foundational law. Through her writing, Butler exposes the claim that we have only two genders, a masculine and a feminine, as a mere fantasy. Now, there are some conclusions that we can draw from this.

First, that culture is the articulation of conventions and norms that are not homogeneous. Their production is activated through practices of exclusion. But, even more, because what is normative is produced by what is counter-normative – heterosexual bodies, to put it crudely, are the outcome of the disavowal of homosexual bodies – this allows the possibility of reciting the norm in a way that what was deemed as unintelligible is produced as intelligible. Butler defines intelligibility in *Undoing Gender* (2004b) as follows, 'intelligibility is understood as that which is produced as a consequence of recognition according to prevailing social norms' (2004b: 3). But this definition is supplemented with a critical reflection. Butler comments that intelligibility based on prevailing social norms does not mean that norms are hegemonic but rather they are restraining (2004b: 3–4). The deconstructive mode that accompanies her work in *Gender Trouble* and *Bodies that Matter* talks of intelligibility of genders that are considered as being unintelligible, but there is still a caveat within her early work that allows us to see that she is talking of a different type of intelligibility. Her intelligible subject, as I indicated in Chapter 2, is one whose intelligibility is formulated through both *res cogitas* and *res extensa*, both mind and body, and comes about through the process of resistance, a resistance of the supremacy of mind over body or vice versa.

Deconstruction, or critique as Butler prefers to call her mode of analysis, enables us to see that what is unintelligible is based on the fantasy of the norm. What becomes politically and philosophically important is to resist[6] this fantasy: to resist the ways in which, both in language but also in materiality, such genders are deemed unintelligible. But resistance is not an agentic act, in the sense that it is not something that bodies autonomously undertake, resistance is the outcome or the product of exposing this fantasy. The effect of this exposition produces an agentic subject, but this production is both local and temporal. It is not the case that, for example, when one is called fat, by simply saying, 'No I am not', one is resisting this allegation. Resistance is more complex, resistance takes place when the norms that produce one are exposed as a fantasy. To do so, one has to answer back in such a way as to undo the presumptions on which a normative understanding of fatness is based upon. This is what, for Butler, constitutes resistance. The agency that emerges out of this resistance is one that is related or located to that specific calling, but at the same time points out that your presumptions of me being fat are based on medical statistics or cultural understandings of fatness that presupposes what fat is. We can say that resistance is the outcome of the effect of reading certain callings differently. Resistance is the reactive undoing of the norm. Resistance can take many forms, from an allegory, to a specific type of denial, as we have seen in relation to Butler's reading of Antigone, to a rereading of Descartes' 'First meditation', to the performances of the army clown at the anti-G8 demonstrations in Edinburgh in July 2005.

Before I proceed to explain the relation between resistance, bodies, norms and power in Butler's work, I want to draw our attention back to her analysis of Descartes' text, for it becomes pertinent to highlight the significance of her constellation of the figural and material body in understanding resistance. She explained how Descartes, in his attempt to discard the material body from knowledge production, reproduces it in another form, as a linguistic figure. The material body then looms out of the text in the form of a figure. In exposing this, she has demonstrated, first, the impossibility of dismembering the body from knowledge production, but also that western metaphysics is contained in or sustained by a fantasy: the fantasy of a rational mind at the centre of the production of intelligibility. Ghostly bodies in the forms of figures always sit upon this rational proposition and expose its inability to sustain its method of question without being mediated by language. Her rereading of this story, queers and queries the text in ways that other philosophers have not done, but, more importantly, allows her to sustain her own method of how bodies are produced. Bodies are produced through exclusion, disavowal. But disavowal, or even doubt in Descartes' case, enables the intelligibility of such bodies, because without them, as either figural or material, intelligibility *per se* could not be sustained. In reiterating all this, what I want to point out – and link up with the next set of points I want to raise – is that while we can undo the norm (the body is not excluded from the meditation), we cannot do without the norm, the norm is what brings us into being. Here, in relation to Descartes, we can say that the norm (reason) has produced us as a rational 'I', that is neither rationality nor materiality, but rather a rational–material figure.

What meaning can we give to the above? Here is a proposition. Butler's 'bodies' are, not pure affect or materiality, they are also rational. They are rational in the sense that they come about through the norm which of course is fantasmatic, but they are enabled by this fantasy of the so-called rational norm. In 'Gender regulations' (2004b: 40–56), in following Foucault, she suggests once more that gender is not regulated only by laws but also by norms. Foucault understands regulation as a practice of disciplinary power that can be historically located and, while within his juxtaposition, we can understand that gender is an instance of this regime, Butler suggests in addition that 'the regulatory apparatus that governs gender is itself gender specific' (2004b: 41). Butler first explains what she means by the norm. The norm, she warns, should not be confused with the rule or the law, '[a] norm operates within social practices as implicit standard of normalization' (2004b: 41).[7] Lawyers engaging in critical theory might find this sentence slightly underinvestigated or impoverished. As lawyers we have been trained to read the law closely, not only to discover the ratios that bind precedent but, moreover, to unveil the normative presuppositions that such precedents produce. Criminal lawyers, for example, are trained to find the very implicit normative values that govern the so-called rational decisions of judges. We are, in other words, well-trained to uncover the normative presuppositions. But Butler is using law here in a slightly different way. As her chapter shows, Butler is out to fight the psychoanalytic understanding of normative production that is invested in the symbolic order (2004b: 43). Moreover, what she is interested in is to demonstrate that

> the notion of culture that becomes transmuted into the 'symbolic' for Lacanian psychoanalysis is very different from the notion of culture that remains current with the contemporary field of cultural studies. . . . I also plan to argue that any claim to establish the rules that 'regulate desire' in an

> inalterable and eternal realm of law has limited use for a theory that seeks to understand the conditions under which the social transformation of gender is possible.
>
> (Butler, 2004b: 44)

In doing so, she proceeds to show how Lacan draws upon Strauss's understanding of the cultural. For Strauss, cultural rules are universal and inalterable (2004b: 45), for Lacan, as she writes,

> what is universal in culture is understood to be its symbolic or linguistic rule, and these are understood to support kinship relations. The very possibility of pronominal reference, of an 'I', a 'you', and 'they' appears to rely on this mode of kinship that operates in as language.
>
> (2004b: 45)

This construction of norms allows a very particular construction of sociability[8] (kinship) that leaves little room for any other form of sociability to come to life and gain intelligibility. Butler, moreover, points out that the symbolic is not the same as the social:

> The symbolic place of the father does not cede to the demands for the social re-organization of paternity. Instead, the symbolic is precisely what sets limits to any and all utopian efforts to reconfigure and relive kinship relations at some distance from the Oedipal scene.
>
> (2004b: 45)

Therefore, in drawing upon the Lacanian understanding of law, which as we have seen is heavily based upon symbolic structures that are considered as being universal, Butler is able not only to cite a difference between the symbolic law and the norm, but to gesture towards the benefit of understanding gender not as the product of law or rules but rather as a norm.

In the same chapter, she explains how she understands gender as a norm. This understanding utilises her concept of gender performativity. Consider her words, for example:

> To claim that gender is a norm is not quite the same as saying that there are normative views of femininity and masculinity, even though there clearly are such normative views. Gender is not exactly what one 'is' nor is it precisely what one 'has'. Gender is the apparatus by which the production and normalization of masculine and feminine take place, along with the interstitial forms of hormonal, chromosomal, psychic, and performative that gender assumes. To assume that gender always and exclusively means the matrix of the 'masculine' and 'feminine' is precisely to miss the critical point that production of that coherent binary is contingent, that it comes at

> a cost, and that those permutations of gender which do not fit the binary are as much a part of gender as its most normative instance.
>
> (Butler, 2004b: 42)

When Butler proposes that gender should be seen as a product of the norm (which she understands to be a process), she does so in order to unveil the fantasy of the sexual difference binary and, most importantly, that the norm cannot render unintelligible intersex and transgender men and women, butch dykes and camp gay men, subjects who do not necessarily fall on either of the sides of the binary, 'feminine'/'masculine'. Butler sustains this observation by suggesting that the norm is not the same as a model. A norm, as she writes,

> is a form of social power that produces the intelligible field of subjects, and an apparatus by which the gender binary is instituted. As a norm that appears independent of the practise that it governs, its ideality is the re-instituted effect of those very practises.
>
> (2004b: 48)

Bodies, therefore, become intelligible, through the norm, but at the moment when they do not enact the norm, they resignify it and, moreover, open up different possibilities for creating livable and viable lives for gendered people.

What is important in all this is not only that Butler provides us with a theoretical framework in which we can see how our political existence as gender subjects is made possible, but, as she herself always contended, she does not foreclose this field of possibilities by telling us what is an intelligible gender. Similarly, Butler is adamant that we should not by any means assume that because a particular resignification of a norm might be contrary to what we aspire, it should be denied for other gendered subjects. For example, in 'Is kinship always already heterosexual?' (2002: 14–44), Butler demonstrates her own reasons for opposing gay marriage, reasons that are not dissimilar to her critique of the Lacanian law, but at the same time she also *refuses* to oppose gay marriage. Such an opposition would institute a belief in the mono-culturalism of the norm and be antithetical to her own method. Bodies should be able to have the lives they aspire to, she would say, as such aspirations are what allow them to have livable and viable lives.

To conclude and to return to Butler's attachment to the body as the vehicle for political life, it is necessary to note that she holds to the position that bodies are dispossessed. Consider her words,

> when we speak about my sexuality or my gender, as we do (and as we must) we mean something complicated by it. Neither of these is precisely a possession, but both are to be understood as models of being dispossessed, ways of being for another or, indeed, by virtue of another.
>
> (2004b: 19)

This dispossessed body, as she writes, does not actually refer to a relationship between me and the other, but rather to an exc-static existence:

> To be exc-static means, literally, to be outside oneself, with rage or grief. I think if I can still speak to a 'we', and include myself within its terms, I am speaking to those of us who are living in certain ways besides ourselves, whether it is a sexual passion, or emotional grief, or political rage. In a sense, the predicament is to understand what kind of community is composed of those who are beside themselves.
>
> (Butler, 2004b: 20)

If one inhabits a dispossessed body, then one's body is never his or her own, nor is it his or her not-own. One comes into being through norms, norms that are linguistic, social, historical, and one by the sheer uninhabitability of these norms resides in them. If this is the case, then one is not also, or should not also, be able to legislate or decide for every other body. The political potentiality of bodies lies precisely here, in their ability to allow those that undo us, resist us, to have their aspirations lived. Resistance, therefore, ends up being the resignification of the ideality of the norm and an aspiration and a continuous possibility for redrafting the parameters of the livable. To have this as a political aspiration also means that philosophically we will have to live with and think through the tension between the material and the cognitive. And this might require us to think again and again about how desire is not monolithic. I sign off by suggesting that Butler's thought provides us with a possible pathway of rethinking how we can resist the totalising and suffocating effects of our political terrains. A pathway that is always open to resistance, not only in the sense of resisting the current geopolitical status quo but also resisting the possibilities, the pathways and propositions that she provides.

Notes

1 The polis ought not to be understood simply as a geographical index, but rather as 'a politically autonomous community of people living together in a defined territory comprising a civic centre with surrounding arable countryside' (Manville, 1990: 53).
2 For a detailed analysis of this trajectory, see Critchley (1993: 200–219).
3 See Derrida (2005).
4 For an insightful discussion of Arendt's somatophobia, see Bell (1999a: 62–84).
5 For more on this, see J A Winders, 'Writing like a man (?): Descartes, science, and madness' (114–140), in S Bordo (ed), *Feminist Interpretations of Rene Descartes* (Pennsylvania: Penn State University Press, 1999).
6 For a sophisticated critique of Butler's concept of resistance see Mills (2003: 253–272).
7 This is a point that I suggest that Agamben does not take. Agamben conflates the norm and the law.
8 For a discussion of the social by her, see Butler (2004b: 47–76).

Chapter 6

Butler's reception

> A trial resembles a play in that both begin and end with the doer not with the victim. A show trial needs even more urgently than an ordinary trial a limited and well-defined outline of what was done and how it was done. In the center of a trial can only be the one who did – in this respect, he is like the hero in the play – and if he suffers, he must suffer for what he has done, not for what he has caused others to suffer.
>
> (Arendt, 1994: 9)

Lois MacNay writes that '[w]ithin the Foucauldian tradition, it is the work of Judith Butler on the performative construction of gender that has had the most influential impact upon feminist understandings of gender identity' (1999: 175). Similarly, Nealon, as early as 1994, writes in the journal *Postmodern Culture* that 'Judith Butler has certainly produced a body of work that matters' (1994).[1] Numerous other scholars, from disciplines as varied as sociology (Bell, 1999a, b, 2002), political science, literature (Berlant, 1997; Sedwick, 2003; Warner, 2001), law (Bottomley, 2004; Conaghan, 2000; Franke, 1997; Halley, 1999; Loizidou, 1999b, 2004; Moran, 2005), philosophy (Grosz, 1994; Hanssen, 2005), geography, cultural studies, critical race theory (Ahmed, 1998), postcolonial theory, gender and sexuality (Halberstam, 2005; Prosser, 1998), have at least since the publication of Gender Trouble (1990), if not earlier, been engaging with her work critically, productively and amicably, taking her understandings of subject formation and moving them within their disciplines in directions that perhaps not even Butler has anticipated. My purpose here is not to offer an analysis of these works. These works share commonalities that I want to just gesture towards: most of them point at the exclusion of certain subjects from the normative terrain (Bell); or challenge in evaluative ways the production of the subject (Braidotti, 2005; Grosz, 1994; Vasterling, 1999); or simply unveil ways in which her concept of performativity can be used (Loizidou, 1999b).

Despite all the amicable and productive responses that her work has given rise to (evidenced by numerous interviews and public lectures), Nussbaum's review of her work published in *The New Republic*[2] in February 1999 challenges this cosy set up and gestures towards the existence of a caustic and unfavourable reception of her work. Nussbaum is Ernst Freund Distinguished Service Professor of Law and Ethics at the University of Chicago. In 'The Professor of Parody' (Nussbaum, 1999a), she undertakes a review of four of Butler's books; *Excitable Speech*, *The Psychic Life of Power*, *Bodies that Matter* and *Gender Trouble*. Her review is rhetorical and undermining towards Butler's work (Bell, 2002: 573–587). In an eloquent and thought-provoking article, Bell correctly observes that the critique centres around the following six issues: (a) Butler's work as professed bears no relation to women's lives nor does it propose any ways of transforming women's lives; (b) her writing is dense and unclear; (c) her propositions are banal and rely on sophistry and rhetoric; (d) her work is unscholarly, lacking sufficient analysis of texts that are being cited; (e) her critique of sexual difference is unconvincing and; (f) her concept of resistance needs to be supplemented by a normative concept of justice (Bell, 2002: 575–576).

Additionally, as Bell suggests, we may form a more profound understanding of the character of the review if we pay attention to where it comes from, to its academic location or context. Bell goes on to locate this caustic response to Butler's work within a particular genealogy. Nussbaum's review belongs, as Bell writes, to an Anglo-American academic tradition which both fears and is hostile towards continental philosophy (2002: 583). Continental philosophy is read as being abstract and bereft of any practical solutions, in our case here of any practical solutions that will benefit the feminist movement. So because of the her suspicion to continental philosophy, as Bell writes, Nussbaum consequently fears that 'the popularity of Butler's work... will dampen feminist solidarity and activism' (2002: 583). It could be said that her review is founded upon reproaching the effects of Butler's work.

Bell's reading of the *New Republic* review reminds us of the pertinence of the genealogical perspective but, additionally, it reminded me of another genealogy, not alien to the one that she proposes but an older one, that shapes and fuels Nussbaum's critique. Nussbaum's method and the substance of her critique owes much to the sixteenth and seventeenth century, common law tradition and, ultimately, legal training. Nussbaum, criticises Butler for offering an unscientific, unsystematic, unpractical, unscholarly, rhetorical evaluation of gender formation. Moreover, she caustically argues that Butler does not take into account questions of gender equality, the victimisation of women and justice. These omissions are put down to Butler's use of an eclectic oeuvre of continental philosophy and method of analysis. In the sixteenth and seventeenth centuries, as Goodrich writes, the teaching and learning of law was still taking place in the Inns of Court (1986, 1990). The study of law was not yet being undertaken in academic institutions. This came much later, in the nineteenth century (Goodrich, 1986, 1990; Rush and McVeigh, 1997). But during these earlier times, a gradual systematisation of the law, primarily due to the availability of printing, begins to take place. What this primarily meant was that law reports were recorded, printed and published by private reporters, such as Coke (Goodrich, 1986: 70). Along with these changes, he writes, a new movement of jurisprudential studies emerges. This movement, rooted in the Inns of Court, promoted the study of law, not in relation to theology, not in relation to rhetoric, not in relation to the civil tradition, but rather in relation to itself. Law is now represented as a discipline of its own, with its own distinct methods of reasoning and argumentation. English law slowly begins to form and in this way develops its own national identity and professional independence. But, simultaneously, the study of law was being undertaken with reference to scholastic literature. As Goodrich writes

> The subjection of common law to the principles of scholastic method enabled the new jurisprudential literature to present a properly doctrinal account of the disparate strands of legal tradition. The common law became in their test a unitary discourse, a professional ecriture, a unique discursive logic, and ultimately an empire of truth supported by a veridical language or orthodoxy that was peculiar to the law alone. In short, the imported and translated scholastic philology enabled the doctrinal systematisers to establish a common law hermeneutic or, by its classical name, a science of interpretation (*scientia interpretationis*). True to its name, the function of such a hermeneutic was to herald to announce the truths of legal discourse in a didactic and oracular way. The truths in questions were drawn from elsewhere, from time immemorial or from divine law, and only doctrine or the peculiar hermeneutic of the common law could safely extract them from their textual custody in the appropriately foreign languages of the ancient tradition.
>
> (Goodrich, 1990: 69)

This new jurisprudence used continental methods of analysis and interpretation. However, this did not mean that there was a massive renaissance of continental jurisprudence but, rather, that something more complex was taking place, namely continental methods of analysis were glossed over or adapted within the national context. We can see that this process intended to immunise common law from any external influences, geographic, institutional, linguistic, etc. (Goodrich, 1990: 70) and, in doing so, simultaneously to utilise this 'unique' legal technique of interpretation to survey the jurisdictional boundaries of law. The effects of legal interpretation would be seen in the production of judgments that were consistent, rational, universal, coherent and above all just.

At the level of method, Nussbaum acts in the spirit of sixteenth- and seventeenth-century jurisprudence. She approaches Butler's work scholastically and searches for its inconsistencies, irrationalities, unscholarly rhetoric and her eclectic adaptation of continental philosophy. Her dissatisfaction with the last issue is developed even more in the second part of the review where Nussbaum accuses Butler of using disparate theoretical perspectives without accounting for their differences, without offering detailed descriptions of received theories, or competing interpretations of those ideas (1999a: 38). Nussbaum perceives Butler's work as being both unsystematic and based upon an incoherent theoretical framework. It seems that Nussbaum was searching for the truth in Butler's book by looking for a sustained and coherent theoretical and scholarly background. This approach to textual reading, I suggest, is very like the jurisprudence described above. There are even more similarities though. While consistency and coherency appear the main tools that she uses to read Butler's work, when it comes to support her own positions, Nussbaum, very much like the aforementioned jurisprudes, draws on referentiality to support the truth of her position. So she draws the truth of her position from other authoritative texts. She calls Butler's work sophistry and cites, for example, Socrates as the main critique of philosophical sophistry (1999a: 40). She points to the unjustifiability of Butler's examples by pointing to empirical and scientific knowledge. If the aforementioned jurisprudes drew the legitimacy of their interpretations from divine law, Nussbaum continues that tradition by drawing upon the most 'divine' law of our times, science. Let us consider some of the uses she makes of the divinity of science. When, for example, she refers to Butler's idea that one comes into being through naming she writes:

> Yet Butler adds to these plausible claims about gender two other claims that are stronger and more contentious. The first is that there is no agent behind or prior to the social forces that produce the self. If this means only that babies are born into a gendered world that begins to replicate males and females almost immediately, the claim is plausible, but not surprising: experiments have for some time demonstrated that the way babies are held and talked to, the way their emotions are described, are profoundly shaped by the sex the adults in question believe the child to have. (The same baby will be bounced if the adults think it is a boy, cuddled if they think it is a girl; its crying will be labelled as fear if the adults think it is a girl, as anger if they think it is a boy.) Butler shows no interest in these empirical facts, but they do support her contention.
>
> (Nussbaum, 1999a: 41)

Nussbaum, as you can see from this extract, accepts that there is some validity to Butler's theory of subject and gender formation as it can be verified by scientific research. Nevertheless, she continues by shedding doubt on all this, by raising her own uncertainty regarding the meaning that Butler wants to give to one's initial entry into the world. So she writes, 'If she means, however, that babies enter the world completely inert, with no tendencies and no abilities that are in some sense prior to their experience in a gendered society, this is far less plausible, and difficult to support empirically' (Nussbaum, 1999a: 41). Her own uncertainty is turned into something that can't be verified by empirical studies. This is not the only time in the review that Nussbaum turns to empirical studies. A page later she not only urges Butler to write about 'real infants' but also accuses her discussion on resistance and agency of being bereft of empirical examples (Nussbaum, 1999a: 42). When in doubt, Nussbaum turns to science and empirical studies.

However, science, the longing for systematicity and consistency and the abjection of continental philosophy are not the only characteristics that attach Nussbaum to this tradition of lawyering. The style of her attack, its dislike of rhetoric bereft of reason and bereft of a justifiable cause, along with her call for clarity of language make this genealogical connection even stronger. One of the things that these jurisprudes objected to was rhetoric. Rhetoric was seen as empty, obscuring the labour of law and obstructing the work of justice (Goodrich, 1990: 93). But it was not all rhetoric that was considered to be doing this. Bad, unstudied rhetoric was the one to be blamed (Goodrich, 1990: 93). As Goodrich writes, '[t]hat rhetoric was essential to law was indisputable. What occasioned concern was that the rhetoric employed was so frequently bad rhetoric' (1990: 93). Manifestations of bad rhetoric, as Goodrich writes, citing Putterham's and Wilson's respective critiques of the state of persuasion in the Inns of Court, are exemplified in the following series of legal practices, '[p]leadings were ambiguous, narrations disordered, figures inappropriate, language "inkhorn" and "powdered," style opaque and topics unseemly' (1990: 93). Not only was it to be blamed, it was seen as jeopardising the legal system. The consequences were devastating for clients who relied on their lawyers for their lives and possessions (1990: 93).

Nussbaum, similarly, attacks Butler's understanding of gender formation and the style in which this is articulated. Butler's 'written style' is described 'as ponderous and obscure' (1999a: 38). Her use of parody obscures the real needs of women, or, as Nussbaum writes,

> For women who are hungry, illiterate, disenfranchised, beaten, raped, it is not sexy or liberating to re-enact, however paradoxically, the conditions of hunger, illiteracy, disenfranchisement, beating, and rape. Such women prefer food, schools, votes, and the integrity of their bodies.
>
> (Nussbaum, 1999a: 43)

She throws at Butler a series of facts that raise doubt as to whether Butler cares about or takes seriously the material conditions of life that constrain our formation as subjects. And, consequently, reads Butler's parodic acts of resistance as analogous to Marie Antoinette's apocryphal line to the starving protestations of the women of France prior to the 1789 revolution, 'Let them eat cake.' In her eyes, Butler is guilty of failing to understand that excluded or foreclosed subjects will not achieve an agentic position through the exercise of parody. Parody, as she writes, can only be a useful act of resistance when one is a tenured professor at a liberal university. (Nussbaum, 1999a: 43)

There is an endless list of examples that situate Nussbaum within the tradition of the sixteenth- and seventeenth-century jurisprudes. In drawing some of these examples to your attention, the aim is not just to highlight this. The purpose is different. It is to focus on the effects of this. The project of these juriprudes was centred, as Goodrich suggests, on the construction and consolidation of the Englishness of common law (1990). They invented ways in which the common law's past could be anglicised. We have seen from Goodrich's analysis of Wilson and Putterham's use of the need for skilled rhetoric an example of how this 'naturalisation' of common law was effected, and also the connection that is made between this and the figure of the victim, or the person who calls the law to assist him/her. Nussbaum likewise accuses Butler of obscuring through her untrained rhetoric the concerns of those that come before the law, the complainants or victims.[3] The victim appears to be central to this campaign of lawyering. Nussbaum accuses Butler explicitly of forgetting the victim and its call for justice. Moreover, rhetorical and academic discourses that place struggles at a local level and suggest that nobody is a victim are considered to be dangerous. At least, that is one way of understanding the caustic nature of the review and Nussbaum's accusatory closing remark, 'Judith Butler's hip quietism is a comprehensible response to the difficulty of realising justice in America. But it is a bad response. It collaborates with evil. Feminism demands more and women deserve better' (Nussbaum, 1999a: 45). Butler is seen by Nussbaum as a collaborator of oppression by suggesting that parodic acts can undo local repression. Nussbaum's attachment to victims' justice turns the review of Butler's work into a trial of Butler. Nussbaum becomes the advocate of minority rights, women's rights, and she presents her case with the support and collaboration of real empirical facts, rigorous scholarship and skilled rhetoric.[4] As you can see, she is explicit as to how she reads Butler's seeming failure to consider the material needs of populations: Butler becomes in Nussbaum's eyes a collaborator with evil.

Let us consider this severe accusation and its effects. Nussbaum's review does not only account for what she sees as the failures of Butler as an established academic, but, rather, it also attributes blame to her. Butler becomes guilty, a collaborator with evil, I presume. This means that Nussbaum sees Butler as being no different from those governments, or political and cultural structures, that maintain women in a position of repression. In this review, Butler becomes a 'criminal'. Looked at from this angle, the review is suddenly seen in a new light. It is no longer an evaluation of ideas, their limits and possibilities, but it takes the form of a trial. Butler is the accused. Nussbaum is the prosecutor. But Butler is not just an ordinary criminal. Butler is more than that. She not only has knowledge of what is evil, she co-operates and collaborates with those who victimise populations that are in need. With this in mind, Nussbaum's attack does not only become an ordinary trial but, indeed, a show-case trial. And she wants to win this textual trial, in the name of the victims, of the ones that have no voice to speak, are too beaten, too exhausted, too hungry for words. But, as Arendt wisely reminds us (in the citation at the start of this chapter) and as Nussbaum forgets, a show-case trial begins with the doer (in this case Butler) and ends with the doer (in this case Butler), it makes the doer suffer but it bears no witness, does not bring to light the sufferings of those that it purports to support. If Arendt is correct, then Nussbaum's attack is meaningless for those that she purports to want to win this battle for.

As I already explained, in *Languages of Law* (1990), Goodrich elaborates exclusively on how modern law and advocates have received from their sixteenth-century brothers an understanding of law as being founded upon reason, coherence and divine authority. Goodrich, though, as I already intimated, suggests that these attachments are not innocent, they have been formed by excluding or casting outside its memory law's own emotional body, and specifically that law is formed not only by those attributes that it includes but also by those which excludes, such as images and signs. Lately, Goodrich (2004: 395–517), has also reminded us of the satirical side of law that gets subordinated in legal scholarship and legal doctrine precisely for the love of rationality. For those old jurisprudes, the body of the victim played, as I suggested, an incidental but important role. It was used as a vehicle, a trope, for promoting the distinct identity of common law. This point is not explicit in Goodrich's account in *Languages of Law*. Although, Goodrich does not write or identify the institution of law, or the legal profession, as putting the figure and body of the victim at the centre of any battle of recognition, nevertheless, when in the *Languages of Law* he writes that,

> [i]n secularised legal terms, the sacrifice founds the authority of law; establishes the state as the social body, the invisible or mystic continuance that was the Crown and became the sovereignty of Parliament. In terms of positive law, the sacrifice is symbolic: prosaically, it simply denotes the subjection of the individual to law, of the singular body to the social, of the physical to the spiritual.
>
> (Goodrich, 1990: 59)

he certainly invokes that there is a sacrificial body at the foundations of law, but he does not purport to suggest that this sacrificial body becomes also a sign for which law fights. In other words, Goodrich does not suggest that a sacrificial body could correspond to the victim who becomes the crusade for lawyers. But I would suggest that we could and can make this connection. The sacrificed Christ returns in the figure of the victim. Law as an institution and a practice becomes a relentless struggle to give a body to the one who has been sacrificed, to reconstitute the victim in the community. *Only* again, as Arendt reminds us, what gets a hearing is not the victim but rather the doer. The doer in this case comes in the figure of law *itself*. Nussbaum's critique of Judith Butler's work, despite its references to the external and material body, despite its scientific groundings, despite its philosophical allusions, produces a meta-narrative that cries out for the survival not of an agonistic feminism but rather of law. It is a struggle for the sovereignty of law.

Now, you might think that I am making a lot of fuss about Nussbaum's style of critique in suggesting that it takes the form of a show-case trial, that in doing so she promotes the sovereignty of law, in both a similar and different way to that of her predecessors. But, if you are still not convinced with all this, consider the analysis below of Vasterling's critique of Butler's work. I pose this comparison because Vasterling's article shares Nussbaum's concerns but the difference in style is remarkable. This difference in style, I suggest, evidences that Nussbaum is not just reviewing Butler's work but that she is indeed putting Butler herself on trial.

At the time she wrote this article, Veronica Vasterling (1999) was an Associate Professor at the Department of Philosophy at the Center of Women Studies at the University of Nijmegen, in the Netherlands. The article under consideration was published in the feminist journal *Hypatia*. She likewise worries that Butler's analysis of the political, despite its aspirations to uproot hegemonic conventions and universal claims, could produce a form of radical inclusive democracy (1999: 33) that might end up having the opposite effects to those to which it aspires (1999: 34), that it mainly ignores that the process of forming inclusivity is always going to be based on some form of exclusivity (1999: 33–34), and 'that the category of "women" is permanently open to different interpretations' (1999: 34). Her concerns, though, are put forward in such a way that she does not appear categorically to denounce Butler's methods or conclusions. On the contrary, her concerns, though insightful and valid, are articulated in the form of worries that Butler might consider and in doing so might strengthen her theoretical position. She also worried, like Nussbaum, that Butler's theory of gender performativity might foreclose different ways of understanding, interpreting and considering the category of 'woman', but at no point does she put her worries as an advocate, nor does she talk of 'woman' as a victim. Vasterling's article offers a critique similar to Nussbaum's, but it comes in the particular form of an offering rather than an attack. It comes in the form of amicable academic discussion without necessarily taking the position of an advocate, without being done in the name of a victim ('woman'), although it is provided and articulated within a feminist philosophical discourse and without being presented as scientific knowledge or positing empirical observations as truth.

Butler does not often get cited in critical legal scholarship. If and when she does, it is always in relation to her understanding of gender formation, or injurious speech, but I would suggest that her biggest contribution to critical legal scholarship lies with her relentless attachment to the material and figural existence of subjects who are and who cannot be victims. Her concept of performativity (gender and otherwise) unveils, indeed, that at the foundations of society lies a foreclosed subject, a foreclosed homosexual subject, a detainee at Quantanamo Bay, *but* it is also a subject that animates the socio-symbolic order, one that exists, lives and engages in practices, which are not normative, but counter-normative. This is a significant difference. As she argued in 'Competing universalities' and *Undoing Gender* (2004b), there is a difference between the norm and its applicability. When a norm can't be applied universally we can say that it gives rise to counter-norms, counter-norms that could compete with universal claims not by demanding to be included, as the excluded Other, but rather as universals themselves. The foreclosed subject, whatever figuration it may take, then becomes not a victim whose inclusion we need to fight for in a community founded itself on that basis. The foreclosed subject is not as Nancy imagines it, a gluing subject, a 'being-with', but, rather, one that always has the potential to counter the universality and establish through this encounter its own agentic position. We just need to think of Butler's exemplary figures to understand that her subjects are not victims. The melancholic drag queen allegorises the fantasy of heterosexual love. Her melancholia, no matter the pain, certainly does not paralyse her. Antigone might take her life, but she does not do so without countering the sovereignty of Creon. The Taliban and al-Qaeda detainees are not victims, 'they can be killed, but they can't be sacrificed'. Butler, of course, desires the creation of conditions for viable and livable lives, but in doing so she does not deny that those whose lives have been foreclosed by the universal laws are victims. Foreclosed subjects have lives, they might be injured, but they are still able to question the conditions that make their lives sometimes unlivable and unviable. They do resist the standards, laws and norms that often suggest that they are not human, they do demonstrate that their lives are worthy, but they do so by exposing not only the unfounded claims of the universal, but also by exposing through their practices that they live counter-normatively. What Butler proposes is not for an all-inclusive radical democracy, as Vasterling fears that she does, but rather for a democracy, if it is a democracy, that deliberates the possibility that lives could be irreconcilable with each other, that we would never understand the life of another. And this should be precisely the basis of our engagement both with the Other and the world.

At the centre of Butler's work lies another important point. If we are to produce and promote a more deliberative work, one precisely that does not act before deliberation or in place of deliberation, we must recognise that all areas that govern life, law, politics, ethics and aesthetics,[5] are inclusively exclusive of each other. This does not merely suggest that they relate to each other. It rather furthers Arendt's proposition, relating to the philosophical–political divisions. All these areas of life might constitute or attempt to constitute their jurisdictions by excluding each other, but these exclusions are exclusions that foreclose the possibilities to answers of how we could create the conditions of more viable and livable lives. If we are to address these questions, then we need to work within the openness that the 'inclusive–exclusive' concept that accompanies the constitution of these areas produces. Nussbaum's critique preserves legal sovereignty, the insularity of law as both a discipline and an institution, and above all collapses and reduces subjects to the same level, by the sheer fact that she presents in the mode of knowability what the Other needs or desires. I am not saying here that Nussbaum is a collaborator of evil, I am just presenting another way of understanding her position and its limitations, the very limitations that Butler's thought at least alerts us to. But if Nussbaum is an old-fashioned jurisprude, to what extent are we, the inheritors of another, minor jurisprudence (a critical jurisprudence), not limiting ourselves to the sovereignty of law, to what extent are we not reducing the Other to the same?

The critical legal studies movement in the United Kingdom passionately engaged with arguing for the inclusion of Otherness in the social–political realm. It did so by introducing into the study of law continental philosophy, aesthetics, cultural studies, political theory, literary theory, feminist theory, sexuality, race and post-colonial theory and history. But despite the intention to unveil the epistemic totalitarianism in law and attempting to demonstrate that the Other is at the foundations of legal formation, they continued reducing the Other to the figure of the victim. It devoiced and defaced the Other and ended in arguing for the law or, as Goodrich has suggested, it ends up demonstrating the critics' love of the law (1999). The works of Douzinas and Warrington (1994, 2000), Motha (2005), Fitzpatrick (2001) and Diamantides (2000) are exemplary of this. Others, such as Aristodemou (2000), Tuitt (2004), Bottomley (2004), Drakopoulou (2000), Goodrich (1990, 1996), Haldar (2004), Cooper (1994) and Conaghan (2000), have promoted an understanding of the subject (whether this comes in the figure of law, women, the refugee, the colonised, the homosexual) *as* agentic. Their work gestures to different possibilities of grasping and grappling with the Other. But, in doing so, they argue either covertly or overtly that agency pre-exists the coming of the subject into being. Consequently, and perhaps unintentionally, and despite their allusions to the importance of language and its metaphorical impetus, they are suggesting that the subject pre-exists language. The subject is the labourer of language.[6] There are some political effects of not taking into account the performativity of language. The subject is returned to a natural, pre-cultural status, the very status that they set up to retreat and retrace – unintentionally invoking the Cartesian mind–body dichotomy.

Moreover, they appear to promote the idea that there is a homogeneous understanding of desire of subjects. In other words, desire *is* presented as being the same for all subjects.[7] It is a desire to be included within the universal of the law. By pointing this out, I have no intention of undermining the work of these scholars, but, rather, to propose that critical legal scholarship in the United Kingdom needs to re-evaluate the very language in which it invokes the agentic subject. Only then, I would suggest, could it open up the space for more livable and viable lives, enable it to think what it means to be human, but also, at a more banal and everyday way, challenge and resist (in the way I suggested in my chapter on politics) the institutional practices of law and its effects, one such effect being, a homogeneous understanding of desire.

The work of Judith Butler has shown how sexual practices enable challenges to the understandings of gender as the formation of sexual differentiation. Her theory of gender performativity has opened up the understanding of gender as a process, as an ongoing process, that shatters and undoes not only our understanding of gender, but also our understanding of universalism, sovereignty, ethics, politics and aesthetics.

Like Foucault, she provides us with a cultural history of the present, one that can most effectively be written and read from the position of the local. In times where universal human rights are used as instruments of governmentality, in times where global capitalism we are told thrives, her work acts as a reminder that if we are to sustain life, and aspire for livable and viable lives, perhaps our agonistic bodies should invest in labouring with the local. This might not be everything, but it is at least something.

Notes

1 http://muse.jhu.edu/journals/postmodern_culture/v005/5.1r_nealon.html
2 *The New Republic*, 22 February 1999, 37–45.
3 Nussbaum argues that her advocacy does not deny claimants any agency, but the sheer fact that Nussbaum argues as if she *knows* what women, or other minority groups, *want*, has the effect of making their agency lose its *gravitas*. This is also the core of Spivak's response to Nussbaum's understanding of what women want (Spivak, 9 April 1999: 43). For a critique of the reduction of every concern and demand to the figure of the victim, see Brown (1995); Berlant (2000); Loizidou (2001).
4 For more about Nussbaum's understanding of victims' rights and agency, see Nussbaum (1999b).
5 Lecture presented at Tate Modern, London, UK on 01/09/04.
6 Goodrich's work appears to be more difficult to categorise in this way. Goodrich, in *Languages of Law* (1990), for example, explicates that there are linguistic resistances that uproot the foundations of law. In this respect, we say that he understands the 'subject' being produced at the moment of resistance, retaining its agency at the moment that it is called into being. Nevertheless, in *Law in the Courts of Love* (1996), when he talks, for example, of the feminine, he adheres to a distinction between the private and the public that betrays a slight construction of a subject that pre-exists language. Having said that, there is a certain poetic tension in both of these representations of the subject which at least gestures that it is impossible to have a universal understanding of the subject, its desires and needs. See Loizidou (2001).
7 See Spivak's critique of the universality of desire (1988: 271–313).

Bibliography

Agamben, G (1998) *Homo Sacer: Sovereign Power and Bare Life*, Stanford, CA: University of California Press

Agamben, G (1999a) *Remnants of Auschwitz: The Witness and the Archive*, New York: Zone Books

Agamben, G (1999b) *Potentialities: Collected Essays in Philosophy*, Stanford, CA: Stanford University Press

Agamben, G (2000) *Means without End: Notes on Politics*, Minneapolis, MN and London: University of Minnesota Press

Agamben, G (2002) 'What is a paradigm?', accessed 1 March 2004, http://www.egs.edu/faculty/agamben/ agamben-what-is-a-paradigm-2002.html

Agamben, G (2005a) *State of Exception*, Chicago, IL and London: Chicago University Press

Agamben, G (2005b) 'State of exception', in Norris, A (ed), *Politics, Metaphysics, and Death: Essays on Giorgio Agamben's Homo Sacer*, Durham, NC and London: Duke University Press

Ahmed, S (1998) *Differences that Matter: Feminist Theory and Postmodernism*, Cambridge: Cambridge University Press

Alderman, N (2006) *Disobedience*, London: Penguin Books

Arendt, H (1970) *On Violence*, San Diego, CA, New York and London: Harcourt Brace & Company

Arendt, H (1990) 'Philosophy and politics', *Social Research*, 57(1), 73–103

Arendt, H (1994) *Eichman in Jerusalem: A Report on the Banality of Evil*, London: Penguin Books

Arendt, H (1998) *The Human Condition*, Chicago, IL and London: Chicago University Press

Aristodemou, M (2000) *Law and Literature: Journeys From Here to Eternity*, Oxford: Oxford University Press

Aristotle (1976) *Nicomachean Ethics*, Thompson, KAJ (trans) London: Penguin Books

Audi, R (2001) *The Cambridge Dictionary of Philosophy*, Cambridge: Cambridge University Press

Austin, J L (1962) *How to Do Things with Words*, Oxford: Clarendon Press

Badiou, A (1999) *Manifesto for Philosophy*, Albany, NY: State University of New York Press

Badiou, A (2002) *Ethics: An Essay on the Understanding of Evil*, London and New York: Verso

Bell, V (1999a) *Feminist Imagination*, London, Thousand Oaks, CA and New Delhi: Sage Publications

Bell, V (1999b) 'On speech, race and melancholia: an interview with Judith Butler', *Theory, Culture & Society*, 16(2), 163–174

Bell, V (2002) 'Feminist thought and the totalitarian interloper: on rhetoric and the fear of "dangerous thinking" ', *Economy and Society*, 31(4), 573–587

Benhabib, S (1992) *Situating the Self: Gender, Community, and Postmodernism in Contemporary Ethics*, New York and London: Routledge

Benjamin, W (1979) 'The task of the translation', in Arendt, H (ed), *Illuminations*, Glasgow: Fontana/Collins

Benjamin, W (2004) 'Critique of violence', in Bullock, M and Jennigs, W M (eds), *Walter Benjamin: Selected Writings Volume 1, 1913–1926*, Cambridge, MA and London: Harvard University Press

Benveniste, E (1971) *Problems in General Linguistics*, Coral Gables, FL: University of Miami Press

Berlant, L (1997) *The Queen of America Goes to Washington City: Essays on Sex and Citizenship*, Durham, NC and London: Duke University Press

Berlant, L (2000) 'The subject of true feeling: pain, privacy and politics', in Ahmed, S, Kilby, J, Lury, C, McNeil, M and Skeggs, B (eds), *Transformations: Thinking Through Feminism*, London and New York: Routledge

Berlant, L and Warner, M (1998) 'Public sex', *Critical Inquiry*, 24(2), 547–566

Bloch, M (1961) *The Royal Touch: Monarchy and Miracles in France and England*, London: Routledge and Kegan Paul

Bloch, M (1976) *The Historian's Craft*, Manchester: Manchester University Press

Bottomley, A (2004) 'Shock to thought: an encounter (of a third kind) with legal feminism', *Feminist Legal Studies*, 12(1), 29–65

Braidotti, R (2005) *Metamorphoses: Towards a Materialist Theory of Becoming*, Cambridge: Polity Press

Braudel, F (1990) *The Mediterranean and the Mediterranean World in the Age of Philip II: Vol.1*, London: Fontana Press

Bredekamp, H (1999) 'From Walter Benjamin to Carl Schmitt, via Thomas Hobbes', *Critical Inquiry*, 25(2), 247–266

Brown, W (1995) *States of Injury: Power and Freedom in Late Modernity*, Princeton, NJ: Princeton University Press

Brown, W and Hartley, J (2002) 'Introduction', in Brown, W and Hartley, J (eds), *Left Legalism/Left Critique*, Durham, NC: Duke University Press

Buell, L (2000) 'What we talk about when we talk about ethics', in Garber, M, Hanssen, B and Walkovitz, R (eds), *The Turn to Ethics*, New York and London: Routledge

Bullock, M and Jennigs, W M (2004) 'A note on the texts', in Bullock, M and Jennigs, W M (eds), *Walter Benjamin: Selected Writings Volume 1, 1913–1926*, Cambridge, MA and London: Harvard University Press

Butler, J (1987) 'Variations on sex and gender', in Benhabib, S and Cornel, D (eds), *Feminism as Critique: Essays on the Politics of Gender in Late-Capitalist Societies*, Cambridge: Polity Press

Butler, J (1990) *Gender Trouble: Feminism and the Subversion of Identity*, London and New York: Routledge

Butler, J (1992) 'Contingent foundations: feminism and the question of "postmodernism" ', in Butler, J and Scott, W J (eds), *Feminists Theorise the Political*, London and New York: Routledge

Butler, J (1993) *Bodies that Matter: On the Discursive Limits of 'Sex'*, London and New York: Routledge

Butler, J (1997a) *The Psychic Life of Power*, Stanford, CA: Stanford University Press
Butler, J (1997b) *Excitable Speech: A Politics of the Performative*, New York and London: Routledge
Butler, J (1998) 'Merely cultural', *New Left Review*, 227, 33–44
Butler, J (1999a) *Gender Trouble: Feminism and the Subversion of Identity*, London and New York: Routledge
Butler, J (1999b) *Subjects of Desire: Hegelian Reflection in Twentieth-Century France*, NewYork: Columbia University Press
Butler, J (2000a) *Antigone's Claim: Kinship Between Life and Death*, New York: Columbia University Press
Butler, J (2000b) 'Competing universalities', in Butler, J, Zizek, S and Laclau, E (eds) *Contingency, Hegemony, Universality: Contemporary Dialogues on the Left*, London and New York: Verso
Butler, J (2000c) 'Ethical ambivalence', in Garber, M, Hanssen, B and Walkovitz, R (eds), *The Turn to Ethics*, New York and London: Routledge, 15–18
Butler, J (2000d) 'Politics, power and ethics: a discussion between Judith Butler and William Conolly', *Theory & Event*, 4(2), http://muse.jhu.edu/journals/theory and event/toc/index.html (accessed on 15 September 2006)
Butler, J (2001) 'How can I deny that these hands and this body are mine?' in Cohen, T, Cohen, B, Miller, J and Warminski, A (eds), *Material Events: Paul De Man and the Afterlife of Theory*, Minneapolis, MN and London: University of Minnesota Press
Butler, J (2002) 'Is kinship always already heterosexual?' *Differences: A Journal of Feminist Cultural Studies,* 13(1), 14–44
Butler, J (2003) *Giving an Account of Oneself*, Assen: Koninklijke Van Gorcum
Butler, J (2004a) *Precarious Life: The Powers of Mourning and Violence*, London and New York: Verso
Butler, J (2004b) *Undoing Gender*, New York and London: Routledge
Butler, J (2004c) 'Judith Butler: reanimating the social', in Gane, N (ed), *The Future of Social Theory*, London and New York: Continuum
Butler, J (2005) *Giving an Account of Oneself*, New York: Fordham University Press
Carrard, P (1995) 'Theory of a practice: historical enunciation and the *Annales* School', in Ankersmit, F and Kellner, H (eds), *A New Philosophy Of History*, London: Reaktion Books
Chrysostally, J (to be submitted 2006) 'Setting the scene', in *The Implications of the Philosophical Critique of Subjectivity for Law with Special Reference to Legal Subjectivity and Sovereignty*, PhD thesis, University of Essex.
Conaghan, J (2000) 'Reassessing the feminist theoretical project in law', *Journal of Law and Society*, 27(3), 351–385
Cooper, D (1994) *Sexing the City: Lesbian and Gay Politics and the Activist State*, New York: Rivers Orams and New York University
Cornell, D (1992) 'Gender, Sex and Equivalent Rights', in Butler, J and Scott, W (eds) *Feminist Theorize the Political*, New York and London: Routledge
Coterrel, R (1989) *The Politics of Jurisprudence: A Critical Introduction to Legal Philosophy*, London and Edinburgh: Butterworths
Critchley, S (1993) *The Ethics of Deconstruction: Derrida and Levinas*, Oxford: Blackwell
Critchley, S (1999) *Ethics-Politics-Subjectivity: Essays on Derrida, Levinas and Contemporary French Thought*, London and New York: Verso
Davis, C and Schleifer, R (1991) *Criticism and Culture: The Role of Critique in Modern Literary Theory*, Essex: Longman

Deleuze, G (1994) *Difference & Repetition*, New York: Columbia University Press
Derrida, J (1976) *Of Grammatology*, Baltimore, MD and London: John Hopkins University Press
Derrida, J (1984) *Margins of Philosophy*, Chicago, IL: University of Chicago Press
Derrida, J (1986) *Glas*, Leave P J and Rand, R (trans) Lincoln and London: University of Nebraska
Derrida, J (1992a) 'Before the law', in Attridge, D (ed), *Acts of Literature*, New York and London: Routledge
Derrida, J (1992b) 'Force of law: the "mystical foundation of authority"', in Cornell, D, Rosenfeld, M and Carlson, G D (eds), *Deconstruction and the Possibility of Justice*, New York and London: Routledge
Derrida, J (2000) *Limited Inc*, Evanston, IL: Northwestern University Press
Derrida, J (2001) *Writting and Difference*, London and New York: Routledge
Derrida, J (2005) *Rogues: Two Essays on Reason*, Stanford, CA: Stanford University Press
Descartes, R (1968) *Discourse on Method and the Meditations*, London: Penguin
Diamantides, M (2000) *The Ethics of Suffering*, Aldershot: Ashgate
Diamantides, M (2006) 'Politicising Levinas: from the desire to escape to the desire to be hostage', in Horowitz, A and Horowitz, G (eds), *Difficult Justice: Commentaries on Levinas and Politics*, Toronto: Toronto University Press
Douzinas, C and Warrington, R with McVeigh, S (1991) *Postmodern Jurisprudence: The Law of Text in the Text of Law*, London and New York: Routledge
Douzinas, C and Warrington, R (1994) *Justice Miscarried: Ethics, Aesthetics and the Law*, London and New York: Harvester Wheatsheaf
Drakopoulou, M (2000) 'Women's resolution of laws reconsidered: epistemic shifts and the emergence of the feminist legal discourse', *Law and Critique*, 11, 47–71
Duttmann, G A (2000) 'Tradition and destruction: Walter Benjamin's politics of language', in Benjamin, A and Osborne, P (eds), *Walter Benjamin's Philosophy: Destruction and Experience*, Manchester: Clinamen Press
Eldeman, L (2004) *No Future: Queer Theory and the Death Drive*, Durham, NC and London: Duke University Press
Felman, S (1975) 'Madness and philosophy or literature's reason', *Yale French Studies*, 52, 208–228
Findlay, N J (2004) 'Foreword', in Hegel, G W F, *Hegel's Phenomenology of Spirit*, Miller A V (trans) Oxford: Oxford University Press
Fitzpatrick, P (2001) *Modernism and the Grounds of Law*, New York and Cambridge: Cambridge University Press
Fitzpatrick, P (2005) 'Bare sovereignty: Homo Sacer and the insistence of law', in Norris, A (ed), *Politics, Metaphysics, and Death: Essays on Giorgio Agamben's Homo Sacer*, Durham, NC and London: Duke University Press
Foucault, M (1980) 'Nietzsche, genealogy, history', in Bouchard, F D (ed), *Language, Counter-Memory, Practice: Selected Essays and Interviews by Michel Foucault*, Ithaca, NY: Cornell University Press
Foucault, M (1988) *The History of Sexuality, Volume 3*, New York: Vintage Books
Foucault, M (1990) *The History of Sexuality, Volume 1*, London: Penguin Books
Foucault, M (1991a) *Discipline and Punish: The Birth of the Prison*, London: Penguin Books

Foucault, M (1991b) *Madness and Civilization: A History of Insanity in the Age of Reason*, London and New York: Tavistock/Routledge
Foucault, M (1992) *The History of Sexuality, Volume 3*, London: Penguin Books
Foucault, M (1997) 'The ethics of the concern for self as a practice of freedom', in Rabinow, P (ed), *Ethics: Subjectivity and Truth: Essential Works of Foucault 1954–1984, Volume 1*, New York: The New Press
Foucault, M (2000) *Aesthetics: Essential Works of Foucault 1954–1984, Volume 2*, Faubion, D J (ed), London: Penguin
Foucault, M. (2001) *Fearless Speech*, Los Angeles, CA: Semiotext(e)
Foucault, M (2002a) 'Governmentality', in Faubion, D J (ed), *Power: Essential Works of Foucault 1954–1984, Volume 3*, London: Penguin Books
Foucault, M (2002b) 'About the concept of the "dangerous individual" in ninteenth-century legal psychiatry', in Faubion, D J (ed), *Power: Essential Works of Foucault 1954–1984, Volume 3*, London: Penguin Books
Foucault, M (2002c) 'The political technology of individuals', in Faubion, D J (ed), *Power: Essential Works of Foucault 1954–1984, Volume 3*, London: Penguin Books
Foucault, M (2003) *Society Must Be Defended*, London and New York: Allen Lane
Franke, K (1997) 'What's wrong with sexual harassment?' *Stanford Law Review*, 49, 691
Freeman, A D M (1994) *Lloyd's Introduction to Jurisprudence*, London: Sweet & Maxwell
Gadamer, G (1975) *Truth and Method*, London: Sheed & Ward
Goodrich, P (1986) *Reading the Law: A Critical Introduction to Legal Method and Techniques*, Oxford: Basil Blackwell
Goodrich, P (1990) *Languages of Law: From Logics of Memory to Nomadic Masks*, London: Weidenfeld and Nicolson
Goodrich, P (1996) *Law in the Courts of Love: Literature and Other Minor Jurisprudences*, London and New York: Routledge
Goodrich, P (2004) 'Satirical legal studies: from the legists to the *Lizard*', *Michigan Law Review*, 103(3), 397–517
Greenblatt, S (1989) 'Towards a poetics of culture', in Veeser, H A (ed), *The New Historicism*, New York and London: Routledge
Grosz, E (1994) *Volatile Bodies: Towards a Corporeal Feminism*, Bloomington, IN: Indiana University Press
Halberstam, J (2005) *In a Queer Time & Place: Transgender Bodies, Subcultural Lives*, New York and London: New York University Press
Haldar, P (2004) 'The jurisprudence of travel literature: despotism, excess, and the common law', *Journal of Law and Society*, 31(1), 87–112
Halley, J (1999) *Don't: Reader's Guide to the Military's Anti-Gay Policy*, Durham, NC and London: Duke University Press
Hamacher, W (1996) *Premises: Essays on Philosophy and Literature from Kant to Celan*, Cambridge, MA and London: Harvard University Press
Hamacher, W (2000) 'Afformative strike: Benjamin's "Critique of violence" ', in Benjamin, A and Osborne, P (eds), *Walter Benjamin's Philosophy: Destruction and Experience*, Manchester: Clinamen Press
Hamacher, W (2002) 'Guilt history: Benjamin's sketch "Capitalism as religion" ', *Diacritics*, 32(3/4), 81–106
Hanssen, B (2005) *Critique of Violence: Between Poststructuralism and Critical Theory*, London and New York: Routledge

Hartouni, V (1986) 'Antigone's dilemmas: a problem of political membership', *Hypatia*, 1(1), 3–20
Hegel, G W F (1975) *Aesthetics: Lectures on Fine Art, Volume II*, Oxford: Clarendon Press
Hegel, G W F (1988) *Lectures on the Philosophy of Religion*, Hodgson, P (ed), Hogan P *et al.* (trans), Berkley: University of California Press
Hegel, G W F (1996) *Philosophy of Right*, Dyde S W (trans), Amherst, NY: Prometheus Books
Hegel, G W F (2004) *Phenomenology of Spirit*, Miller A V (trans), Oxford: Oxford University Press
Heidegger, M (1962) *Being and Time*, New York: Harper & Row
Heidegger, M (1969) *The Essence of Reasons*, Evanston, IL: Northwestern University Press
Heidegger, M (1977) *The Question Concerning Technology and Other Essays*, New York: Harper & Row
Heidegger, M (1985) *History of the Concept of Time: Prolegomena*, Bloomington, IN: Indiana University Press
Heidegger, M (1988) *Hegel's Phenomenology of Spirit*, Bloomington, IN: Indiana University Press
Heidegger, M (2004) 'Letter to humanism', in Krell, F D (ed), *Martin Heidegger: Basic Writings*, London and New York: Routledge
Hobbes (1972) *Leviathan*, London: Collins/Fontana
Honic, B (1992) 'Toward an agonistic feminism: Hannah Arendt and the politics of identity', in Butler, J and Scott,W J (eds), *Feminists Theorise the Political*, London and New York: Routledge
Hyppolite, J (2000) *Genesis and Structure of Hegel's Phenomenology of Spirit*, Evanston, IL: North Western University Press
Irigaray, L (1985) *Speculum of the Other Woman*, Ithaca, NY: Cornell University Press
Irigaray, L (1993a) *Sexes and Genealogies*, New York: Columbia University Press
Irigaray, L (1993b) *An Ethics of Sexual Difference*, London: Athlone Press
Isaac, C J (1992) *Arendt, Camus and Modern Rebellion*, New Haven, CT and London: Yale University Press
Kant, I (1982) *Critique of Pure Reason*, London: Macmillan Press
Kaplan, M (1997) *Sexual Justice: Democratic Citizenship and the Politics of Desire*, New York and London: Routledge
Kojeve, A (1980) *Introduction to the Reading of Hegel: Lectures on the Phenomenology of Spirit*, Ithaca, NY and London: Cornell University Press
Lacan, J (1992) *The Ethics of Psychoanalysis, 1959–60*, London: Tavistock/Routledge
Lacoue-Labarthe, P and Nancy, L J (1997) *Retreating the Political*, London and New York: Routledge
Levinas, E (1998) *Otherwise than Being: Or Beyond Essence*, Pittsburgh, PA: Duquesne University Press
Loizidou, E (1997) 'A phantasmatic moment: the defense of in-sanity', *Law and Critique*, VIII(2), 115–140.
Loizidou, E (1999a) 'Sex @ the end of the twentieth century: some re-marks on a minor jurisprudence', *Law and Critique*, 10(1), 71–86
Loizidou, E (1999b) 'The trouble with rape: gender matters and legal "transformations" ', *Feminist Legal Studies*, 7(3), 275–297
Loizidou, E (2001) 'Learning pain: poetry in emotion', *Liverpool Law Review*, 1(23), 179–185

Loizidou, E (2004) 'The love bug and the melancholic drag queen or a reflection on the cultural political "grounds" of subjects as sexual', *Journal For Cultural Research*, 8(4), 447–466
Macalpine, I and Hunter, R (1991) *George III and the Mad-Business*, London: Pimlico
MacIntyre, A (1998) *A Short History of Ethics*, London and New York: Routledge
MacNay, L (1999) 'Subject, psyche and agency: the work of Judith Butler', *Theory, Culture and Society*, 16(2), 175–193
Malabou, C (2005) *The Future of Hegel: Plasticity, Temporality and Dialectic*, London and New York: Routledge
Manville, P B (1990) *The Origins of Citizenship in Ancient Athens*, Princeton, NJ: Princeton University Press
Miller, J H (1987) *The Ethics of Reading*, New York: Columbia University Press
Mills, C (2003) 'Contesting the political: Butler and Foucault on power and resistance', *The Journal of Political Philosophy*, 11(3), 253–272
Moran, L (2005) 'What's home got to do with it? Kinship, space and the case of family, spouse and civil partnership in the UK', *Yale Journal of Law and Feminism*, 17(1), 269–295
Motha, S (2005) 'Guantanamo Bay, "Abandoned Being," and the constitution of jurisdiction', in McVeigh, S (ed), *Jurisprudence of Jurisdiction*, London: UCL Press
Nancy, J-L (1994) 'Corpus', in MacCannel, F J and Zakarin, L (eds), *Thinking Bodies*, Stanford, CA: Stanford University Press
Nancy, J-L (1997) *Being Singular Plural*, Stanford, CA: Stanford University Press
Nancy, J-L (2002) *Hegel: The Restlessness of the Negative*, Minneapolis, MN and London: University of Minnesota Press
Nealon, J (1994) 'Postmodern culture', accessed on 22 Nov 2006, http://muse.jhu.edu/journals/postmodern_culture/ v005/5.1r_nealon.html
Nietzsche, F (1998) *On the Genealogy of Morals*, Oxford and New York: Oxford University Press
Nussbaum, C M (1999a) 'The professor of parody: the heap defeatism of Judith Butler', *The New Republic* (22nd February) 37–45
Nussbaum, C M (1999b) *Sex and Social Justice*, Oxford and New York: Oxford University Press
Phelan, P (1997) *Mourning Sex: Performing Public Memories*, New York and London: Routledge
Plato (2005) *Symposium*, London: Penguin Books
Prosser, J (1998) *Second Skins: The Body Narratives of Transsexuality*, New York: New York University Press
Rabinow, P (1997) 'Introduction', in Rabinow, P (ed), *Ethics: Subjectivity and Truth: Essential Works of Foucault 1954–1984, Volume 1*, New York: The New Press
Roteinstreich, N (1963) 'On the ecstatic sources of the concept of alienation' in *Review of Metaphysics*, 16(3), 550–555
Rush, P, McVeigh, S and Young, A (eds) (1997) *Criminal Legal Doctrine*, Dartmouth: Ashgate
Searle, R J (1969) *Speech Acts*, Cambridge: Cambridge University Press
Sedgwick, E K (2003) *Touching Feeling: Affect, Pedagogy, Performativity*, Durham, NC and London: Duke University Press
Siegle, L (2005) 'Kids are alright', *The Observer* (6th February) 56
Sophocles (1984) *The Three Theban Plays: Antigone, Oedipus the King, Oedipus at Colonus*, Fagles, R (trans) London: Penguin Books
Sorel , G (1961) *Reflections on Violence*, New York: Collier Books

Spivak, C G (1976) 'Translator's preface', in Derrida, J (ed) *Of Grammatology*, Baltimore, MD and London: John Hopkins University Press

Spivak, C G (1988) 'Can the subaltern speak?', in Nealson, C and Grossberg, L (eds), *Marxism and the Interpetation of Culture*, London: Macmillan Education

Spivak, C G (19 April 1999) 'Martha C. Nussbaum and her Crtics: and Exchange', *The New Republic*, 220(16), 43–45

Spivak, C G (2003) *A Critique of Postcolonial Reason: Toward a History of the Vanishing Present*, Cambridge, MA: Harvard University Press

Steiner, G (1986) *Antigones*, New Haven, CT: Yale University Press

Taylor, C (1999) *Hegel*, Cambridge: Cambridge University Press

Tuitt, P (2004) *Race, Law, Resistance*, London: The GlassHouse Press

Vasterling, V (1999) 'Butler's sophisticated constructivism: a critical assessment', *Hypatia*, 14(3), 17–38

Warner, M (2001) *Publics and Counter Publics*, New York: Zone Books

Weber, S (1992) 'Taking exception to decision: Walter Benjamin and Carl Schmitt', *Diacritics*, 22(3/4), 5–18

Weisberg, R (1992) *Poethics*, New York: Columbia University Press

Winders, A (1999) 'Writing like a man (?): Descartes, science, and madness', in Bordo, S (ed), *Feminist Interpretations of Rene Descartes*, 1999, University Park, PA: Penn State University Press

Zizek, S (1999) *The Ticklish Subject: The Absent Center of Political Ontology*, London and New York: Verso

Index